LLOYD GEORGE'S TADA

LLOYD GEORGE'S TADA

- the one father he never knew!

Peter Rowland

PublishNation
London and Cardiff

ISBN: 978-1-291-82828-3

'Of the many difficulties which afflict the biographer, the moral difficulty must surely be the greatest. By what standard, that is to say, is he to judge the morals of the dead? By that of their day, or that of his own? Or should he, before putting pen to paper, arrive at some absolute standard of right and wrong by which he can try Socrates and Shelley and Byron and Queen Victoria and Mr Lloyd George? The problem, though it lies at the root of biography and affects it in every fibre, is for the most part solved or shelved by taking it for granted that the truth was revealed about the year 1850 to the fortunate natives of the British Isles, who need only in future take into account circumstances of date, country, and sex in order to come to a satisfactory conclusion upon all cases of moral eccentricity submitted to their judgement.'

- Virginia Woolf, *Times Literary Supplement*, December 1922, unconsciously juxtaposing two names from two very different periods between which, however improbably, a link did indeed exist.

CONTENTS

PREFACE AND ACKNOWLEDGEMENTS

If the words of the old song are to be believed, Lloyd George knew everybody's father but his own. Not altogether surprising, perhaps, since Britain's future Prime Minister was only sixteen months old when William George died. Chatting to Herbert Lewis (his best friend) in December 1907, he confessed that he had no more than 'a faint recollection' of his parent. He marvelled that William had such 'a very inadequate knowledge' of his native language - 'He never spoke Welsh at all' - but was evidently pleased to learn that he resembled his father in appearance. [1]

He would also have been pleased, presumably, that his spectacular by-election victory of April 1890, making him M.P. for Caernarvonshire District Boroughs, was responsible for shedding enhanced lustre upon his father's memory. A contributor to the *Pontypridd Chronicle* spent a little while investigating the antecedents of this 'young man from Criccieth ... suddenly brought into prominence' and reported that he was the son of another young man who, despite ill-health, had had an 'illustrious' teaching career and been struck down in his prime. A summary of that career, not totally inaccurate in its details, was provided. 'We have here', declared the excited investigator, 'an illustration of the law of convergence and development. The neighbourhood that produced an advanced intellect in one instance will fan the flame and set others ablaze.... Show us a talented son, and we will point to a talented parent on one side or the other, and if on both sides all the better. The son is the development of the mental and moral qualities of his predecessors.... The son of William George, Trecoed, has already distinguished himself in the path of eminence marked by the father and judiciously directed by a careful mother. The Lloyds of Criccieth and the Georges of Trecoed are centred in the robust intellect of the Baptist, the lawyer, the temperance advocate, and the M.P. for Carnarvon.'[2]

To strike a more mundane note, the son also seems to have benefited from some of the items in his father's library. Chief among these was the English translation of an eight-volume history of ancient times by Charles Rollins, originally published in the 1730s, which Lloyd George claimed to have read in its entirety. A volume or two of bound copies of a weekly journal called *The Examiner*, which told him all he wished to know about the American civil war, and a Victorian *History of England* 'which was rather good', apparently completed his literary inheritance. [3] These were the only English books that he recalled from his childhood although there were, in fact, many more (not least fourteen volumes of *The Penny Cyclopaedia*).

William George would have been gratified to know that he had managed, indirectly, to make a contribution to his son's early education. 'He should have been a preacher,' an emphatic old gentleman from Pembrokeshire told Herbert Lewis. 'They said he was a man of great personal fascination, They used to crowd round him and he would talk to them by the hour.' *'Pan yr oedd ar ei draed yr oedd y lle yn berwi drwyddo'* the old man had exclaimed - 'When he was on his feet, the whole place was buzzing.' [4] All of which might have led Lewis to conclude that it was not only in physical appearance that Lloyd George resembled his father, for by 1907 the 'whole place' - whether it be a platform in a village hall or the Chamber of the House of Commons - was indeed 'buzzing', in eager anticipation, when the President of the Board of Trade rose to speak, aware that either verbal fireworks or some light-hearted knockabout fun (most probably a mixture of both) were sure to follow.

By June 1914, as both a dynamic Chancellor of the Exchequer and an ardent campaigner for Land Reform, David Lloyd George was rarely out of the spotlight. The Prime Minister, Herbert Henry Asquith, was content to let him occupy this position, confident of his own ability to exercise a restraining hand should circumstances require it. In 'a manner cool and calm', to quote the words of another contemporary song, he exercised a policy of benign tolerance so far as his chief lieutenant was concerned, taking an avuncular interest in whatever scheme that adroit tactician might be currently devising but observing him, in effect, with a certain measure of amused detachment. From Oxford, on Whit Sunday, he forwarded to his lady-love, Venetia Stanley, what he thought was probably the longest letter that Lloyd George had ever written with his own hand, and asked her to either destroy it or to keep it, as a curiosity, in a very safe place. The letter in question (running to 175 words) had been written from No. 11 Downing Street two days earlier, on 5 June 1914, and concerned a plan for tightening up party organisation in the country at large. [5] It has proved impossible to discover what Lloyd George himself was doing on 7 June 1914, but since it was a Sunday (and a special one at that) we must assume that he went to chapel - and we must also assume that at some stage he reflected on the fact that it was now fifty years, to the very day, since his father had died. One hopes that there would have been a certain degree of solemnity in his behaviour that day, and he may have been a little quieter than usual. But, with the best will in the world, it cannot be guaranteed that this was so.

One hundred years on, a vast amount is known about Lloyd George himself and one might almost doubt whether there is anything basically fresh still awaiting discovery. A renewed interest in the Great War will doubtless shine the spotlight upon him yet again, however, and fresh evaluations and debates about the Welsh Wizard will be triggered off when the events of December 1916 are re-scrutinised some two years hence. But information about his father, William George, has continued to be in short supply, even though (to adopt the phraseology of that excited *Pontypridd Chronicle* correspondent, probably speaking more truly than he realised) he trod a 'path of eminence' and prepared the way for the triumphs of his eldest son. It is hoped that the account which now follows, designed to mark the 150th anniversary of William's death on 7 June 1864 and charting what was indeed a path of eminence, will prove illuminating (and even, at times, entertaining) to a wide range of readers, both English and Welsh. There may be surprises in store for some of them. I have endeavoured, so far as the material currently available permits, to bring William back to life as a rounded figure, so that he may take his true place as the founder (with Betsy Lloyd as consort) of the Lloyd George dynasty and, despite an impressive career cut tragically short by illness, be recognised as a remarkable person in his own right.

My greatest indebtedness in undertaking this venture has been, first and foremost, to the George family, who, following the death of Dr W.R.P. George in 2006, entrusted his papers to the National Library of Wales for cataloguing and safekeeping. They included those of his grandfather, William George, the subject of this book. I am also immensely grateful to Mr Philip William George, the son of Dr George and great-grandson of William, for his assistance and advice on several matters. The papers relating to William George are a small treasure-trove, and his *Student's Journal*, in particular, contains some fascinating and tantalising information. But it is a matter of serious regret that some of the documents which Dr George drew upon in 1976, when writing *The Making of Lloyd George* (including, it seems, substantial sections of the *Journal*) have apparently disappeared. One hopes that this material is still extant, in some form or other, and will one day re-surface, but it does mean that there are, for the moment, several perplexing lacunae in the story of his life which it might otherwise have been possible to fill.

A second huge debt of gratitude must be to Mr Henry Harrison, who is related by marriage to the Lloyd George family. At the invitation of the late Owen, 3rd Earl Lloyd George, he undertook in the 1990s the immense task of sorting out the complexities of that family and establishing (in the days before the internet got into its stride) the precise relationships between its various members and branches and the dates of births, marriages and deaths, so far as they could be established, over a period of time ranging from the late eighteenth to the late twentieth centuries - not to mention the location and size of sundry farms and estates, with a plentiful supply of maps, photographs and documents buttressing the family trees and, underlying everything, an interesting narrative. *Hanes Teulu Lloyd George Family History*, first printed for private circulation in 1999 (but with copies made available to the British Library and the National Library of Wales and other reputable bodies, plus legitimate researchers), is an awe-inspiring achievement. 'I am', he says modestly, 'neither a genealogist nor a historian - merely an amateur.' [6] One is tempted to emulate the Churchillian exclamation - 'Some amateur!' For he succeeds in clarifying a tremendously complex and confusing picture, shining a torch into areas which had previously seemed impenetrable. I doubt whether I could have threaded my way through the earlier part of this book without the guidance of his astonishing and painstaking monograph. I am also very grateful to him for his assistance and advice on various matters (and reaction to sundry ideas) which came to light during my own researches, and for his general encouragement - I hope that this finished production does not fall too far short of his expectations and standards.

I am much obliged to the staff of the National Library of Wales for allowing me to examine the papers of William George and also for their patience and diligence in dealing with the host of queries with which, from afar, I subsequently plied them. I am also grateful to Dr J. Graham Jones, until recently senior archivist and Head of the Welsh Political Archive at the Library, for his encouragement. I must acknowledge my indebtedness to Pollinger Ltd, acting as literary agent on behalf of the Earl of Lytton, for allowing me to examine some of the papers of Lady Byron relating to educational matters (part of the Lovelace-Byron Deposit) in the Bodleian Library, Oxford, and to the staff of that Library for their courtesy and assistance.

Mr Simon Hancock, Curator of the Haverfordwest Museum, has provided me with much valuable advice and assistance during the past few years and I am also grateful to Miss Nikki Bosworth, an archivist with the Pembrokeshire Record Office, for coming up with the answers to what had originally seemed intractable questions and for supplying, at the same time, some very useful background information. Mr John Aaron via Mrs Shâron Barnes, Office Manager for the Evangelical Movement of Wales, Bridgend, made a determined effort to identify the particular 'Great Gun' to whom William had listened, with much admiration, at a Methodist Association gathering at Pwhlleli in 1858 and the Rev. Martin Spain of the Tiers Cross congregational church pointed me in the right direction for finding out a little more about its Minister in 1861 and very kindly explained to me the significance of the word 'Listeners' in its census return for that year. So far as the Manchester-based calico print works of Thomas Hoyle & Sons are concerned, I am greatly indebted to both Dr Philip A. Sykas of the Manchester School of Art and to his colleague, Mr John Beckett, for a fund of fascinating and very helpful information.

Others who have assisted with information and advice are Christopher Davies, publisher of *The History of Education in Wales* (1978), Lynn C. Francis, Principal Archivist of Caernarvonshire, Anghared Meredith, Archivist and Records Manager of Harrow School, Mr Derek Rees of the Haverfordwest Civic Society, Rebecca Shields of West Glamorgan Archives Services and Miranda Tennant acting on behalf of Queen Elizabeth Grammar School, Wakefield. I am grateful to Tracey Jennings (and her mother) for deciphering some very ancient shorthand, much of it rather baffling, and to the Cymen Translation Company for rendering into English the relevant part of a long article about Lloyd George and his forbears written by the Rev. Henry Rees in 1909 - and also the 'buzzing' remark made by that emphatic old gentleman from Pembrokeshire quoted above.

Nearer home, I must once again thank my cousin, Katie Constable, for solving (after hours of research on the internet) some family relationship problems which had eluded even the vigilant scrutiny of Henry Harrison (although we never did quite solve the mystery of just how many wives the voracious Benjamin Williams might have got through in his later years - a question best left unanswered, perhaps) and I am also extremely grateful to my friend Beryl Porter for having helped me in the time-consuming task of deciphering the 1839 entries in William's *Student Journal* - although there were occasional differences of opinion, and some of the passages and allusions proved (as will be seen) totally beyond us. Needless to say, I take sole responsibility for all the shortcomings of the book and for any errors that appear in the text - and am not remotely sanguine enough to assume that there will not be any! (Like Henry, I do not claim to be much more than an amateur, having spent most of my career as a local government officer.) I must also apologise to anyone whom I have inadvertently excluded from the list of acknowledgements set out above. But I would be grateful if any omissions or mistakes could be brought to my attention and will certainly endeavour to ensure that the record is corrected at the first available opportunity. And additions, in the way of fresh information, would also be most - and, indeed, rather more - welcome. Other than that, all I can do (rather like a waiter whipping off the lid of a tureen, with the air of an impresario, before beating a speedy retreat) is to say 'Enjoy!'

Peter Rowland
Wanstead, London
March 2014

NOTE

Six people called William George appear in the narrative that follows, although two of them only very briefly.   To avoid confusion, the classification and explanatory details that follow may prove helpful.

William 1 (1747 - 1839):

The patriarch of Tresinwen, grandfather of the subject of this book.

William 2 (1786 - 1853):

Fourth son of William 1, a mariner known as Wil Siors Bach and uncle of the subject of this book.

William 3 (1815 - 1818):

First son of David George, grandson of William 1 and pre-deceased brother of the subject of this book.

William 4 (1821 - 1864):   **Second son of David George, grandson of William 1 and the subject of this book.**

William 5 (1865 - 1967):   Third son of William 4, the subject of this book.

William 6 (1912 - 2006):   Son of William 5 and grandson of William 4, the subject of this book - William Richard Phillip George, Archdruid of Wales, 1990-93; referred to hereafter as either W.R.P. George or Dr George.

BY WAY OF INTRODUCTION

With an astonishing faith in either my ability or gullibility - almost certainly the latter - a very persuasive American publisher once sweet-talked me into writing a new biography of David Lloyd Gorge. It was the autumn of 1968, and the world (as George Cole's Arthur Daly would have said) was my lobster. My first book, an account of the last Liberal Governments, covering the period from 1905 to 1910, had just been published and had been quite well received. A sequel, covering the period from 1911 to 1915, was taking shape and a third volume (*The Coalitions, 1915 - 22*) would complete the trilogy. Suddenly cutting across all this there came a bright and breezy letter from a representative of the New York publishers of book No. 1 (lagging about four months behind the British edition) asking whether I would like to try my hand at 'a really good biography of Lloyd George (especially from his downfall over Chanak until his last gasps in the Commons as caught so forcefully by [Harold] Nicolson and others).' [1]

It was a totally unexpected proposition. Strictly speaking, as a young man of thirty serving as a junior administrative officer with the Greater London Council, whose delvings into historical manuscripts and literary activities were a strictly leisure-time pursuit - and who, moreover, still had much to learn - I ought to have declined the invitation by return of post. Prudence suggested that I should wait until I was forty or fifty before, with the accretion of greater layers of wisdom, knowledge and judgement, I attempted a major production of this nature. On the other hand, I currently had zeal and energy (or, if it be preferred, 'the towering confidence of youth') which might well have evaporated once those distant shores of caution and maturity had been reached. [2] I had already covered five years of Lloyd George's ministerial career in the first volume of *The Last Liberal Governments* and was about to tackle the next five in the second volume, while the final seven would obviously be the centre-piece of *The Coalitions* (a volume which in the event, never materialised). Perhaps, after all, I was not so ill-equipped for the task as I had initially thought? - and it was an opportunity which might never come again. But I remained in two minds for a while. What finally determined matters was that my wife urged me to take up the challenge, giving me her fullest backing and support (plus invaluable advice and her typing skills) throughout. My employers indicated, after some hesitation, that I would be permitted to take a certain amount of unpaid leave providing that the quality of my admin. work on their behalf did not suffer as a consequence.

So the plunge was taken and a contract signed. I agreed to produce a new 'cradle to grave' biography of Lloyd George similar, in scale, to Lord Blake's recently-published biography of Disraeli (which had run to 818 pages - my own production, albeit with smaller print, would exceed that total by 54). It was, moreover, an opportune moment for such a book to appear, for the Lloyd George papers (which Lord Beaverbrook had clutched tight to his chest during his lifetime) had now been made available to *bona fide* researchers in the newly-established Beaverbrook Library at the *Daily Express* buildings, following the death of his lordship, and their custodian was the renowned and almost legendary A.J.P. Taylor, a displaced person from the official world of academia, who was zealously engaged in producing a massive biography of his mentor. A further huge batch of Lloyd George family papers became available to researchers, a little while later, at the National Library of Wales.

As my American publisher had indicated, there was clearly a gap to be filled. It was fourteen years since Frank Owen, at Beaverbrook's command, had produced a lengthy but melodramatic biography of Lloyd George (*Tempestuous Journey*). Prior to Owen, there had been an 'official' biography by Malcolm Thomson in 1948 and an independent assessment by Thomas Jones in 1951 - two useful but relatively short books - and long before them there had been a distinguished interim biography by Herbert du Parcq (1912-13) which made good use of some early George family papers. A volume drawing upon all the latest available information could well become a best-seller.

As soon as my second book on the Liberal Governments had been completed, the new biography had my undivided attention. It was finished in the spring of 1975 and came out at the end of that year - twenty-one years after Owen's. Intended to be entertaining, as well as enlightening, this too was quite well received. Taylor and Blake both wrote very kind reviews, in the *Observer* and *Sunday Times* respectively, and there was an equally flattering one from John Grigg (now at work on his own multi-volume biography of Lloyd George) in the *New Statesmen*: he continued to praise it during the twenty years which followed. Indignant spluttering came, however, from some of the younger, University-based historians, on whose toes I had evidently trodden. Part-time historians with the temerity to venture on to what they regarded as their own exclusive territory were not welcome! Their ire had doubtless been fuelled by a remark of Taylor's - 'Professional historians must tremble at competition from an amateur of such stature.' (Mischievous comments, designed to stir up hornets' nests, were his stock-in-trade.)

The book was probably too long (although my publishers had resisted the idea that it be issued as two separate volumes) but it managed to cover, in the five years or so which had been available to me, all the salient points of Lloyd George's career in some detail and remains a reasonably comprehensive survey of a fascinating man. Almost forty

3

years later it has become something of a period-piece in its own right, but it did manage to fill a distinct gap, the sales were good and people claim, even now, that they have enjoyed reading it. The American whiz-kid responsible for commissioning it had soon shot off to a different publishing house (and in due course would set up one of his own) but was pleased with the finished product. On his next visit to London he took my wife and myself out to a sort of night-club ('The War Room') and chortled when I made what he wrongly interpreted as an acerbic remark - 'Gee, I guess you're still sore at me over that Lloyd George deal!' - from which I gathered, belatedly, that I had evidently done the work for what he regarded as peanuts. (He then moved on to sketching out a new project, which was designed to make all our fortunes - helping a certain well-known lady to write her memoirs - but I was able to turn down this particular idea with no qualms whatsoever and our paths have never crossed since.)

In 1981 the book formed the basis for a nine-part BBC television series, with Philip Madoc in the starring role and a specially-commissioned signature tune from Ennio Morricone, no less. The script was by Elaine Morgan, a well-known dramatist at that time, with an accompanying 'tie-in' paperback by David Benedictus. Mr Benedictus warmly acknowledged that both she and he had 'drawn heavily' upon my 'weighty biography' (an acknowledgement already made, indeed, by Ms Morgan in a private letter to myself). There was much that I recognised and it was curious to hear, for instance, the text of a forgotten Gladstone speech, which I had laboriously quarried out of the archives, being declaimed by none other than Roland Culver! But there was no remuneration forthcoming and my name never appeared in the list of credits that followed transmission of each episode - an omission for which, on the whole, I became rather thankful, since their quality was distinctly variable. (The role of accredited 'historical advisor' was filled by A.J.P. Taylor, who had evidently pocketed the cheque and turned a blind eye to a good many things.) Watching the brilliant television series about John Adams a few years ago, with tremendous emphasis being placed, right from the outset, on the fact that it was based on the biography written by David McCullough, I was able to reflect that such matters were handled a little differently nowadays. [3]

I encountered one particular mystery, when working on the very first chapter of the book - on the very first page, indeed! - that I was totally unable to solve satisfactorily at that time. Starting truly at the outset, as it were, I had obtained a copy of the certificate of marriage on 16 November 1859 between Lloyd George's parents - William George and Elizabeth Lloyd - only to be pulled up short by the description of William George's marital state as that of 'widower'. *So there had been a first Mrs William George!* This came as something of a bombshell. There had been no mention of any such lady in the biographies by du Parcq, Thomson, Jones or Owen. An outline of William George's career had been sketched out by du Parcq, so far as it could be reconstructed, but he was totally silent about this particular personage - the reason being, I speedily realised, that he had no idea that she had existed.

But somebody who *did* casually mention her, except that I had temporarily forgotten this passage since reading his memoirs *My Brother and I* (1958) some years earlier, was William George the Second (1865 - 1967) - second surviving son of the first William, born eight months after his father's death, and brother of David. When sketching out his father's career, he writes: 'According to a romantic and well-authenticated anecdote in the family, an invalid lady became so lovesick of him that her doctor advised my father that she would surely die unless he married her - which he did! I am afraid that she did not live long afterwards because she died some years before he married my mother.' [4]

So here was some self-confessed 'anecdotal' evidence of the first wife's existence, presumably passed on to him by either his mother or by Uncle Lloyd. It will be convenient, although jumping very slightly ahead in strict chronology, if we also consider at this stage a paragraph which appeared in *The Making of Lloyd George* (1976) by W.R.P. George - William George the Third (1912 - 2006), son of the second William George and grandson of the first:

> I was told by my father that he [the first William George] married a widow many years older than himself in Haverfordwest. She was in some way connected with the premises where he established his school [in April 1854]. Her name was Mrs Brown and she was consumptive. My father told me that she had fallen deeply in love with William George.... There is nothing [in my grandfather's papers] to support the oral tradition in the family that he did not expect Mrs Brown to live more than a few years and that he married her out of pity. The probability is that he married her when he was thirty-two and when she had lost the lustre and beauty of her first youth. She probably was, like himself, in poor health, and this may have been a bond between them. In fact, she died within two or, at most, three years after their marriage. [5]

It will be noted that this second account, although also emanating from William George the Second, varies from its predecessor quite considerably. (A possible explanation for this apparent discrepancy, coupled with a suggestion that two separate stories have been conflated, will be set out later for the reader's consideration. For the moment, he or she is simply asked to bear in mind the obvious reflection that family tales or legends are passed on by word of mouth, not written down. Names are not spelt out, only uttered aloud, and there is a strong likelihood that if the name uttered - with a characteristic Welsh lilt - had actually been 'Baron' or 'Burun', or something similar, that it would have sounded like 'Brown' to the young William George and this is how he would remember the name for the rest of his life.)

In 1971, wishing to establish the identity of this first wife once and for all, I thought it would be a comparatively easy task. All one had to do was to check through the hefty volumes stacked at Somerset House containing indexes to the marriage registers, discover which one of them related to William George, obtain a copy of the certificate, note the name of the wife and then ascertain, as a totally separate exercise, when she had died. Nothing could be simpler!

In fact, I soon found that this was going to be a time-consuming and monumentally frustrating exercise. Bearing in mind that William had apparently been born in 1820, and that his second marriage took place in November 1859, I decided that he was unlikely to have married before his nineteenth birthday and that adequate time needed to be allowed for the unfortunate lady to breathe her last and be buried for a respectable period before Wedding No. 2 could took place. This being so, then the marriage must have occurred between 1 January 1839 and 31 December 1858 - a period of twenty years. I discovered to my horror, after drawing up an initial list of William Georges, that the total number who had got married in England and Wales during this period totalled 280 (an average of 14 a year, 15 in 1845 being the highest individual total and 8 in 1843 being the lowest). Even so, I was not immediately discouraged because I was equipped with an outline knowledge of where the very mobile Mr George had been during this period - London, Liverpool and Wales (with

Haverfordwest a crucial name to bear in mind). This narrowed the field slightly, and (to select half-a-dozen names at random) places such as Hemel Hempstead, Cheltenham, Salisbury, Hatfield, Marlborough and Nottingham could be ignored - or, at any rate, set to one side for the time being. One of those discounted in this fashion, as seeming intrinsically unlikely, was a marriage in central London at the ultra-fashionable St George's, Hanover Square in the second quarter of 1855: this had clearly been a 'high society' event, and it was most improbable that a humble schoolteacher from Wales could have been the groom.

I was based, at that time, in London's County Hall, on the south side of the Thames, so it became a regular lunchtime routine to cross Waterloo Bridge and walk to Somerset House, located in the Strand, to pursue my task of 'find the lady'. In the event, I made eight-five attempts to pinpoint the date of that first marriage. For a small fee, one was able to submit, to the patient authorities behind the cubby-holes, a 'Marriage Verification Quote' in which were posed three questions for cross-checking: Was the bridegroom a schoolmaster? Was he the son of David George, a farmer? Was he born in 1820? Back there came, as the weeks went by, a host of discouraging answers - although some of them were, in themselves, quite interesting. The professions of some of the William Georges I encountered were those of labourer, plasterer, painter, collier, wheelwright, cabinet maker, grocer, tailor, draper, mercer, farmer, shipwright and mariner - and one of them, clearly a cut above all the rest, was simply 'a gentleman'. In the whole of this collection I discovered only one William George who might, just conceivably, be my quarry,

In the course of seeking copyright clearance for some of the material I was using, I wrote to Lady Olwen Carey-Evans on 1 November 1973, by that time Lloyd George's one surviving daughter, to ask (among other things) whether she

8

happened to have any information about the first Mrs William George. She replied on 18 November stating that a search for information about the lady was 'being done now' but that at present neither she nor her cousin (i.e., W.R.P. George) was able to enlighten me.

The amount of time that I had so far devoted to trying to track down the elusive lady was proving wildly disproportionate, of course, to the main project. I eventually decided, though not totally convinced of my wisdom in doing so, that William George, of 'full age' and son of a farmer called David George, had married a lady called Anne George (possibly a relative) at St Martin's, Haverfordwest on 20 April 1841. The only problem in adopting this conclusion was that the groom was described as a 'labourer', not a 'teacher', on the certificate. It was conceivable, however, that he had not secured a teaching post at that point in time and was simply filling in with some temporary employment on the family farm.

In 1976, however, when W.R.P. George's *The Making of Lloyd George* was published, it became obvious that my guess had proved incorrect, for in 1841 William George had been pursuing his studies at a teachers' training college in Battersea. The mystery of the identity of the first Mrs William George remained unsolved, although W.R.P. George had narrowed it down to the mid-1850s and had put forward the name of Mrs Brown, a widow (presumably wealthy) who had been involved in the establishment of the new school at Haverfordwest at which William would preside (for a couple of years) as headmaster. And yet, however hard I tried, I could not quite believe in Mrs Brown. She somehow did not ring true and this was, after all, no more than hearsay evidence. From a highly respected source, admittedly, but hearsay none the less - and if this was really her name, why had it not been mentioned by William George when he wrote *My Brother and I*?

9

During the next thirty years I often pondered on the identity of the Unknown Lady - a companion piece, as it were, to the Unknown Warrior - and even made one or two additional (but equally unsuccessful) attempts to locate her. For it could be argued that her death had been indirectly responsible for changing the history of the world - and for this alone, if nothing else, she surely merited a mention somewhere or other. If the first Mrs William George had not left the earthly scene when she did, then her widower would not have been free to marry Elizabeth Lloyd. If her widower had not married Elizabeth Lloyd, then there would have been no such person as David Lloyd George - and if there had been no such person as David Lloyd George then Great Britain, in all probability, would have been denied the benefits of a rudimentary pre-1914 Welfare State and would have been defeated in the First World War. So just who was this Unknown Lady?

It is time to return, for the very last time, to A.J.P. Taylor. One of his dictums had been: 'All secrets are in print if you know where to look.' And if I had happened to looked at page 23 of a book called *Old Haverfordwest*, written by a Mr W.D. Phillips and published in that town in 1925 - a reprint of articles which had appeared in the *Pembroke County Guardian* - then I would have found the answer to my question (or half of it, at any rate) gazing me in the face.

William David Phillips had been born in Haverfordwest in 1846 and had lived and worked there all his life. In the words of his son, 'He had a long and varied career, including being clerk with William Davies, solicitor [and a Liberal M.P. in the 1880s], accountant, landlord of the Salutation Hotel, auctioneer, valuer, estate agent, insurance and general commission agent.' [6] He also had a very wide circle of acquaintances. There was, in short, not much that happened in

Haverfordwest between December 1853, when the railway reached the town amidst scenes of much jubilation, and the time of his death in June 1926 that Mr Phillips, as man and boy, had not been aware of.

In February 1924 he began penning a series of recollections for the *Pembroke County Guardian*. The seventh of these articles was entitled 'Mr D. Lloyd George's Associations with the Town'. Though hazy about the precise dates, which he did not attempt to define, he recalled that Lloyd George's father had kept a school in Upper Market Street. He added:

> During this time Mr William George became acquainted with a Miss Huntley who, with her companion, Miss Legge, then resided in Haverfordwest. The acquaintance ripened into friendship, and ultimately into something stronger, and they afterwards married. Mrs George, however, died a year or two after her marriage. She was buried in St Thomas' Churchyard, Haverfordwest.

At the end of the book several pages were taken up by a list of its subscribers. In that list appeared an entry for 'George, Right Hon. D. Lloyd'. For the first time, in all probability, William George's most famous son now became aware of the surname of his father's first wife - for Phillips had been unable to remember Miss Huntley's Christian name. Lloyd George may well have lost no time in passing it on to his brother, for apart from anything else he was aware that the second William contemplated writing a biography of their father. This was a project that had been under consideration since 1922. The chances are, however, that this second William George had already seen the article when it appeared in the *Pembroke County Guardian* on 21 March 1924. But, in

11

any case, he had no need to note the name for himself, for he knew it already. Among the papers relating to his father one finds a couple of pages on which he had pencilled down, apparently on 6 November 1922, some preliminary notes (based largely on information supplied by his mother-in-law). He lists some of the places where his father was known to have lived or taught - Liverpool, Pwllheli, Rawtenstall (which he spelt, as it is pronounced, 'Rottenstall'), Manchester and Bulford. Then he came to Haverfordwest and jotted down some notes in shorthand - and the name 'Huntley', written out in full, appears halfway through them. [7]

In the event, William George's full-scale biography of his father never materialised. By the time he came to write *My Brother and I* thirty-five years later he had evidently forgotten both his earlier notes and *Old Haverfordwest.* In summarising his father's career, he contented himself with simply quoting the 'romantic and well-authenticated' family anecdote recorded above. His own son, W.R.P. George, had no knowledge of the Phillips book and subsequent biographers of Lloyd George, including the present writer, were equally unaware of its existence. Somebody who rediscovered it, however, was Mr H.W. Harrison, who, at the invitation of the late Owen, 3rd Earl Lloyd George, compiled for private circulation in 1999 a monograph about the Lloyd George family (*Hanes Teulu Lloyd George Family History*). He not only rediscovered the Phillips articles - he also discovered Miss Huntley's first name as a result of consulting the Registers of St Thomas, Haverfordwest, and was able to establish the precise date of her death at the early age of 35. She had been William's wife for no more than eight months - and it was subsequently established that they were the couple married at St George's, Hanover Square in the spring of 1855, whom I had recklessly discounted when sifting through my original list of 280 William Georges.

So the last crucial scrap of information about the mysterious life of William George (or so it then seemed to me) had finally come to light. Long before learning of the existence of Selina Huntley, however, I was beginning to suspect that the life of William George could well be an extremely interesting story in its own right - and that it might possibly contain a few surprises. It is hoped that the readers of the pages that will follow will agree, in due course, that there was adequate justification for this initial surmise. (Rather more, indeed, than the most sanguine of researchers could have anticipated.)

1 - THE FORERUNNERS

What was probably the very first potted biography of William George appeared in the *Pontypridd Chronicle* in May 1890, an account which was promptly reproduced in Welsh newspapers elsewhere. Its author is unknown. Mr W. George, it explained, father of the newly-elected M.P. for Caernarvonshire Boroughs, who had been born in Manchester but hailed from Fishguard,

> was the son of Mr George, of Trecoed farm, and grandson of William George of Tresynwen farm, a deacon of the Baptist Church for over 40 years, and a landowner.... We are informed that Mr W. George was of delicate health, and of a studious disposition. When at a Grammar School at Haverfordwest, the lady where he lodged made a serious complaint against him, that he would burn a whole wax candle in a night - bothering his head with books continually; and when on one morning he was heard reading *Paradise Lost*, the pious old lady protested that he would never go to heaven because he was reading so much of hell....
>
> After years of training at Haverfordwest, he entered a seminary in London, where he remained for eight years, for a part of which time he occupied the position of assistant tutor in the Metropolis of the world. Leaving London, he had the charge of a large school in Liverpool, under a committee of influential gentlemen. One prominent member of this committee was Mr Martineau, father of the celebrated Harriet Martineau. He was also intimately acquainted with this distinguished authoress. Declining health occasioned his leaving Liverpool and coming home, where he remained for about a year, till his strength was

recruited.   About 1851 he established a private Grammar School at Haverfordwest. Here again, his health failed, and he removed to North Wales, where he made there acquaintance of Miss Lloyd, a native of Criccieth. They were married in 1860. Now comes his connection with Manchester.   Mr George accepted charge of a large school there, which position he retained for a few years, during which period D. Lloyd George was born. The father's constitution again gave way, and he returned to Pembrokeshire and took a small farm called Bwlford, near Haverfordwest, where he spent the remainder of his illustrious life in the quiet repose of a small dairy farm. A promising career was, however, intercepted by death on 7 June 1864, when W. George was only 44 years of age. His tombstone is now in Jordanston graveyard, within three miles of Fishguard. But he has left a better monument than the stone: he left behind a son then but a babe in arms, in the person of D. Lloyd George. [1]

By January 1909 D. Lloyd George had become a dynamic and multi-talented Chancellor of the Exchequer and a leading member of Mr Asquith's Liberal Government. That month there was published in the Welsh magazine *Seren Gomer* a long article about him contributed by the Rev. Henry Rees of Pwllheli. Not only did it cover in glowing terms the career to date of its subject ('our hero') but it also supplied brief accounts of the lives of his parents. The section on William George, when translated into English (and with some explanatory remarks about the Unitarian religion omitted), ran as follows:

William George hailed from an old Pembrokeshire Baptist family. He was born in Trecoed, one of the main farmsteads in the Fishguard area, in the year 1820. His parents were David and Mary George. His mother was a faithful and hard-working member of the old Baptist Church at Llangloffan. Trecoed was a preaching station, the pulpit being one of the main pieces of furniture in the house, and the travelling preacher was welcomed there as one of the family. It was in this environment that William George was brought up and he was trained in the healthiest principles of Nonconformist religion in Wales.

He was a man of average height but was strongly built with broad shoulders and a thin, pale face; a high, wide forehead; large, lively eyes indicating a quick and penetrative mind; a heart full of tenderness and sympathy; and all his gestures were quick, strong and determined. This was the man as he was described to us by someone who knew him well: '*Dyn ydoedd, dianwadal / Rhyw un dyn! i'w air yn dal.*' ['He was a man who was not fickle, A man who was true to his word.']

He was brought up to go into the educational profession. He served as a teacher for some time in London, and afterwards in a school in Liverpool which was under the auspices of the Unitarians. He himself was not a Unitarian, nor did he teach Unitarianism.... During his stay in Liverpool he formed a friendship with one of the clearest and most inspired thinkers of the nineteenth century - a man who left a deep and lasting influence on the literature and theology of his age - none other than Dr Martineau, the world-renowned Unitarian minister and teacher, and he continued to correspond with him for the rest of his life.

After leaving Liverpool he spent a short time running a Grammar school in Haverfordwest, but around 1857 he settled in Pwllheli as Headmaster of Troedyrallt British School. He proved himself to be an unparalleled disciplinarian, bringing order instead of disorder to the work of the school. He was an excellent musician and it is said that he was the first to teach the principles of the tonic sol-fa in the town. He was also a regular and committed teacher of a class of young men at the old Pentrepoeth Chapel Sunday School and some of his pupils remain to this day who hold his memory in high respect. They bear witness to the fact that he was a robust and principled thinker whose debating and reasoning skills were without equal. He was here when Dr Owen Davies was starting to preach, and he prophesied that the young man would become a man of importance and influence in his denomination, and of great service to his nation and country. During his time in Pwllheli, he married Elizabeth, daughter of Dafydd Llwyd of Llanystumdwy.

Around the end of the year 1859, he left for Newchurch, in Lancashire, and he and his family attended the Baptist Church at Cloughfold, a name that is renowned among Welsh Baptists due to the connection with Dr Abel Parry and the church in later years. In Newchurch, their daughter Mary Ellen (Mrs Phillip Davies, Criccieth) was born on 8 November 1861. He was here for only three years, as his health deteriorated. He was persuaded by Dr Morrell, the famous Inspector of Schools and English Grammarian, who was also a close friend of his, to take charge of an important school in Manchester for a few months until a suitable teacher could be found, and he agreed, and it was there, during this short stay, that David Lloyd George was born on 17 January, 1863.

During the same year, he and his family moved to Pembrokeshire, and he took a lease on a farmstead named Bwlffordd, approximately four miles from Haverfordwest, half way between Haverfordwest and Milford. He devoted himself to applying his scientific knowledge to agriculture and he was soon succeeding in the work, but oh! He was struck down in less than two years. He died suddenly of *pneumonia*, 7 June 1864, whilst still a young man of forty four, at 'Alban Hefin' (Summer Solstice) a time of life and hope! The lease and the property were sold and the widow and the daughter Mary Ellen and son David Lloyd came to live at Llanystumdwy with the grandmother and uncle and it was there, after his father had died, that the youngest son, William, was born on 23 February 1865.

It is clear from the above that our hero's father was a man of extraordinary intellectual and educational attainment, and that he was blessed with a robust humanity, or he would not have been able to fill the positions noted, or indeed gain the respect, trust and friendship of men of importance, learning and influence such as Dr Martineau and Dr Morell. [2]

Most of the source-material for this article would have been derived partly from William's favourite niece, Anne Williams, partly from his three children, recalling information told to them by their mother (who had died in 1896) and partly from Richard Lloyd, William's brother-in-law. Three years later, in 1912, Herbert du Parcq wrote a detailed biography of Lloyd George which incorporated into its opening chapter an account of William George written by Anne Williams. She was 74 by then and it is not clear whether she had produced it especially for du Parcq or whether it had been penned earlier. Totalling almost 800 words, it runs as follows:

William George's great-grandfather lived at Tresinwen, a farm on the North Pembrokeshire coast, on part of the land of which the new Strumble Head Lighthouse is built. Both he and his wife Anne were very highly esteemed by all in the neighbourhood and the country round. They were Baptists, and used to ride on horseback every month to the old chapel of Rhydwilym, of which they were members, to the Communion Service. They had two sons, David and Timothy. David, after he was married, went to Trecoed to live on a large farm a few miles from Fishguard. Both he and his wife were well known for their good and virtuous lives, and their hospitality, especially to ministers of the gospel, was unbounded. They had two sons, William and John. The elder son, William (the Chancellor's father), although he liked the country and loved nature, yet greatly disliked the idea of being only a farmer. His ambition, above all things, was to become a scholar, and he tried to draw his brother John into his way of thinking, telling him what a poor thing life would be for him if he remained all his days 'with his nose in the soil'. His mother was very anxious that he should go in for the medical profession, and he became apprenticed (as was the custom in those days) to Dr Miller of Haverfordwest; but the drudgery of the surgery did not suit his taste, especially as the doctor kept him too busy at work to admit of his having any leisure for study. The doctor also complained that he burned too much candle after he retired to his room for the night. William, therefore, sought a better chance of indulging his literary taste by entering a school in London as an articled pupil or pupil-teacher. He remained there for some years, and from there went to

Liverpool, where he remained for eight years as head master in charge of a school. While here he became acquainted with, and afterwards became a great friend of, Dr Henry Martineau and his daughter Harriet.

He used to spend his holidays at his home at Trecoed, making a round of visits to his many relatives and friends around. He was well up in affairs of State and current events, and especially well versed in politics, and an excellent talker - in fact, a brilliant conversationalist, genial and humorous withal, and possessing a very engaging manner, so that he was much sought after by all, especially the well-educated families, throughout the whole of North Pembrokeshire.

He was very fortunate in his marriage, and although short, his married life was exceptionally happy. In a letter to his mother he said he had been lucky enough to win one of earth's best and fairest daughters, and one he felt sure his mother would be proud to welcome as a dear daughter. Alas! that joy was not realised. His good mother, to whom he was very much devoted, died within a year after his marriage. Through some neglect he did not receive the news of his mother's death until it was almost too late for him to arrive at he funeral. He arrived at Trecoed just as the funeral cortège was leaving the house, and, the nearest station being sixteen miles away, the poor fellow had to walk all the way to his old home, after a long tedious journey, because no conveyance had been sent to meet him, although there were plenty of horses on the farm, and a trap as well. As soon as he arrived, he joined the procession, which meant another mile to walk, as the mother's coffin was carried to the cemetery by the tenants and servants at their express wish, to pay her a last token of respect.

He (my uncle) never could have properly recovered from that tremendous strain upon his body and mind, because it was not long after this trouble that he retired from school life. The prospect of a restful holiday at Trecoed had now been lost to him, together with the joy of personally introducing his dear wife to his mother. Consequently, he evidently bethought himself that a little farmhouse of his own would be the next best thing.

I had the pleasure of seeing them settled in their new home at Bwlford and of holding the infant David Lloyd George in my arms when he was three months old; his little sister Mary was then toddling about the room, being about fourteen or fifteen months old.

William George's death was caused by a chill taken while out gardening on a damp day, and pneumonia set in and took him away in less than a week after he was taken ill. [3]

Some of her information may, conceivably, have come from William himself but at one point she clearly drew upon the memories of his brother, who had died in 1907. It is a warm-hearted, honest account, written to the best of her ability, but there were various matters (such as the places where William studied and where he himself taught, not to mention his first marriage) about which she apparently knew nothing. Du Parcq, while incorporating it wholesale into his book, was able to draw upon the article written by Rees and to supply some supplementary information (based largely on family letters) and several useful dates, but it was basically Anne's account - some of it amounting to little more than hearsay evidence - to which most subsequent biographers of David Lloyd George turned during the sixty-five years which followed when seeking to produce potted summaries of William's life.

The George family, while fully co-operating with du Parcq's researches in the first instance, were greatly troubled by the publicity his four volumes subsequently received and reached the conclusion, within a very short space of time, that he had revealed far too much about their antecedents and private lives. They apparently banished his *magnum opus* from their bookshelves and would pretend, henceforth, that it had never existed. The corollary of this was that they were obliged to ignore its contents, however helpful, when working on narratives of their own.

There should also be noted, in passing, a further biography of Lloyd George by J. Hugh Edwards, the first volume of which was published in 1913. This is less informative, on the whole, than du Parcq's, and only of marginal importance. One is aware of a great deal of padding and a good many adjectives, but (apart from some helpful photographs, not seen elsewhere) there are occasional fresh snatches of information which catch the eye. On William's career after leaving Haverfordwest, we are told: 'He spent some years in London as a tutor in a private school, and while he imparted information on the one hand he at the same time replenished his own, day after day. From London he left to take charge of a school in Liverpool.' There is a quotation from a jubilant letter which he sent to 'a relative in Pembrokeshire' on the day David Lloyd George was born and a brief account of William's life at Bulford, both of which we will come to in due course. [4] The 'relative in Pembrokeshire', and cautious purveyor of snippets of information withheld from du Parcq, could only have been Anne Williams.

Anne was the daughter of William's sister Gwenllian (later known as Mary) and therefore the cousin of his children, one of whom (born posthumously) was another William. In July 1910 she also became this younger William's mother-in-law. In 1922 William Jnr decided to write a biography of his father and asked her to tell him all she remembered. She supplied him with what was, in essence, a much shorter version of the account printed by du Parcq. In the event, William abandoned the proposed biography and it was not until he wrote *My Brother and I* that Anne's second account (or a portion of it, at any rate) saw the light of day. The only respects in which it differs from its predecessor, penned at least ten years earlier, is that she now refers to William's employer as 'Doctor Mills' and suggests, rather more strongly, that it was William who took the initiative in terminating the apprenticeship, as he found the surgery duties 'irksome' and 'complained that they left him very little time for private study:'[5]

In the meantime W.D. Phillips, in *Old Haverfordwest*, had set down some statements of his own - which, for the most part, went unnoticed by the world at large. 'Mr William George', he told his readers,

> was the eldest son of Mr David George, of Trecoed, in the parish of Jordanston, near Fishguard. He was of a literary turn of mind, and although pressed to stay at home and manage the farm, he would not do so. He was articled to Dr Brown, of Haverfordwest, with the view of becoming a doctor. His bent, however, was for literature, in the pursuit of which he spent so much midnight oil that Dr Brown, realising that his inclinations were not for physic, advised his parents to let him pursue his literary studies. Mr George accordingly took up the position of tutor in London. Whilst there he became acquainted with Messrs. Murray (the well known publisher). He had access to the libraries and lectures, and thus acquired a profound knowledge of literature in its widest aspect. After remaining in London for about ten years, reasons of

health compelled him to return home, and for a few years he pursued his studies in his more congenial native air. He then opened a private school at Llysronen, Granston, near Mathry.

The accuracy of much of the preceding account is a wee bit questionable, for Mr Phillips (like many another Welsh story-teller, from Giraldus Cambrensis onwards) tended to succumb rather easily to the temptation of vivid and vigorous embellishment, but then comes the information about William's first wife that is genuinely fresh and would not be found anywhere else for more than seventy years. His brief outline of the remaining years of William's life is reasonably accurate, although he insisted that it was at *Manchester* that William made the acquaintance of Dr Martineau, 'the well known literateur [*sic*], with whom he became closely associated in the various branches of his work' - a wonderfully vague statement! [6]

As we have noted, W.R.P. George was not acquainted with *Old Haverfordwest* and its revelation about Miss Huntley. But when he wrote *The Making of Lloyd George*, and supplied a summary of his grandfather's early life, he acknowledged (without evincing any real curiosity in the subject) that William must have gone to school somewhere or other. He then reverted to Anne's earlier account (evidently sneaking a look at du Parcq) and to the name of 'Dr Miller':

> Contrary to the natural expectations of the family of widowed mother and sisters, William took no interest in farming. After leaving school he was apprenticed to a Dr Miller of Haverfordwest at the age of seventeen. It was the custom at that time for youths to work in a druggist's store before entering medical school to sit examinations. But William did not meet with Dr

Miller's approval because of his habit of burning the midnight oil to read books, thus making him less lively than he should have been in performing his chores in the store. He left Dr Miller to become apprenticed to a draper in a village five or six miles away. As he was of delicate health, his mother bought him a pony so that he could ride to and from his work. However, this way of life did not suit him as he was too tired to study when he got home. [7]

Dr George's account is a rehashed version of the one written by his grandmother in 1912 but expanded in three respects. He states that William was aged seventeen when he was apprenticed to Dr Miller and reveals, for the first time in a book, that William worked in a draper's shop after parting company with the doctor. Pinpointing William's age as seventeen was probably no more than a reasonable guess, and in 1916 some local Haverfordwest newspapers had excitedly publicised the revelation of his apprenticeship at a draper's shop - reports which may have been the prime source of Dr George's information in 1976. [8] The story about the pony is the only truly new scrap of information. Some twenty years later, however, assisting Mr Henry Harrison in his magnificent compilation of basic data about the Lloyd George family, Dr George amplified his account rather more significantly. After six months working as an apprentice to the doctor, he stated, William 'gave it up and spent a similar period acting as traveller for the General Store at Mathry, then as an assistant to a draper who lived in a nearby village'. [9] Maddeningly, the sources of this supplementary information are not known but they do have an undoubted ring of authenticity.

In 1976 Dr George also reproduced some potions of a journal which William started in 1839 and was also able to supply a considerable number of extracts from letters which he had written to members of his family and to friends, not to mention his ruminations on various matters, which greatly helped to build up a more convincing portrait of the man. As already noted, however, the details of the first marriage were still unknown to him at that time. (But redressing the balance with gusto almost thirty years later, a junior member of the family, a Mr Robert Lloyd George, would confidently assert that William had married *twice* while still in his twenties but that both his wives died childless. Whether the unfortunate young ladies in question were a Miss Ogmore and a Miss Pritchard will have to remain a matter for speculation.) [10]

So here we have five mini-biographies of William George produced over a period of eighty-six years. (And there may, of course, have been one or two more which have escaped notice.) They all tell what is basically the same story of a hardworking, conscientious young man cruelly beset by ill-health but they differ on details and dates. The *Pontypridd Chronicle* sheds fresh light - indeed, the *only* light - upon William's schooldays before it becomes slightly woolly about subsequent events. The Rev. Rees draws attention to Trecoed's function as a preaching station, a reference found nowhere else, while Anne Williams speaks from personal recollections - especially about the funeral of Mary George - but is hazy about her uncle's earlier life. (And oddly, like the *Chronicle* writer, she describes Harriet Martineau as the daughter of the Unitarian divine - who was a James, not a Henry - rather than his sister.) W.D. Phillips comes up with some emphatic assertions, most of them questionable but incorporating, it must be acknowledged, some factual nuggets of crucial importance. (It will be noted that by this time the complaint about too much candle-wax being consumed, originally attributed to his Haverfordwest landlady, has now been transferred to the local doctor - be his name Miller, Mills or Brown - to whom he had been apprenticed.) William's grandson ponders and probes over a long period of time, sometimes going back on himself and sometimes (as will be seen) going seriously astray in his conjectures, but he eventually supplies us with information about a pony and a couple of shops *not* in Haverfordwest where William was employed which seems to ring true - even though his source-material has proved elusive.

Not the least of the challenges for a fresh biographer of William George is the need to separate fact from fiction - and to bring to light, at the same time, some information that is genuinely new. 'Hearsay evidence', if it is the only kind available, is still better than no evidence at all. It undoubtedly helps to fill a void, provided its tentative nature is recognised, and where documents have totally disappeared from the record then the historian is obliged to fall back on cautious conjecture and to assess the likelihood of what may or may not have happened. But he should also treat with respect the work of those who have gone before him (who, in this instance, are primarily Henry Rees, Anne Williams and Dr George), however limited the range of their information might have been, and not to dismiss too casually the work of his forerunners. His own work may very well prove, after all, to be very far from the last word, and merely a link in a chain. For pioneering, in the last analysis, is an on-going activity.

2 - THE SON AND HEIR

William George was, like the second of his three sons, a heaven-sent replacement. An earlier William had died on 10 February 1818 at the age of three and his parents, David and Mary George, would have been anxious for a new son and heir to take his place - and, in due course, to inherit the management of their farmstead of Trecoed in the parish of Jordanston in north Pembrokeshire. Just how long they had to wait is uncertain, because there is no record of when the second William arrived. It is usually assumed that the event took place in 1820, for this is what the legend on his gravestone implies - 'departed this life June 7th 1864 aged 44' - but for the reasons set out in Appendix I it is far more likely that the year in question was 1821 (or even, just possibly, 1822). In the circumstances, while having sounded that initial note of caution, and accepting that in all probability the matter will never be resolved, it would seem practicable to proceed on the basis that he was born in 1821.

So far as the actual month is concerned, it is just possible that the event took place towards the end of May. A diary for 1839 was commenced at the beginning of June rather than January (and so too was one for 1842), which suggests that the notebook (a *Student's Journal*) may have been a birthday present from his mother. And he recorded on 20 May 1850 that his weight was 9 stone 10lbs, which may have been a way of marking a birthday. But this is no more than a tentative conjecture.

The place of his birth is not in doubt - or not, at any rate, quite so much. It would definitely have been in Jordanston, but whether at Trecoed or at an adjoining farm called Pantycoch, immediately to the north, will in all probability never be known. Precise data, once again, is lacking, but the indications are that his parents were married by

1803 (David having been born in 1782) and began their life together at Pantycoch, the 150 acres of which he leased from the Vaughan estate. His wife Mary, the daughter of William and Martha Charles, was a year younger than himself. Their first two children (Anne and Hannah) were born in 1804 and 1807 respectively. Two more daughters would follow (Phebe, in 1810 or thereabouts, and Gwenllian in 1813) before William, their short-lived first son and the first to bear that name, arrived in 1815. Martha, another daughter, had been born by 1819 and the second William, the subject of this biography, then arrived on the scene. Hannah, although only 13 (one year older than the minimum permitted age), married David James in January 1820 and they eventually took over the lease of Pantycoch. David George, who had still been its lessee in 1817, seems to have taken up the lease of Trecoed (a farm of 306 acres, roughly twice the size of Pantycoch, also part of the Vaughan estate) by 1821. One or other of these farms, in short, was the place where Mary George, in her late thirties, gave birth to the second William. [1]

The two people who would have loomed largest in his life, at such time as understanding began to dawn, would obviously have been his mother and father. Next came four sisters and then the servants employed in the house. For the house, in the first instance, comprised the whole of his world. As he began cautiously toddling about the farmyard, so he would have become aware of the people working for his father, who would greet him kindly but with a certain amount of deference - for he was, after all, an embryonic 'young master' - and this was the point at which he probably realised that he was in a land in which two different languages flourished. (In the first instance, however, he himself spoke nothing but Welsh.) And then, with horizons expanding still further, and after registering the existence of another sister and her husband, there would be two or three uncles and aunts and a batch of cousins to take into account - and finally, but far from least, two very venerable and perhaps rather awesome grandparents to be visited on special occasions and to be treated with a great deal of respect. (Moreover, and wonder of wonders, he would discover that his grandfather had exactly the same name as himself.)

It was a great deal for a small boy to absorb. And a great deal, by the same token, for the readers of this biography to absorb, especially since the author is obliged to confess that none of these people (apart from William's mother) will impinge on our narrative for very much longer. But the information needs to be placed on record, even though the scenes and the people of his childhood would play only a very limited part in William's life after he reached manhood, for we need to understand the world and the traditions in which he grew up.

By 1820 his grandfather, the elder William - although he had still another nineteen years to live - was already the majestic patriarch of the George family. Born in 1747, probably in the parish of Puncheston, he relinquished care of a family farm (Fagwrfran) to his (younger?) brother John in the 1780s and moved a few miles north-west to the parish of Llanwanda. He held the tenancies (or part-tenancies) of one or two different farms in that parish before acquiring, at a date unknown, that of Tresinwen, a substantial holding of 320 acres lying immediately south of Strumble Head and just over five miles from Trecoed. He had also (in 1780 or thereabouts) acquired a wife some five years younger than himself called Mary. Following David's arrival in 1782, she had presented her husband with three more sons - William, John and Timothy (born in 1786, 1789 and 1791 respectively) and two daughters (Anne and Mary, born 1787 and 1795 respectively).

So, on his father's side alone, William had three uncles and two aunts.

Uncle William (another namesake, but known locally as Wil Siors Bach) was a mariner away from home for much of the time, but he had married a Martha Evans in 1800 and they produced six children (four boys and two girls). Nothing is known of John and it is probable that he died young. Timothy lived at Tresinwen, where he assisted his father in running the farm. In due course he would take over the tenancy in accordance with the Welsh system of gavelkind, which (the exact opposite of its English counterpart) recognised the younger rather than the elder son as the natural heir. He had married a Mary Davies in 1817 and they are said to have had four children (two boys and two girls) during the four years which followed. On the assumption that Uncle Wil and his family were also living in the immediate area, William would have had a considerable number of cousins to play with. Aunt Anne had married a Joseph Owen in 1808 but little more is known about her, and nothing at all is known about her sister Mary. But they too might still have been living in the area.

William's mother was the daughter of a farmer living at Trefgarn Owen in the parish of Brawdy, six miles from Trecoed, and according to W.R.P. George had been a governess prior to her marriage. She had four brothers and one sister. Information about the Charles family is sparse, but it is reasonable to conclude that, in addition to a squad of Georges, young William came into occasional contact with relatives on his mother's side of the family - including, in particular, a cousin called Thomas Nicholas, whom we will meet again later on. [2]

Since the seventeenth century, ownership of the Jordanston estates had been vested in the Vaughan family who resided at Jordanston House, about half a mile from Trecoed. Thanks to the researches of Major Francis Jones, we know that in 1803 Gwynne Vaughan, as lord of the manor, 'leased the farm of Trecoed and four fields in the demesne of Jordanston, and three cottages and gardens, to Peter Meyler of Letterston, for three lives, at a yearly rent of £240, rendering two hens at Christmas, the carriage of two cart-loads (each cart containing four barrels) of coal or culm from Fishguard to Jordanston House, and six men to make hay for one day at Jordanston.' [3] This particular Vaughan died in 1808 and it is highly probable that his son, an unmarried gentleman of the same name, imposed similar feudal conditions on David George at such time as the latter took over the lease.

Jordanston was (and is) a quiet part of the world. A contemporary gazetteer records that it contained 157 inhabitants (rather more, indeed, than one might have expected). 'It appears to have derived its name from an ancient family estate within its limits, and is pleasantly situated in the north-western part of the county, being intersected by a stream which falls into the river Hog. The surrounding scenery is agreeably diversified, and the views of the adjacent country comprehend a pleasing variety of interesting features.' The church, located in close proximity to Jordanston House and dedicated to St. Cwrda, was 'a small neat edifice, appropriately fitted up for the performance of divine service, but not distinguished by any interesting architectural details.' [4] This account indicated that it was primarily a rural area and no mention was made of a cluster of ancient slate mines, located a few miles to the east, which were still being worked.

It must be assumed that Trecoed was a typical 'mixed' farm for that part of Pembrokeshire. Drawing somewhat hazily upon information from a much later period, and noting that about twenty fields, of very differing shapes and sizes, came to be pretty evenly divided between pasture and arable, it clearly possessed some livestock, in the form of cattle and sheep (supplemented, perhaps, by a few goats and pigs), but keen attention would be concentrated upon the annual harvests of corn, wheat and barley. The farmhouse would have been large, even then, capable of providing a roof over the heads of at least ten people at any one time and of being extended as the need arose. It would eventually develop into quite a formidable establishment. The census return for 1841, the first to shed any light on the matter, reveals that seven young people were employed there (three men and four women, most of them in their early twenties), but there were by then only three members of the family in residence. During the second half of the 1820s (when a series of wet summers resulted in very poor harvests, farmers' incomes dropped alarmingly and Pembrokeshire banks failed) one assumes that the number of servants would have been rather less, for the four daughters would have played a crucial role in helping to run the place and it was only as they married, and moved elsewhere, that the need for a fresh pair of hands, imported from outside, would have arisen. The number of servants-cum-farm workers present when William was growing up probably did not exceed four or five. He would have been trained to assist them in such basic tasks as feeding the chickens, with the well-intentioned but ultimately unsuccessful aim of gradually absorbing him into the administration of a family business which was arguably heading for a precarious and uninviting future. While lacking the precise words with which to put such a realisation into speech, it may have dawned on him, even then, that he was not cut out to be a farmer's boy.

In a sense, as well-established tenant farmers, the Georges could be regarded as constituting the next level down from 'the gentry' (as represented by the Vaughan family). Tradition had it, indeed, that the Georges had been among the Flemish supporters of Henry Richmond at the battle of Bosworth, and were rewarded for their services with grants of land in Pembrokeshire, but modern researchers, carefully scouring the records for chapter-and-verse, have been unable (as yet) to confirm this. Early biographers of David Lloyd George automatically referred to William's grandfather as a 'Yeoman' farmer, which has a splendid ring to it. But, although baritone voices might still occasionally proclaim the virtues of 'the Yeomen of England', summoning up an image of an army of John Bulls, pitchforks at the ready to repel invaders, we hear virtually nothing about 'the Yeomen of Wales'. The word has, in any case, rather lost its meaning in the twenty-first century. In more modern parlance, his grandparents might be regarded as trend-setters - or, at the very least, as senior and much respected members of the community. They set 'the tone' of their immediate neighbourhood. They were devout Baptists, as were their immediate descendants, and apparently rode on horseback every month to Rhydwilym Chapel at Llandissilio in Carmarthenshire, more than 20 miles away. It is probable that they contributed handsomely in 1828 to the building of Harmony Chapel at Pencaer, a short distance to the east of Tresinwen, where both of them would be buried.

Simple geography would form part of William's elementary education (a subject to be considered in more detail in our next chapter) but he would soon learn that he lived in a very mountainous country called Wales, to the west of - and governed by - a much bigger but less mountainous country called England. A little later, he would find that he lived in the southern half of Wales, in a county known as Pembrokeshire (the former kingdom of *Dyfed*). Then, as a further refinement, he would eventually discover that Pembrokeshire was itself unofficially divided into two parts, north and south, and that he himself happened to be located in its northern portion. This would be more than enough information for a youngster to absorb before reaching, say, the age of ten.

Pembrokeshire was, and is, quite unlike any of the other Welsh counties, for it is bounded by sea on its northern, western and southern sides. It juts out from Wales in much the same way as Cornwall juts out from England, apparently straining wistfully in the direction of Ireland, *fons et origo* of the Celts, and seeking to disassociate itself from its more immediate neighbours of Ceredigion (or Cardiganshire, as it was then known) and Carmarthenshire. A maritime county, its coastline of 170 miles and innumerable bays and sandy beaches was fast making it an intriguing and satisfying place for tourists and holiday-makers. 'The soil of Pembrokeshire', *Pigot's Directory* recorded in 1835, 'varies considerably, including the extremes of good and bad, with all the intermediate gradations: its surface is generally hilly, but not mountainous, and rendered fruitful by its numerous streams. The north-east portion is the mountainous tract, affording good pasturage to flocks of sheep. This part of the county also abounds in coal, and its coasts with iron-stone.' [5]

Exploring the southern coastline from east to west, one travels through the fishing village of Saundersfoot, the town and harbour of Tenby and the small resort of Manobier before reaching the major port of Milford Haven, located in close proximity to Pembroke Dock and Pembroke itself. The concave western coast embraces St Bride's Bay, with Haverfordwest and its castle almost ten miles inland from its midway point, and the miniature cathedral of St David adorns the point where the coastline zooms out again before swinging round in a north-easterly direction towards Strumble Head and the small resorts of Mathry and Goodwick. Then comes Fishguard, a favourite port for visitors to Ireland, and thence to the less well-known harbour of Newport. Cemaes Head marks the easterly termination point of the north Pembrokeshire coast.

Daniel Defoe, in the 1720s, had found Pembroke, and the port of Milford Haven, 'the most flourishing town of all

South Wales' and thereafter 'went to Haverford, or by some call'd Haverford-West'. He discovered 'a better town than we expected to find, in this remote angle of Britain; 'tis strong, well built, clean and populous.' After visiting St David's, 'or St Taffy's, as the Welch call it', he noted that 'the country begins to look like Wales again, dry, barren and mountainous'. Following the coastal route to Newport, which would have taken him within striking distance of Jordanston, he remarked that the country was rugged and mountainous and that 'the hills even darken'd the air with their height'. [6] The hills to which he referred were presumably the Preseli Mountains, some twelve miles east of Jordanston and the source, it has been claimed, of the stones from which Stonehenge was created. Ninety years later, starting out from his home at Fishguard, Richard Fenton embarked on Defoe's journey in reverse. A survey of Goodwick, only a short distance from his own doorstep, gave him pause for thought. 'The whole region round', he reflected, 'is a barren heath, secluded from the haunts of man, on which a few miserable sheep pick a scanty subsistence. Yet here are springs of the most delicious water, some known to ebb and flow, and the situations seems particularly adapted to druidical rites'. He rhapsodised over the cathedral of St David's, where the country's patron saint had established his see more than a thousand years earlier, and was greatly impressed with Haverfordwest, hailing it as 'indisputably the largest and most central [town] in the county.' [7] (It would eventually supplant Pembroke as the county's official heart of government.) Virginia Stephen, staying at Manorbier in 1908, would note that it was 'a lean country, scarcely inhabited' with 'green & gray sand hills, sprinkled with sheep, which is just colonised by a dozen sky gray cottages.' In 1934 she too found herself at Goodwick, and blithely informed her nephew that Wales was 'full of sheep and salmon rivers'. [8]

The country was indeed traversed by rivers, chief among which were the western and eastern arms of the Cleddau, starting from Milford Haven, which extended north-westwards and north-eastwards almost as far as the boundaries of the county would permit, but another line of division, albeit totally invisible, was of equal importance. This was the one that divided south Pembrokeshire, largely English-speaking (where the Charles family lived), from the largely Welsh-speaking northern part of the county (where the George family lived). It has been referred to as 'the landsker line', but there has been much uncertainty as to when this term came into general use - if, indeed, it ever did - and it is highly unlikely that the description would ever have been familiar to William. [9] It might be regarded as an intangible version of the Berlin Wall but the important thing to note is that south Pembroke came to be known as 'Little England beyond Wales', where (in theory) all the English-speaking inhabitants of the county clustered and as the place where visitors from England felt most at home.

The county has its place in history. The Normans had built castles at Pembroke, Tenby and Haverfordwest. Young Henry of Richmond, with an appointment to keep at Bosworth Field, landed at Milford Haven in August 1485 and marched off via Haverfordwest, while a motley band of Frenchmen, in a moment of madness, landed at Fishguard in February 1797 and attempted their own invasion of England - surrendering, after a few days, to the local militia reinforced by indignant local residents. The colourful notion that William's ancestors had assisted in the defeat of King Richard III has already been touched upon, but there is perhaps rather more justification for assuming that members of the George family were involved, in some way or another, in suppressing the very last invasion of the British Isles.

There would be one more addition to the family at Trecoed, for in 1826 or 1827 Mary George (now into her mid-forties) gave birth to her final child. It proved to be another son, and the proud parents named him John (presumably after his deceased uncle). So William was no longer the youngest member of the household. (And as it happens, though nobody knew this at the time, John was destined to be the *true* heir.)

But disaster now struck. David George died on 7 May 1828 at the age of forty-six, the cause of his death not being recorded. His widow, with two young sons and four daughters with which to cope, endeavoured to manage the farm single-handed to the best of her ability but it was an unequal struggle. On 1 April 1830 she married Benjamin Williams from the parish of Castle Blythe, aged thirty-two and some sixteen years her junior. (She signed the marriage register with her mark, which casts a shade of doubt on the notion that she had once been a governess.) In effect, Benjamin now assumed control of the farm, although the lease remained in Mary's name for another twelve years.

Two of her daughters, Hannah and Phebe, married in 1831 and a third, Gwenllian, in 1834; Martha would not follow suit until 1840. John, throughout the 1830s, would be growing up and making himself useful at Trecoed, in much the same way (we assume) as his elder brother had done during the 1820s. But this confronts us with an unpalatable truth, namely that the history of William George during the first nineteen years of his life is an almost total blank. There are only three things which we know for sure. The first is that he was a voracious reader, absorbing virtually anything that came his way - 'poor Mother', he recalled in 1862, 'often used to wonder what pleasure I had in reading "that old newspaper".' [10] The second is that, until the age of nine, he was fluent in the Welsh language (knowing scarcely a word of English) and had virtually forgotten his native tongue ten years later. The third is that he found the notion of spending his adult life working on a farm totally repugnant.

So where did he learn to read? And how is it that he was, by the age of eighteen, speaking impeccable English, reading Bulwer Lytton's latest novel, and displaying a startling degree of knowledge about the world in general? The answers to these perplexing questions must be sought in our next chapter.

3 - THE SCHOOLBOY AND THE APPRENTICE

We do not know how or where William George was educated. But encountering, as we will very shortly, a youth who is obviously intelligent and equipped with a wide English vocabulary, it is clear that the quality of education he received was remarkably high. The period of that education presumably occurred between 1826 and 1836 and the primary facilities available to him during that period must be largely a matter of conjecture.

In the very first instance, William would presumably have been educated at home, picking up knowledge from his mother and his sisters. It is improbable, for the reason already indicated, that his mother had been a fully-fledged governess, as claimed by Dr George, but she may well have been a nurse-maid or nanny in a large house for a year or two, equipped to relate simple stories and perhaps even able to impart some elementary information to her son. From the age of seven or eight, however, William would have needed more professional tuition. Jordanston was a parish, not a village, and there is no record of anything equivalent to a village school ever having existed in close proximity to Trecoed. We do possess some 'snapshots', however, of the local facilities - further afield than Jordanston - that were available at the beginning of 1847 and the chances are that those facilities were not wildly dissimilar from those which existed ten or twenty years earlier.

Before perusing the snapshots in question, however, it may be helpful to put them in context - to display them in an album, as it were - and to have some idea of the general level of education reached in the Principality by the 1830s.

Wales was, traditionally (and perhaps unfairly) regarded as a 'backward' area when it came to education, a state of affairs which the controversial Blue Books of 1847 would seemingly confirm. But it was not from want of trying.

In the eighteenth century the 'circulating' schools pioneered by Griffith Jones, and continued by Madam Bridget Bevan of Laugharne after his death, had made an impact and their effect lingered on in many areas, even though the funds available for that movement were in short supply after the 1790s: 'Mrs Bevan's charity schools', as they came to be known, remained in existence and were still a very active force in the land fifty years later. The original 'charity schools' had emanated with the Society for the Propagation of Christian Knowledge (SPCK) in the early eighteenth century, but were confined largely to England. Griffith Jones tackled the problem of Wales, with its thinly-spread population and mountainous terrain, by the ingenious notion of schools which would 'circulate' rather in the manner of a travelling circus, regularly spending three months in a particular locality, usually in the winter time. Dissenters, as well as Anglicans - and adults, as well as children - were made welcome and the schools proved immensely popular.

By the dawn of the nineteenth century there was a growing feeling that the subject of education should be treated on a more systematic and national basis. A London-based Quaker, Joseph Lancaster, pioneered in 1806 a system of non-denominational schools which should be available to all, and made earnest attempts to publicise his methods. But there were limits to what could be achieved by one man, however industrious: in 1811 his work was taken over by a committee which developed into the British and Foreign Schools Society (BFSS) in 1814. Its 'British' schools met with the approval of Whigs, Radicals and dissenters (of whom there were now a vast number in Wales). The Church authorities, alarmed by Lancaster's activities, and the prospect that the prestige of their own schools would now be actively challenged, meanwhile established, in 1811, the National Society for Promoting the Education of the People in the Principles of the Church of

England. It redoubled its efforts to build 'National' schools in which all pupils, whatever their religion, read the Bible and learnt the catechism and the liturgy of the Church. They were warmly supported by the Tories.

Two great societies thus battled for supremacy in the sphere of education, and in 1833 the Government acknowledged that the State also had a role to play - a moral responsibility, indeed - in shaping the nation's future. It made available, from the national exchequer, the sum of £20,000 to supplement private subscriptions towards building schools for the poorer classes. Throughout the remainder of the 1830s this annual sum would be steadily increased, although the BFSS was none too pleased to find that, in the early years at any rate, 80% of the funds made available went towards Anglican projects.

And then, of course, there were 'the others' - a vast number of tiny schools and academies (sometimes amounting to no more than somebody's front room), especially in the towns. 'There is no satisfactory means', Paul Langford has remarked, 'of estimating the numbers educated in private schools, or even the number of schools themselves. They sprang up and withered away wherever individual enterprise and public interest dictated.... Whatever the curriculum, these were in the strictest sense commercial activities. There were no charters, no rules, no governors: only the individual educational entrepreneur offering his [or her] services in a highly competitive but ever-expanding market.'[1] He is writing of the eighteenth century, but his comments are equally applicable to the greater part of the nineteenth. (Dickens, in 1838, would be drawing attention to the dubious educational standards maintained by some of the notorious 'Yorkshire' schools, as exemplified by Mr Wackford Squeers.)

At which point, we can return to those 'snapshots'. Working clockwise, the parish of Jordanston was surrounded by six others - Manorowen, Llanstinan, Letterston, Mathry, Granston and St Nicholas. Early in 1847 a squad of Government Commissioners would carry out a detailed and systematic examination of what facilities were then available in Wales, county by county, on a hundreds and parish basis. [2] We find that, as was the case with Jordanston itself, there were no schools in Manorowen, Granston or St Nicholas. But Llanstinan, Letterson and Mathry did have some facilities to offer.

At Llanstinan, the Commissioner, David Lewis, noted that there was 'a substantial schoolroom built in a corner of the churchyard.... The only furniture there was a long table and two small benches. This table when I entered was covered in earthen pots belonging to the master, who also uses the building as a dwelling house. In one corner of the room was a wretched bed supported by two small benches. There was a small fireplace in the room. The children were not present. The master some years ago had been a master of one of Mrs Bevan's charity schools'.

William Morris, investigating Letterston, found that the school consisted of one room, equipped with a desk and four benches. 'The principal supporter of the school is Charles Matthias, Esq, of Lamprey Court, near Pembroke, who pays £6 a year for teaching poor children of the parish. The master spoke English tolerably well. He had been a prisoner in France for nine years, and while a prisoner he acquired such information as he possesses'. The scholars were the children of farmers, mechanics and labourers. 'The master said that a great many parishioners are too poor to pay the smallest sum for their children's education.'

Lewis reports that, on 19 January, he visited the Rehoboth day-school in the parish of Mathry. 'It was held in the Independent Chapel. The children had not been in attendance for the last five weeks on account of the severe

43

weather. There was no school furniture in the chapel. The master told me that the boys were in the habit of writing on the seats of the pews. The master, who was also minister of Rehoboth Independent Chapel, was far from being conversant with the English language.' The following day he called at a day-school at Harmony, near to Tresinwen. 'It was kept by a very ignorant young man who had previously been a sailor.' Six pupils were present, two of them aged 15 and 20. They knew nothing of the Old Testament and their knowledge of the New Testament proved to be very muddled. A boy studying arithmetic was unable to subtract a farthing from £1,000: 'the way he attempted it was by reducing the £1,000 into farthings, and then he could not tell me the remainder.' Two other children, aged about six and eight, were grappling with Charles Vyse's *Spelling Book*, first published in 1776.

It is conceivable that William attended a school of this nature at some stage but, clearly, they were none of them particularly impressive. One question needing to be considered is his social status at this time. The death of his father in 1828, and his mother's marriage to Benjamin Williams two years later, meant that he was a semi-orphan and, in a sense, surplus to family requirements. A perpetual bookworm, with no great interest in farming or the outdoor life, he was clearly something of a cuckoo in the Trecoed nest. Relations between himself and his step-father, despite good intentions, may well have been strained. Could he have been regarded (in modern parlance) as a charity case and eligible for attendance at a free school for hard-up scholars?

The likelihood is that his grandfather, the senior William George, came to the rescue. (He might even have acted in concert with William's *other* grandfather, assuming that the latter was still alive.) All other things being equal, and given that he was evidently a lad of quite remarkable intelligence - just like his cousin Thomas Nicholas, indeed, who was meanwhile being educated at a prestigious grammar school in Liverpool - special measures seemed called for. It would be reasonable to suspect at this point that William became a boarder at Haverfordwest's illustrious Free Grammar School, founded in 1488 (and destined to last for almost five hundred years). We know from contemporary reports by the Charity Commissioners that there were 70 free scholars in 1835, one of whom (in this scenario) might have been William, and by 1847 there would be only three paying scholars, the rest of the pupils being admitted free of charge. (There were no boarders by that time.)

Lewis submitted a series of written questions to James Thomas, the headmaster, in 1847. In response to the first, asking what subjects were taught, there came the reply: 'English grammar, history and geography; Latin and Greek; Euclid, and in some cases the elements of logic. The upper boys read Euripides, Homer, and Greek Testament; Horace, Virgil; [Thomas Kerchever] Arnold's *Latin and Greek Exercises*. They usually do hexameters and pentameters from [Robert] Bland.' Boys were admitted to the school from the age of eight onwards, he explained, and were 'very irregular as to their time of leaving'; some left very soon, some stayed eight or nine years.

It was not quite the centre of excellence, however, that these initial replies had implied. Asked whether the managers of what was both a public and a charity school were enabling it to meet its full potential, there came a rather disillusioned reply from the headmaster. 'As a school for providing a cheap classical education for the children of respectable parents,' he conceded, 'it might be much benefited by the corporation's declining to send boys of so low a station in life, and who come very ignorant, and often cannot find books to continue their studies; in which case they often abruptly leave just at the time when the master expects to see some fruit, or at least some promise of fruit, from his labours.' 'I believe', he added, 'the letter of the law is kept by the corporation. In my opinion, however, they have acted very injudiciously, lowered the character of the school, and deprived the master of all hope of increasing his income by pay scholars of a respectable class. A stock of good elementary books would be the best thing (under circumstances) to make the school more efficient.'

'Some stay eight or nine years.' One would like to think that William, classified as a 'scholar of a respectable class', was one of those who did. From the biographer's point of view, this would be a very convenient way of accounting for those 'lost' years of the 1830s - for the period from 1828 to 1837, say. Haverfordwest was in the southern half of Pembrokeshire, where - in theory - the residents spoke nothing but English. William himself, writing in 1858, declared that although Welsh was his mother tongue, and he had known very little English before his ninth birthday, he had spoken almost nothing but English *since* that birthday. 'The English language', he said with assumed ruefulness (for he was addressing a Welsh Baptist Minister at the time), 'has done with me what the English people have done with our country - taken possession of the richest and largest part of it. No sooner do I use two or three Welsh words than their bolder English brethren thrust forward and the poor timid Taffies shrink back to hide themselves and I cannot, in spite of the utmost effort, find them again in time.' [3]

We have, too, the assertion in the *Pontypridd Chronicle*, to the effect that he attended the town's grammar school, lodged with 'a pious old lady' and studied *Paradise Lost*. There is, however, one huge objection to the notion that he was attending Haverfordwest Free Grammar School *throughout* this period. For in 1862, reassuring Richard Lloyd that fifteen-year-old David Lloyd Jones (for whom he was then acting in *loco parentis*) was coping very well in a strange part of the country, he recalled how he himself 'went to London when I was younger than David, & I well remember how wretched I felt for the first few weeks'. He then 'got better' but in the first instance it had been a 'bitter experience'. 'All who go out to the world to fight their own way must go through this hardening process,' he robustly reflected, '& the sooner the better. The griefs of early life are often very bitter but they are almost always of very short duration in comparison with those of after years.' [4]

This letter, if it is to be taken literally, drives a coach-and-horses through the accepted idea of how William's life developed after his boyhood at Trecoed. He is asserting, at the very least, that he had taken up residence in the Great Wen at the age of fourteen and had been domiciled there for many weeks. Now it may be, of course, that he was greatly exaggerating, as a means of putting his brother-in-law's mind at rest, and that he was referring to his stint at the teacher's training college in Battersea which he would join early in 1841. But a difference of six years (between the ages of fourteen and twenty) is quite considerable and, from all we know about him, William was not by nature an untruthful man. The age of fourteen, moreover, is slightly late in he day for such an education to commence, and he may well have been sent to London at the age of twelve (i.e., in 1833). Unless further evidence on this subject comes to light, all one can do is to note the existence of this letter and the fact that it casts serious doubt on the theory that he was living in Haverfordwest, or in close proximity to Trecoed, throughout the 1830s. He could well have been at a boarding school in London for much of this period. (His mother would have been gratified, for such an establishment would clearly have been superior to the one in Liverpool to which her nephew had been sent: the possibility of sibling rivalry cannot be discounted.) And this may even have been the time when, in the words of W.D. Phillips, William 'had access to the libraries and lectures' the capital had to offer.

One thing of which we can be certain, however, is that the love of learning, which had been an intrinsic part of his make-up from the very outset, was now developing at a rapid pace. His studies as such were far from over, and he may have been slowly reaching the conclusion that only if he himself became a teacher would he be able to fulfil his potential and be truly satisfied. But teachers were not necessarily held in high regard at that time and his mother apparently had a rather more ambitious plan in mind for her son's advancement. For we must return to the story that, when his schooldays came to an end, she arranged for him to be apprenticed to a doctor in Haverfordwest - to Dr Miller or Mills, according to Anne Williams, or to Dr Brown if the Phillips account is followed.

The records for Haverfordwest in 1833, embodied in an edition of *Pigot's Directory*, show that there were three physicians and nine surgeons resident in the town at that time. The three physicians bore the surnames Harries, Morgan and Reynolds; the nine surgeons, ranging from John Tasker-Evans to William Warlow, included in their ranks a certain George Millard, based in the High Street. There was no-one called either Miller or Brown. Nor do those names feature in the list of the town's nine 'Chymists and Druggists'. The equivalent directory for 1844 lists, rather surprisingly, no physicians at all, while a list of eight surgeons includes most of the 1833 names. George Millard, now based in Market Street, is still there, but on this occasion - as would be appropriate for someone scheduled to become the town's mayor two years later - his middle name, Llewellin, is supplied. A surgeon called James David Brown, based in Tower Hill (whom we will meet again), is a newcomer, but he was almost William's contemporary.

The notion of a 'Dr Brown' cannot be totally ruled out, but he does not appear in the town's 1841 census returns and preference should probably be given to Anne William's slightly more reliable recollections. (Phillips was not necessarily infallible on such matters.) The strong likelihood is, therefore, that it was George Llewellin Millard (1794 - 1862) who became William's first employer and that, many years later, his name would be imperfectly recalled as either 'Miller' or 'Mills' by William's niece.

If Dr George's assumption about dates is roughly correct, it would have been in 1837, roughly coinciding with the accession of Queen Victoria, that William went to work in Haverfordwest. John Brown, one of his contemporaries, has provided a good eye-witness account of the town as it looked to a keen-eyed youth in the 1830s. (Born in 1817, or thereabouts, he would eventually succeed his father as the town's wine merchant.) The little burghers who ran the shops, he recalled in 1882, 'seemed to me all short, little, fat men, who, one would think, had been run in a mould; and their "good condition", as we say, was doubtless occasioned by their sticking so close to business and taking little exercise. In these shops you might get supplied with calicoes, striped cotton, groceries, etc. There were two or three proper drapers' shops, but the common people were generally dressed in homespun articles, and but few affected broadcloths or silks. The masters were always behind the counters, or in the small rooms behind their shops, overlooked by a small glass door, from early morn to dewy eve;' - clearly, he too had studied *Paradise Lost* - 'for as trade was not very pressing, they did not require many holidays. The shops were fitted up in comfortable style, with deal counters and shelves, and small windows, as unlike as possible to the establishments of today.' [5]

There is obviously little that one can add to Anne William's basic account of William's short-lived apprenticeship to a doctor in Haverfordwest. The probability is that his mother did indeed wish him to pursue a career in medicine, since farming did not appeal, but that William himself very soon made up his mind that he wanted to become a teacher. Haverfordwest was presumably a town that he found quite agreeable, for he would return there in the mid-1850s.

So it can be surmised that late in 1837 or early in 1838 William and the doctor parted company, to their mutual relief, and that William now embarked on an onerous programme of study. 'I have taken all knowledge to be my province,' Francis Bacon had declared in 1592 - adding for good measure, five years later, 'Knowledge is power.' [6] Slogans such as these could well have appealed to the very ambitious, conscientious young scholar, as he redoubled his efforts to complete what was evidently some kind of preordained syllabus. In the meantime, he had to earn a living, for it was impossible that his mother and his grandfather should go on supporting him indefinitely, and in the absence of any other information we may cautiously accept Dr George's statement that he now became a traveller for the General Store at Mathry for another six months or so. Mathry is a small coastal village, located on a hilltop to the west of Fishguard. If William was helping to deliver the shop's wares to people in the neighbourhood, then this may be the occasion when the pony proved a very useful asset. For reasons shortly to become apparent, the notion that, later in 1838 or early in 1839, William became an assistant to a draper can also be cautiously accepted - but it was evidently *not* on a full-time basis, and the suggestion that it was located 'in a nearby village' is questionable. [7]

William's grandfather and namesake, the patriarchal William George of Tresinwen, died on 10 April 1839 (almost four years after his wife) at the impressive age of 92. It is conceivable that he made special provision for his semi-orphaned grandson in his will but we have no means of knowing whether this was the case.

Frustratingly, the greater part of our narrative, up to this point, has been taken up with surmise and speculation. Suddenly, but for a limited period only, the mists clear away. William, and the world which he inhabits in the early summer of 1839, become unbelievably crystal-clear. For, by a huge stroke of luck, his diary for June and the first week of July still exists. The entries give a reasonably detailed account of what he was doing during those weeks and his frame of mind. He emerges as a well-read, anxious, conscientious and hard-working young man, albeit sanctimonious and self-conscious - and pining for a decent girl friend to whom he can pour out his hopes, ambitions and worries. It tells us a great amount although tantalizingly silent on the matter of precisely where he was living. For the moment, however, in the chapter that follows, William is able to speak for himself for the very first time, and we must seek to derive whatever benefit and clarification we can from his remarks.

4 - A STUDENT'S JOURNAL

Towards the end of May 1839, a month after the death of his grandfather, William acquired a small notebook measuring 7.5 by 4.5 inches with the words *Student's Journal* on the cover. It may have been a (birthday?) present or it may, for reasons to be explained in a moment, simply have caught his eye in a stationer's shop-window. He made daily entries in it very conscientiously for three weeks, slackened off in the fourth, resumed it briefly in the fifth and then - while ending on a note of jubilation - completely lost interest. There would be no more entries made in 1839 - nor, indeed, in 1840 - but he would still use it thereafter, primarily as a record of his expenses in the 1840s. (He may also have used it for its original purpose when he resumed keeping a diary in 1842, a subject to which we will return in due course.) A summary of its contents, in the form in which it currently exists, will be found in Appendix II. [1]

The notebook ran to 138 numbered pages. Pages 37 to 108 are now missing, as are fourteen others, but one assumes that the official diary element occupied pages 2 to 104 (the remaining thirty-four being left blank). The pages on the left-hand side (*verso*) of that element were divided into four sections (for Monday, Tuesday, Wednesday and Thursday) and those on the right-hand side (*recto*) into three sections (Friday and Saturday being allotted the same space as their predecessors and Sunday, as a day of rest and serious meditation, being granted a double-portion). The printers had headed *verso* pages with the words '**Day of**' and *recto* pages with '**183-**', leaving the diligent student to fill in the blanks. With the end of the 1830s almost in sight, it is very likely that the price of this little notebook had been drastically reduced: William, who always invested his pennies very carefully, might well have thought it a bargain.

So far as the first week was concerned, he christened page 2 by heading it '2nd **Day of** June 1839' - a slightly unfortunate beginning, since the Monday of that week was actually the 3rd. (He had it right for the following Monday - 10th June - and continued correctly so far as subsequent *verso* pages were concerned.) The entries are written in pencil and in very small script on the first three days (almost equivalent to hieroglyphics on microfilm), but thereafter they tend to become shorter and the size of the writing increases. Unfortunately, there are places where the writing develops into an elongated scrawl and, with sundry abbreviations, becomes extremely difficult to decipher. William also started jotting down items of expenditure in whatever space remained after his main entry. W.R.P. George perused this journal in 1976 and quoted several extracts from it in *The Making of Lloyd George*. [2] It was an admirable piece of pioneering work but Dr George's transcriptions were sometimes abridged, sometimes edited and sometimes wrong. (But it should be emphasised that the present writer, despite having devoted much time to studying the text with the aid of a magnifying glass bearing Baker Street antecedents, and deriving great benefit from the suggestions of a very patient friend, lays no claim to infallibility. There are two or three sentences which have obstinately refused to yield up their meaning and, with the best will in the world, can only be reproduced as they apparently stand for others to ponder upon and exclaim '*Eureka!!!*' as enlightenment dawns.)

The entries for the first week, which reveal that William was working in a store (though not on a full-time basis) and reaching the end of a rather unhappy involvement in amateur theatricals, run as follows:

[*Mon, 3rd June*] Today began a very eventfull week. The morning was spent between attending to my duties at the store and preparing myself for the theatrical performances tomorrow evening. Spent an hour alone after dinner in rehearsing my part. From that till six I was again occupied in preparing as before. After tea I attended the rehearsal at the Theatre which lasted till near ten o'clock; did not get on very well with my part. I have not bustle and energy for it!

[*Tues, 4th June*] This morning again I was occupied principally in preparation for the performance in the evening. Spent some time in rehearsing my part; found that it did not at all suit me; and I was very low spirited in consequence. After dinner, I spent some time in the store, went to the Theatre to rehearse my part & got through rather better than the previous evening. Still I greatly fear a failure. Took some stimulants in the evening hoping that I should get on better, but overstept the mark and I did it much worse than at either of the rehearsals.

[*Wed, 5th June*] Got up this morning at a late hour and with a severe headache. Felt deeply mortified at my failure on the previous evening, for I cannot conceal the fact from myself any more than from those who witnessed it that it was a failure. I derived however some consolation from the fact that some of the leading qualities of the character of Capt. Levant are those which it is no misfortune I do not possess. In the evening I attended the fireworks at the bowling green in company with my friend Mr Brett.

[*Thurs, 6th June*] The whole of this day was spent in the usual monotonous routine of business, untill the evening when I went to the Harmonia Society's concert.

[*Fri, 7th June*] This morning I was principally preoccupied in business during the morning [*sic*] & part of the afternoon. Read very little & that little was of a desultory character. Find that the proceedings of the last fortnight has [*sic*] unsettled me very much. In the evening I attended the meeting at the Theatre.

[*Sat, 8th June*] This morning I was occupied in business as usual.

[*Sun, 9th June*] The greater part of the morning I spent in arranging my books, after which I dressed and took a short walk before dinner. After dinner I spent some time at my a/cs. That done, I went for a long walk which I enjoyed very much, the weather being delightfully fine, but still I derive nowhere enjoyment, I am not happy, I want enthusiasm, energy, and *uniformity*. I have [done] little today but intend beginning in earnest tomorrow and to go on with my German & French untill Mr W's return when I shall begin Maths. Thus ends the History of the first week of my Journal; it contains nothing but paltry commonplaces, but I hope that in a little bit I shall improve.

Introspection already looms large, in short. The information gained from this first week's entries tell us that William was working at a store while pursuing academic studies, that he was based in lodgings (perhaps, indeed, the home of the store-owner) where breakfast and dinner were supplied on a regular basis, that there were fireworks on a bowling green, that he had a friend called Mr Brett and that there was a meeting of the Harmonia Society.

And, of course, that he was involved with a Theatre (always mentioned with a capital T). Although he had obviously not been at his best in his most recent performance, his desire to tread the boards (as we will see shortly) would remain unabated. (Sadly, it has proved impossible to identify the play in which 'Capt. Levant', the gentleman with the dubious qualities, featured. An *HMS Levant* had been captured by the United States in February 1815, at the very tail-end of the naval war, and while she undoubtedly possessed a captain, and the situation was certainly dramatic, there does not appear to be any record of a stage play resulting from this event.)

The opening words of Sunday's entry are ambiguous. They suggest, on a first reading, that William already possessed a small and extensive private library and that arranging it to his satisfaction had taken up most of the morning. Subsequent journal entries raise the strong possibility, however, that the word 'books' simply refers to the accounts of the store where he worked during the week: Sunday was a 'day of reckoning' in a purely commercial sense. (There was evidently no question of going to chapel, let alone church - for the moment, religious observance did not loom high among his priorities.)

Despite a question-mark hanging over that initial word 'books', literary matters certainly held an interest for him, as the two opening entries of the following week make clear, and the United Abstinence Society [3] is now mentioned for the very first time:

> [*Mon , 10th June*] Was called this morning at 6 intending to get up, but could not muster resolution enough and fell asleep again. Got up at 8 after breakfast went to business, where I cont'd untill dinner, went to Mr Walker, took up *The Man of the World* which I read through, liked the character of Egerton

very much, should like to play part! I went to the dancing class. 7 [o'clock] U.A. Society mtg. 9 [o'clock]. Fireworks in the garden. Paid [*Journal ?*] 19/-, U.A. Soc. 1-0, Fireworks 19-6.

[*Tues, 11th June*] Got up at 6 with intention of going to bathe, but afterwards thought it too cold. Went for a walk on the bank, on my return copied *Ernest Maltravers* till breakfast. Store till dinner. I went to the gardens in the evening. Heard a lady play on the musical glasses very beautifully but was deprived the pleasure by the insulting conduct of a fellow towards Miss P. which made me unhappy the rest of the e'ning.

The Man of the World (which takes at least ninety minutes to read) was a comic five-act play by the Irish actor Charles Macklin, written in the early 1760s but not staged at Covent Garden until 1781 (having met, initially, with the censor's disapproval). It is a fast-moving, extremely enjoyable piece of work, very nearly in the same league as *She Stoops to Conquer* and *The School for Scandal*. In the original production Macklin himself played the title role, a scheming Scottish M.P. called Sir Pertinax Macsycophant who has acquired his fortune, over many years, by bowing and scraping to complacent superiors, taking advantage of their carelessness and always having an eye to the main chance. His current plan is to obtain control of the estates of Lord Lumbercroft, a good-natured but heavily impoverished spendthrift, semi-intoxicated for much of the time, which will give him (among other things) possession of three parliamentary seats. Charles Egerton is actually Sir Pertinax's elder son, but has recently adopted his mother's maiden name in order to inherit an estate from his great-uncle (who detested the thought of its passing into the hands of anyone called Macsycophant). He is a pleasant, lively, well-educated and clean-living young man. Sir Pertinax wants him to become more politically active, in the family's interest. He also intends him to marry the daughter of Lord Lumbercroft, as part of the deal about to be formally concluded with that gentleman, but Egerton is in love with Constantia, his mother's penniless ward, and has no intention of plighting his troth with Lady Rodolpha Lumbercourt.

Everything works out well for all parties in the end, for it turns out that Lady Rodolpha is actually in love with Sir Pertinax's *other* son (whom we never meet), and aspersions cast by the wicked old schemer at Constantia's virtue prove to be totally unfounded. Egerton's virtue is sharply contrasted with his father's cunning: he makes it clear that he is anxious to obey his father so far as he reasonably can, but will do nothing in 'direct opposition to my character and my conscience'.

> SIR PERTINAX. Conscience! Why, ye are mad! Did ye ever hear ainy mon talk of conscience in poleetecal matters? Conscience, quotha? I hai been in Parliament these three and thratty years, and never heard the tarm made use of before - sir, it is an unparliamentary word, and ye wull be laughed at for it - therefore I desire ye wull na offer till impose upon me wi' sic phantoms, but lat me ken yeer reason for thus sleeghting my freends and disobeying my commands. Sir, gi' me an immediate and an axpleecit answer.

> EGERTON. Then, sir, I must frankly tell you, that you work against my nature; you would connect me with men I despise, and press me into measures I abhor; would make me a devoted slave to selfish leaders, who have no friendship but in faction - no merit but in corruption - nor interest in any measure, but their own - and to such men I cannot submit; for I know, sir, that

the malignant ferment which the venal ambition of the times provokes in he heads and hearts of other men, I detest.

Sir Pertinax accuses his son of being mad, for expressing these and similar sentiments, but Egerton triumphs in the end, being united with Constantia and (as we have seen) not being too badly off so far as worldly goods are concerned, and brings the proceedings to an end with the following reflection:

My scheme, though mocked by knave, coquet, and fool,
To thinking minds will prove this golden rule;
In all pursuits, but chiefly in a wife,
Not wealth, but morals, make the happy life. [4]

One can understand, in short, why this is a character whom William would have been extremely happy to portray on the stage. His idealism, combined with his practicality, held obvious attractions. William was doubtless yearning to leap to the defence of Miss P. in much the same way as Egerton had come to the defence of Constantia.

And there was an almost parallel fictional case which he was absorbing at this time.

Ernest Maltravers, by Edward Bulwer Lytton, had been published in three volumes in 1837. It is a High Society novel covering a period of almost twenty years. To be more precise, it is only *half* a novel, for it was continued in another three volumes entitled *Alice.* It tells the tale of a young couple (he very rich, she very poor) who fall in love and beget a child - although the hero, in noble ignorance, does not realise this at the time. But they are then abruptly separated, rediscovering each other (after many vicissitudes) only in the final chapters. Whether William was able to get through all six volumes we will never know. But the story evidently appealed to him. Its hero, when the tale begins, is an intelligent student returning to his native land after studying at Göttingen, still intent upon mastering Shakespeare and Schiller. He is only eighteen years old, so this is clearly someone else with whom William would have been able to identify.

One assumes that William had borrowed *Ernest Maltravers* from a branch of Mudie's circulating library. We know that on 11 June he copied out certain passages which caught his attention - and he would do so on the following day as well. The likelihood is that one of those passages would have been the following:

> We are apt to connect the voice of Conscience with the stillness of midnight. But I think we wrong that innocent hour. It is that terrible 'next morning' when reason is wide awake, upon which remorse fastens his fangs. Has a man gambled away his all, or shot his friend in a duel - has he committed a crime, or incurred a laugh - it is the *next morning*, when the irretrievable Past rises before him like a spectre; then doth the churchyard of memory yield up its grisly dead - then is the witching hour when the foul fiend within us can least tempt perhaps, but most torment. At night we have one thing to hope for, one refuge to fly to - oblivion and sleep! But at morning, sleep is over, and we are called upon coldly to review, and re-act, and live again the waking bitterness of self-reproach.

And perhaps also the following sentiments:

> Nine times out of ten it is over the Bridge of Sighs that we pass the narrow gulf from Youth to Manhood. That interval is usually occupied by an ill-placed or

disappointed affection. We recover, and we find ourselves a new being. The intellect has become hardened by the fire through which it has passed. The mind profits by the wrecks of every passion, and we may measure our road to wisdom by the sorrows we have undergone. [5]

Thereafter (to the eyes of the present author, at any rate) uplifting passages and solemn words of guidance and caution seem in rather short supply, but William may well have found one or two more to stand him in good stead.

Somebody else who read *Ernest Maltravers* at about this time, together with other works emanating from the same pen, thought that Lytton's books were amusing but totally unrealistic - and, indeed, positively dangerous if taken too seriously. 'He affects a contempt for the frivolities of the pursuits of men - [he sets his hero] above the power of ambition.... I think his novels are calculated to injure a very young man. They would be apt to make him think he could be every thing at once, & lead him really to be nothing. A man consumes his nights in the deepest studies - is a Platonist - an historian - a poet - knows every species of language, literature & science', dressing exquisitely, wooing effortlessly and excelling in all encounters with all adversaries. So thought Anthony Trollope (six years older than William) in 1840 [6], and much of this description of a would-be heroic figure, geared to overcome all eventualities, could certainly be applied to William in the years that lay immediately ahead.

The remaining entries for that week in June 1839 run as follows:

[*Wed, 12th June*] Miscellaneous reading till breakfast. French class till nine, attend the Algebra eleven for the first time. Made some more extracts from *Maltravers* in the afternoon. Went to the dancing at 4, went through a variety of exercises. Saw Miss H. in the evening; felt much concerned about her. Have a great [inclination] to write her or grandmother a letter of advice, anonymously.

[*Thurs, 13th June*] Rose at 8. German 9 to 10 a very interesting lesson. Mr G gave us a new version of the cheap Bauer story. Encouraged me to attend the lesson. Think that if I persevere and endeavour to distinguish myself[,] but [*sloth*?] will render any application much the poorer. About 11 started off quite unexpectedly on an excursion down the river in company with my friends Charles Anthony & W. Ward, enjoyed ourselves very much, I was in tolerably good spirits considering I got very wet coming back. Spent 2/6.

[*Fri, 14th June*] Rose this morn'g at 8, rather tired, but the morning being wet felt heavier than I otherwise should have done. Went after breakfast to Mr L. Tonight I began taking medicament, am full of hopes of a speedy & *effectual* cure. Business. Algebra at 11 to 12 - begin to feel a pleasure in it already[,] am determined to go on now with energy I had - by 3 months I shall be able to teach others as well as myself. Aft'n business, & miscellaneous reading. Paid for boots [*or* books?]. [*Minute record of several items of expenditure follow.*]

[*Sat, 15th June*] A dull monotonous day spent chiefly in business. Washing 1/6.

[*Sun, 16th June*] The whole of the morning was employed at the books. Felt rather happier than usual.

Had a misunderstanding with Mr R respecting some cash which however was soon explained. When there is no empathy [?] the slightest incident will rouse angry feelings. In the afternoon, being very fine went for a walk in company with Messrs. Crouch, R. Walker, & Ward (G.). Conversed about a great many things on the way but chiefly of a light hearted nature. X [*name indecipherable*] made one witty remark on being asked whether he should prefer a prostitute or a woman of Religious sentiments for a wife, he replied that if she was so high in heaven as I am deep in hell, I would prefer a religious woman.

It is clear that William was attending classes on a regular basis (French, Algebra and German are those specifically mentioned) but the words that leap out are those he wrote on 14 June: 'by 3 months I shall be able to teach others as well as myself'. These confirm, so far as confirmation is still required, that he was definitely following a specific syllabus of some kind and was confident that, by September 1839, he would have become a qualified teacher. (He had also signed up for dancing classes, evidently being keen to master the social graces, but it is improbable that these featured in any official curriculum.)

The entries for the following week run as follows:

[*Mon, 17th June*] Spent the morning between business and Algebra. I was occupied nearly the whole of the afternoon in translating the German Fables. After the U.A. meeting went to the Theatre. When we came home we had supper after which we had some very agreeable conversation. Music [*accompanying salad?*] with Mr HH, he gave some usefull advice I think. Sub. U.A. 1/6 [one shilling and sixpence]. Theatre 6.

[*Tues, 18ᵗʰ June*] Was too lazy to enter the particulars in this evening, and I have now forgotten them. But this much I recollect, that I was rambling about the best part of the day from one thing to the other, and consequently did but very little of anything. I must undergo a radical change before I can do any good at my present pursuits. Monthly Mag 2/6 Shakespeare pt. 2/6.

[*Wed, 19ᵗʰ June*] An uneventfull day. Got up rather late, spent the morning pretty much in the usual way, learnt very little from my books. In the evening went to the Theatre. After we returned we spent a very agreeable hour in [*Myra Hof? Major H of?*] Peterboro's company. Paid H. Hill 1/6 Theatre 1/-.

[*Thurs, 20ᵗʰ June*] Returned from walking at 8. Had not been to bed all night. Slept till near 11.

[*Fri, 21ˢᵗ June*] Rather late getting up, hardly got over the late *sprees* yet. Am very sorry that they should have occurred and particularly that I should have taken any part in them. Have some thoughts of going to New Zealand, think it desirable to encourage the diary. Maths signs feel more indefinitely [*sic*]. Theatre 2/- for the last time, a while.

[*Sat, 22ⁿᵈ June - entry largely blank, apart from two or three words starting 'DV' - the writer was perhaps indisposed - and references to expenditure on gloves and to having received the sum of twelve shillings and fourpence.*]

[*Sun, 23rd June - in a very large but almost indecipherable scrawl*] Engaged at my a/cs all the morning. Did better. Suffered from a severe headache & went for a walk in the aft'n - obliged to go to bed after tea. I had another walk in the evening, met Miss R. & she still exercises an influence over me which is larger to my impure qualities than before & hate [?] my not being on terms of intimacy with a better [girl].

There are some intriguing hints and allusions in these entries. It would be going much too far, probably, to say that (despite the example of Ernest Maltravers) William was tentatively seeking to sow wild oats in the summer of 1839. But he had certainly been caught up in one or two 'sprees' - one of them of the all-night variety - and he had dallied, against his better judgement, with the mysterious Miss R., while regretting that he was unable to find anyone 'better'. It may be that he sometimes felt he had been leading a life that was too staid and studious, and whimsically considered going off to New Zealand as a means of enlivening his diary entries. He was at a volatile age, swinging from one mood to another (from recklessness to repentance, say) and much inclined to severe self-criticism. In the entries for Monday and Wednesday it is interesting to note that the word 'we' suddenly appears, with no kind of explanation offered, which suggests that there was a fellow-lodger (presumably another student) with whom he kept regular company: it may be that the jobs at the stores were shared equally between them.

The reference to purchasing a Shakespeare 'part' is also interesting. There was a family story to the effect that an enterprising publisher issued a new edition of the bard's works in monthly parts, rather similar to the manner in which *The Pickwick Papers* had been issued, and that William walked many miles to the one particular newsagent's shop which happened to stock it every time a new instalment came out.

[*Mon, 24th June*] Still very unwell. Have done very little today, am getting on very slowly with the algebra. Have no business of longing for bed now although in way this state of my health is some excuse. Mr Hunter [?] came in evening to take subscription of the U.A.S. Am Fool enough to be so weak as to feel an[n]oyed because Miss PH did not come   This is any thing but dignified or elevated.   [*Marginal note*: Rec'd 7/6.]

[*Tues, 25th June*] Got up late. My cold not much better yet. This illness makes me more irresolute than ever. Always too weak for food. Never am active and well, it is now quite important. But I must hope I get well, and then if I don't do something I don't deserve to live.

[*Wed, 26th June*] Felt pretty much the same as I did yesterday when I got up this morning. Spent nearly the whole of the day at my labours but made much better progress. I do not yet practically practise my french, excellent opportunity.

There are no further entries for the remainder of this week.   One would like to think that William devoted the greater part of it to practising his French pronunciation.
A new month now dawned.

[*Mon, 1st July*] There is a very marked improvement in my health. Have left of[f] back medication. I still continue very unsettled in my pursuits. Went in the evening to the U.A.S. meeting. U.A.S. 1/6

[*Tues, 2nd July*] Spent the morning at my lessons and store. In the aftern^n went out fishing in company with Messrs R.W. & B.W. Passed it very pleasantly. Our conversation was unserious & unprofitable. Spent the evening in walking & talking, etc.

[*Wed, 3rd July*] This morning I spent in translating – made but little progress. My radical defect is a want of unity & continuity of purposes. This is partly constitutional & partly owing to my not having any being to whom I am strongly attached, on whom my affections are centred instead of wandering about.

[*Thurs, 4th July*] The first thing I did when I came downstairs this morning was to eat my breakfast, which before I have [skimped], after that mathematics. In the afternoon I went up the Mindak [?].

The diary suddenly comes to an end, so far as 1839 is concerned. Underneath these final four entries, however, there is written in ink the Roman numeral 'I' followed by the letters '**D.L.B.C.**', some mysterious hieroglyphics culminating in an exclamation mark and yet more hieroglyphics terminated by another exclamation mark. It is obviously a jubilant proclamation of some kind and, even at first glance, can only be interpreted as tantamount to an announcement that William has passed his exams with flying colours and that he is now able (in theory, at any rate) to go forth and teach.

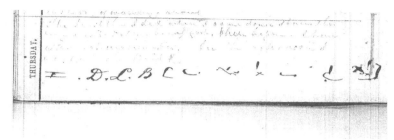

At a second glance, however, and with the aid of an expert on the intricacies of Pitman's shorthand, it is possible to be a little more specific. William is gleefully awarding himself a batch of spurious academic honours (First Class), on the grounds that these seem 'appropriate', and concluding with sentiments on the lines of 'Let feasting commence!'

Presumably this jubilant entry was made in September. It is conceivable that William now returned home in triumph to Trecoed, brandishing his qualifications, and that he endeavoured to establish a small school at nearby Llysronen. Before following him there, however, and ascertaining how the venture developed, we must pause for some final reflections on what the diary entries quoted in this chapter have to tell us.

William was working at 'the stores' on a very casual basis, but perhaps more regularly than initial impressions may suggest. Wednesday appears to have been his definite 'free' day (or could Wednesday have been a general 'early closing' day in that part of the world?) but during that first week of June it is clear that he otherwise attended at the stores on every day of the week and was preoccupied with balancing its accounts on the Sunday. In the second week he worked at the stores on only four days (Monday, Tuesday, Friday and Saturday) but was again attending to its books on the Sunday. In the third week, however, he is present only on the Monday, although once again sorting out the accounts on the Sunday, and thereafter was indisposed for much of the time. He returned to the stores on Tuesday, 2 July, but only for the morning, and

68

then the diary peters out. Payments received of twelve shillings and sixpence on 22 June and seven shillings and sixpence on 24 June presumably relate to the hours that he had worked. Otherwise, his time was much taken up with lessons - French, German and Algebra - and the notion of somebody working his way through college, to adopt a twentieth century idiom, becomes overwhelming. It may be, as already suggested, that a fellow-student (the other half of the mysterious 'we', possibly Mr Brett) took over when William was away and that the post of assistant was handled on job-share terms. Failing this, he presumably arranged things with the owner of the stores (Mr R.?) on an *ad hoc* basis.

His leisure-time (leaving aside fishing trips and dance classes) was taken up primarily with two institutions, the United Abstinence Society and the Theatre. The first of these met every Monday evening, one gathers, and the weekly subscription to their funds was one shilling and sixpence. (At the time when William was indisposed, zealous Mr Holland made a point of visiting his lodgings to collect it.) Payments made to the Theatre apparently varied, ranging from one to two shillings, depending (one assumes) on what particular entertainment was on offer. Sometimes it may have been a play-reading in which those present participated, at other times there might be a small cast of visiting performers to entertain them.

We become acquainted with several people, although the problem of deciphering William's handwriting makes it difficult to be sure that the right names have been bestowed upon them. Mr W. evidently teaches maths and he may well be the Mr Walker referred to on 10 June. (Perhaps he was also the R. Walker mentioned on 16 June and the R.W. referred to on 2 July, although one suspects the latter more likely to have been a young man of William's own age - perhaps the son of the first Mr Walker - rather than his tutor.) Mr G. teaches German and Mr L. is either the local doctor or a chemist. The other friends listed by the diarist are Charles Anthony, W. Ward, G. Ward, Crouch and somebody with the initials B.W. ('Messrs. Crouch, R. Walker, & Ward (G.)' looks at first glance like 'Miss Crouch, R. Walker, etc' but the light-hearted banter about the prostitute and the woman of religious sentiments is unlikely to have taken place in the presence of a young lady - unless she was well out of earshot - and, with some hesitation, the reading of 'Messrs.' has therefore been adopted.)

William, a sensitive youth with unsullied ideas of what was noble and honourable, was nevertheless developing an interest in the opposite sex. We have noted his admiration for Miss P. on 11 June (it is not clear whether she herself was the talented performer on the musical glasses on that occasion) and his strong inclination, uneasily suppressed, to rush to her defence when a churl insulted her. He was also tempted, the following evening, to send an anonymous letter to either Miss H. or her grandmother, proffering advice as to what was right and seemly: he evidently felt that Miss H. had been indecorous in some way. It may be that Miss P. and Miss H. were one and the same, for on 24 June - when Mr Hunter came to collect the U.A. Soc. subscription - William bitterly regretted that he had not been accompanied by Miss P.H. (clearly, either his daughter or his sister). As someone with whom to dally in moments of weakness, there was always Miss R., the attractive young lady with the dubious reputation, but William was conscious that he needed to find someone 'better', someone on whom his affections could be centred instead of 'wandering about' and someone to whom he could pour out his hopes and ambitions.

Finally, there remains the mystery of where he actually *was* in the summer of 1839. As noted earlier, W.R.P. George thought that his grandfather had been a draper's assistant in 'a nearby village'. But he failed to grasp that William was working his way through college and, with weekly classes to attend, was only employed on a part-time basis. With so much going on at the *locale* in question, and so many people with whom the diarist comes into contact, the conclusion must surely be that he was living in a town rather than a village. (Although the Harmonia Society responsible for giving the concert on 6 June may have been linked to the Harmony Chapel - a surmise which it has proved impossible to confirm one way or the other - which would suggest that he was not too far away from home territory.)

All that he himself actually tells us about his surroundings is that there are some gardens, a bowling green and a theatre. This raises the possibility that he was back in Haverfordwest, for there is a strong probability that the town had a bowling green (as well as several drapers' shops). But, seemingly, it did *not* possess a theatre in 1839 - nor is there any record of celebrations marked by fireworks taking place on the evening of 5 June 1839. [7]

Yet, while Haverfordwest did not have a fully-fledged theatre at that time, there had been talk over the years of one being established there. Proposals had been mooted in 1807 and in April 1810 Edmund Kean gave his postal address as 'the Theatre, Haverfordwest'. This indicates that a hall designed for entertainments did actually exist by then - or Kean may simply have been indulging in a moment of self-deceptive grandeur. But this is an isolated reference. There was a mention in 1829 of 'a commodious new theatre in the centre of Haverfordwest' but this too is only a fleeting citation. Cecil Price has recorded that, by 1844, there were only five theatres in Wales - at Aberystwyth, Abergavenny, Brecon, Carmarthen and Wrexham. And another historian of the Welsh theatre, Peter Davey, has referred (for reasons unknown) to the 'bigotry' of Haverfordwest in 1840 against theatricals. [8]

Much depends, obviously, on whether William was speaking of a genuine purpose-built theatre, recognised by all and sundry, or a local hall which, informally at any rate, served as such. The fact that he always uses a respectful capital T when writing the word would seem to be the deciding factor. On the assumption that he was still in Wales at this time, there is a case for concluding that he is referring to the theatre at Aberystwyth (the nearest of those listed), which had been built in the early 1830s. By road, the distance from Trecoed to Aberystwyth would have been formidable; even by sea, if one set out from Fishguard, it was 50 miles away. This was, at that time, quite a daunting journey. On the 'plus' side, however, it must be remembered that Aberystwyth would become the natural location for the University College, Wales in 1872, just over thirty years later, and it might well have been regarded, even in the late 1830s, as an embryo centre of learning.

Another conjecture, perhaps, is that - in view of the very strong trade links between Haverfordwest and Bristol - William might have left the Principality for a second time and gained further experience of life in an English city. [9] The eighteenth century Theatre Royal, which would eventually became known as the Bristol Old Vic, would certainly merit a capital T in any written references to it. (And the surnames of the people he refers to in his diary would seem to be English rather than Welsh.)

A geographical clue lies, obviously, in that mysterious word 'Mindak', which suggests either a hill or a river. But unless more decisive evidence ever emerges, it will have to be acknowledged that the basic mystery of William's whereabouts in 1839 - whether in Aberystwyth, Haverfordwest, Bristol or a small village near his home, as claimed by Dr George - will have to remain unsolved.

In the seventh of the articles about old Haverfordwest which he contributed to the *Pembroke County Guardian*, W.D. Phillips claimed that William had, at a relatively early stage in his career, 'opened a private school at Llysronen, Granston, near Mathry'. This statement was challenged a little while later by a columnist in the *South Wales News*, who stated that such a school had never existed. In another article (his seventeenth), many weeks later, Phillips triumphantly smote his critic into the dust by declaring that he had 'made the statement on the authority of one of the pupils of Mr William George, and who was in the school he held at the farm of Llysyronen, near Granston. So that's that!' [10]

The precise location to which Phillips is referring is not clear, unfortunately, and investigation is not helped by the fact that he used different spellings on each occasion, with an additional 'y' appearing in the second version. The fact that he suddenly describes it as a farm, however, rather than a village or hamlet, is significant in itself. No farm of that name exists in the twenty-first century, although there are certainly several farms in the area, and one assumes that a change of name has taken place during the past ninety years.

Granston is only two miles from Trecoed. It may have been at a later date that William taught here, but it is more realistic to assume that, after triumphantly passing his exams in the autumn of 1839, he returned to the family home and was anxious to begin his teaching career without delay. With friends at Granston willing to assist, he was presumably permitted to establish himself for several hours each day in a room at the farmhouse itself or in a nearby barn. *The Topographical Dictionary of Wales* tells us that, in 1833, the parish has a population of 195 inhabitants, that it is 'intersected by the turnpike road leading from Fishguard to St. David's, and is watered by a small stream, which, after flowing through it, falls into the sea near Aberbâch. The surrounding scenery is not distinguished by any peculiarity of feature, though from the higher grounds some good views are obtained over the channel and the adjacent country.' [11]

Mention of turnpike roads is a timely reminder of that curious phenomenon of the army of transvestite protesters responsible for 'the Rebecca riots' which erupted in parts of Pembrokeshire in the summer and autumn of 1839 and would continue, both here and elsewhere in Wales, until turnpikes were formally abolished in1844. In November 1839 troops had to be called out when the Chartists attempted to seize control of Newport. William's views on their activities are unknown, but they were an obvious symptom of current discontents in his part of the world. Agriculture was in dire straits from 1839 to 1841, as a result of a succession of very bad harvests, and farmers were finding it almost impossible to make a good living.

For the old order was now changing with a vengeance. 'A nation of countrymen', a historian born fifty years later would observe, 'was slowly turning into a nation of townsmen. Unsuccessful farmers were drifting into towns and setting up in business; their labourers were hewing coal or digging cuttings for the railways; and unnumbered children enjoyed the benefits of two hours' schooling in return for their nine hours in a mill. But half England' - and, for that matter, rather more than half of Wales - 'still lived in the country, and more than half was country-born. It was still a pink-cheeked population. For though the towns were growing fast, their growth was fed by a long stream of rustic immigrants. The countrymen were moving into town beneath a spreading pall from the blast-furnaces. It was an age of movement - of canals out-pacing waggons and of railways challenging canals. Long-necked locomotives puffed their way along five hundred miles of rail; excited speculators lent, promoted, borrowed, and intrigued for at least a thousand more; and burly men in corduroys swung pickaxes, as they bridged and tunnelled England into a new shape.... The roads were emptier, as stage-coaches were taken off. The Tally-ho left for the last time, and the wheelers stamped no more outside the posting-houses. But the dwindling traffic moved faster, where the bagman in his gig dashed past on his way from town to stock his country customers, who would not have to wait for the slow recurrence of a country fair. All the world was moving faster now, when Irish butter came in steamboats and men began to talk of "getting up the steam" and "railway speed" and whole factories were operated by steam-power. It was an age of wheels - of wheels spinning at pit-heads as the winding gear brought up the cages loaded heavily with coal and blackened colliers, wheels grinding into tunnels and along railway embankments, wheels humming endlessly above the bowed heads and the busy spindles of north-country mills.' [12]

William probably never visited a mine but ahead of him lay experience in London, in towns and villages in Lancashire, Leicestershire and Yorkshire, where mills and canals would flourish and factories would operate around the clock. Railways were a benefit of which he would take full advantage. He would encounter both extremely rich and extremely poor people. And he would also help, in passing, to teach some of those impoverished children.

5 - 'NORMAL' LIFE AT BATTERSEA

By 1840 Benjamin Williams was fully in charge of Trecoed, with his wife (in her late fifties) and young John (now aged 13) being assisted by two farm labourers and a maid-of-all-work who would help Mary in the house. It is doubtful whether William would have had much to contribute towards its running, apart from a substantial portion of the income which he would earn as a teacher. But did that income really amount to much? Nothing whatsoever is known about what he was doing in 1840 but it could well have been the case that the classes we assume he held at Llysyronen were not a great success. Let it be surmised, as a starting-point, that he managed to secure eight or nine pupils and that their parents were prepared to pay modest sums towards their tuition. By the time he had acquired a bench for them to sit on, provided them with slates, and found a table or desk for himself, it is hard to see his initial outlay being speedily recouped. Even if he were allowed to use the facilities at the farm rent-free, a very small income would be all that could be guaranteed for a good many months. He would have found it difficult, moreover, to re-acquire the Welsh language in its full fluency, having become 'Anglicised' during his absence from relations and friends. He would now be speaking it with a certain amount of hesitancy. Despite the familiarity of his surroundings, he had become a foreigner, a stranger, in their midst. For all we know, this particular enterprise may have lasted for no more than a few weeks - and it was apparently followed by others which were equally unsuccessful.

What we do know, however, is that by the autumn of 1840 William was in a state of utter despair and frustration. And then, perhaps as a result of perusing 'that old newspaper', hopes of making a successful career from school-mastering were suddenly given fresh impetus. For it was announced that a certain Dr James Kay, in partnership with Edward Carleton Tufnell and with the full support of officialdom, had established at Battersea in south-west London the very first teacher-training college for young men - a 'Normal' school (echoing a French term originating in Rheims in 1685, with the foundation of the École Normale) which would set the 'norm' for how children in Great Britain ought to be taught henceforth. In great excitement, and with bated breath, William wrote to Dr Kay asking whether he could be allowed to enroll as a student. It was, seemingly, the last throw of his dice.

'When I applied to Dr Kay for admission to this institution,' he recalled at the end of 1841, 'I confess that I had but a very faint hope of success. I was an utter stranger to him, and I must add that my means were very limited. I made the application as an experiment - a last desperate experiment - to obtain what I had so long desired; for I had long wished to become a teacher and I felt that this wish had in great measure been responsible for destroying my usefulness in other pursuits. I had formed a thousand schemes to attain my object but all had failed, and I had almost given up in despair, when I heard of this Institution. I then determined to make another attempt, thinking that if I failed, it would be only adding one more disappointment to the many I had already experienced. I did so, and great was my surprise at all the success I meet with; and whenever I think of the manner in which I made myself known to Dr Kay, and how little there was to recommend me to his notice, I am convinced that nothing but a very deep interest in the cause with which his life is identified, could have induced him to avail himself of the services of such a humble instrument to assist in carrying out the good work.' [1]

Sadly, the actual letter does not appear to have survived. It would presumably have given a very useful résumé of

William's early life, including his brief period of apprenticeship to a doctor. But Dr James Kay, his senior by seventeen years, probably recognised a kindred spirit, for in many respects his own career had not been totally dissimilar. It is essential, for the purpose of setting William's own subsequent career in its relevant context, that a little time be devoted to summarising the progress to date of Kay's. [2] Born into a well-established textile family in Rochdale, he had left school in 1819 but found that a career in the family's concerns did not appeal to him. He then worked in his uncle's bank for about three years but that too did not appeal. In 1824 his father eventually agreed that he should go to Edinburgh to study medicine. A student at the University until 1827, he made a name for himself as a diligent researcher and was soon recognised as a highly intelligent man, capable of sustained periods of hard work - but also as someone who was highly strung.

Beginning as a resident clerk at Edinburgh Royal Infirmary, he decided to pursue a career in Manchester and became one of the two doctors at a newly-established dispensary designed primarily for the benefit of the 'deserving poor'. He developed into a radical campaigner, writing articles and pamphlets, and was actively involved in the agitation for parliamentary reform. A cholera epidemic led to a change of direction, for the Privy Council set up an advisory Board of Health in 1831 and Kay joined its Manchester branch. He published in 1832 a book about the moral and physical condition of the city's working class, producing tables and visiting a vast number of dwellings in the course of his investigations. Cholera reached Manchester soon after and he played an active role in fighting it, sometimes facing much opposition. He founded the city's Statistical Society, taking a very close interest in lives of the poor, and in May 1835 applied to become honorary physician at Manchester Royal

Infirmary. His failure to obtain this post resulted in a deep depression and he experienced something very close to a nervous breakdown.

An abrupt change of direction now followed. A Poor Law Amendment Act passed in 1834 had transferred responsibility for poor relief from individual parishes to proposed Unions of parishes. A Commission was set up to bring this about. Kay successfully applied for the post of Assistant Commissioner in Suffolk in the summer of 1835 and took over Norfolk as well a few months later. He toured the parish workhouses, establishing Unions against much local hostility, and made it a personal crusade to eradicate pauperism. To this end he took a tough line with the paupers, being a keen advocate of the policy of 'Treat 'em mean, keep 'em keen.' His superiors were awed by his frenetic activity and in 1838 they entrusted the London district to him as well. He became increasingly interested in the education of pauper children - 'Catch 'em young' being, in effect, another of his policies - and visited an experimental school at Ealing Grove established by Lady Byron (of which there will be more to say shortly) and also schools at Hackney Wick and Chiswick. He worked in close association with Edward Tufnell, the Assistant Commissioner for Kent, and together they studied educational developments in Edinburgh and Glasgow - where, respectively, John Wood and David Stow were putting new ideas into effect. He was particularly impressed by Stow's Glasgow Normal Seminary.

This triggered off a new crusade. Kay felt that workhouse schools, especially those in London, were of no practical benefit and simply created a fresh generation of felons and vagrants. What was needed was a fresh start! In Tufnell's company, he continued to visit schools in England and paid brief visits to Holland and Belgium. With all the energy and dynamism of the newly-converted, he was once again carried away with enthusiasm. 'Wood, Stow, Lady Byron and the industrial schools of the Children's Friend Society', R.J.W. Selleck has written, 'jostled continental reformers such as Labarre, Prinse, Pestalozzi and de Fellenberg, as Kay raided them for ideas.' [3] His *Report on the Training of Pauper Children*, published in 1838, estimated that there were more than 44,000 workhouse children in England, many of them orphaned. He urged that district schools of industry be set up to equip them for useful life in community and that they be taught the 'three Rs' plus carpentering, tailoring and shoemaking for the boys and domestic management for the girls.

To demonstrate the efficacy of his theories, Kay was keen that a 'model' school, run on the principles enunciated, be established without delay so that it might serve as an example for other schools - or, as the next best thing, that an existing school be taken over and reorganised on these progressive lines. And, clearly, this new establishment would need to be staffed by the best possible teachers. By now a fully committed disciple of Stow, Kay was convinced that such teachers came solely from Scotland. This may have been the case, but the problem was that not enough of them wanted to work in England. Once again, falling back on the next best thing, Kay reached the conclusion that English (and Welsh) teachers would have to be specially trained in order that they might reach the standards set by their Scottish counterparts. A 'norm' would thereby be established. England's first Normal school, he proclaimed, would be 'an institution for the instruction of teachers in the theory of their art and in the matter of instruction.' [4]

Kay was by now uniquely qualified to bring such a venture to a fruition, for he had the ear of central Government - although the Government in question was, at this point in time, an extremely weak one. The Whigs were still theoretically in office, under the leadership of Lord Melbourne, but their parliamentary majority had dwindled to what was almost vanishing point. Ministers, especially Lord John Russell, were anxious to do something in the way of educational reform, over and above making annual grants made towards the building of schools for the poorer classes, and this would have been the ideal moment to create a Ministry of Education. But, given the precarious state of their fortunes, such a proposal (arousing the ire of the Church of England and the Tories alike) would have been highly controversial and would most certainly have led to their defeat in the House of Lords. As the next best thing, however, and as a way of by-passing the Upper Chamber, it was decided in February1839 that a committee of the Privy Council headed by Lord Lansdowne should be set up. This was, in effect, a Ministry of Education in embryo (and would, in fact, gradually become known as the Education Department). It was created by Queen Victoria on 10 April and met for the first time the following day. Kay, while retaining his post with the Poor Law Commission, took on the role of secretary.

A minute published by the Committee of the Privy Council on Education three days later, written by Kay, stated that they had approved a scheme to establish a Normal School and a Model School. The Normal School would be one 'in which candidates for the office of teacher in schools for the poorer classes may acquire the knowledge necessary to the exercise of their future profession, and may be practised in the most approved methods of religious and moral training and instruction.' [5] The Model School would be a boarding school with accommodation for at least 450 children (consisting of 120 infants, 200 boys and girls receiving 'ordinary' instruction and fifty boys and fifty girls receiving 'superior' instruction) plus 150 or 200 children attending on a daily basis. This did *not* mean, however, that central government itself would pay for these establishments, simply that they approved of them in principle and would be happy to make a small contribution to their running costs once a private sponsor had come forward.

No private sponsor materialised, however, and Kay and Tufnell eventually decided that they themselves would have to share this role - although many private individuals, including the Bishop of Durham, the Earl of Chichester and Lady Byron, would contribute towards the running costs. The only problem that remained was that of finding premises at a suitable location. In 1838 it had seemed that a pauper school at Norwood in south London (the School of Industry) would fit the bill. But, on closer inspection, it fell short of what was required. In the autumn of 1839, however, the Queen's chaplain and the vicar of Battersea, the Rev. Robert Eden (distant connection of a future Prime Minister), volunteered to make his village school available for the project and Kay accepted his offer with alacrity. It was agreed that Eden himself, a High Church minister but a moderate liberal, would oversee religious instruction. Somebody else recruited to the teaching staff (though not on a full-time basis) was a young man called John Hullah, fast becoming known as the country's leading authority on musical tuition and a promising composer in his own right. (Encountering a Miss Fanny Dickens at the Royal Academy of Music, he had collaborated with her brother three years earlier in writing an operetta entitled *Village Coquettes* which had proved very popular.)

With a very modest initial complement of both pupils and staff, the new Battersea education complex cautiously opened for business in February 1840. Kay, accompanied by his widowed mother, sister and brothers, had moved into an old manor house known as the Terrace House, in close proximity to vicarage and school, where Tufnell joined them. A dozen boys, most of them orphans aged about 13, and all of them transferred from the Norwood establishment, took up residence at the Model School. They were accompanied by one of their masters, a young Scotsman called Walter McLeod (trained by David Stow), who became headmaster. There would be twenty-four such pupils by the end of the year. Not initially proclaimed, however, but an integral part of Kay's scheme, was the notion that they should all be regarded as potential members of the Normal School - destined to become, literally, pupil-teachers. In theory, they were embarking on an onerous five-year course. During the first three years they would study the art of teaching. At the age of 18 they would graduate to the Normal School and practise their newly-acquired skills at the Model School which they had just left. Examinations would follow, and they would then (if successful) be appointed 'assistant teachers' in selected pauper schools - with remuneration which would increase from year to year - and becoming eligible for full professional status at the end of a further two years.

In the first instance, however, a batch of young men were needed (in modern parlance) to kick-start the Normal School. These young men, ranging in age from twenty to thirty, would be required to stay there for at least one year and were to be nominated by personal friends of Kay or Tufnell 'or to be trained for the schools of gentlemen' with whom they were acquainted. By the end of 1840 nine were in residence - 'a number accumulated [so Kay explained] only by very gradual accessions, as we were by no means desirous to attract many students until our plans were more mature'. [6]

It had been assumed, it seems, that these young men, or students, would be equipped to exercise their newly-acquired teaching skills at the drop of a hat- which would then be refined into something far more sophisticated. But theory did not correspond with practice. Kay ruefully acknowledged, in January 1841, that some of these young men, despite having 'been in charge of village and workhouse schools', had 'frequently been found even worse prepared than the boys of thirteen years of age.... Their acquaintance even with rudimental knowledge would not bear the test of slight examination. With pupils and students alike, it was therefore found necessary to commence at an early stage of instruction, and to furnish them with the humblest elements of knowledge. The time which has elapsed since the school has opened' - i.e., the whole of 1840 - 'ought therefore to be regarded as a preparatory period'. It was now intended, he explained, to divide the residents of the establishment into four categories - (1) 'the preparatory class' of students and pupils, who would become (2) 'candidates' for teaching status if awarded a proficiency certificate at the end of their first year, who in turn would become (3) 'scholars' if passing another examination at the end of their second year and who would be recognised as (4) 'masters' if passing a final examination at the end of their third year. [7]

The foregoing paragraph needs to be borne in mind when considering William's initial status at the Battersea Normal School. He arrived there in his twentieth year, taking up residence early in 1841, and in the census return of 6 June he is described as a 'pupil-teacher' rather than a master. There might be an element of surprise in such a grading for he had, after all, passed exams in the autumn of 1839 which apparently qualified him to teach, and it is very possible (but not absolutely certain) that he had been running that small school at Llysyronen in 1840. For reasons that will be explained shortly, it is assumed that he was now being given an accelerated passage (or 'crash course') through the various grades described by Kay and that he would, in fact, have reached the status of 'master' by the end of 1841 - another instance, it would seem, of practice not being quite in line with theory on those occasions when an exceptionally talented student appeared on the scene.

The census return for this unique Battersea establishment, providing as it does a bird's eye-view, deserves closer attention. There was, first, the Terrace House (separated, presumably, by a red brick wall from the scholastic buildings) in which Kay lived with his mother, his sister and two brothers, as well as Tufnell, their domestic needs being catered for by three female servants and a lad (the 'boots'?) aged fifteen. Kay and Tufnell, although the founding fathers and actively involved in determining the guidelines for their schools, were not teachers in their own right but 'superintendents'. Their official status, so far as the census was concerned, remained that of Poor Law Commissioners.

Then comes the return for the Normal School, which housed thirty-six male individuals on that particular night. In terms of age, the oldest of them was aged 40 and then came seven young men (five aged 20 and two aged 25) and twenty-seven teenage boys (two aged 13, six aged 14 and nineteen aged 15) and one boy (William Bragg) who, at the age of eleven, had not yet reached the status of teenager. Five of the men were designated as 'school masters' while the other three, comprising William plus a young man of his own age and another one five years his senior, were described as 'pupil-teachers' - as were all the twenty-eight boys. One of the masters, Benjamin Horne aged 25, had been mentioned by name in Kay's report (being singled out for special responsibilities); so too had been a Mr Tate, but he does not appear in the census return drawn up six months later - perhaps he had been replaced by the forty-year-old gentleman, John Mitchell. 'Superintendents' had a part to play in making announcements, a description which could have encompassed Eden and McLeod as well as Kay and Tufnell. (McLeod, aged

24, does not feature in this particular return, as he was living in the High Street with his sister.)

As an all-male establishment, the Battersea community was almost monastic in character. (The only female member of staff was a matron who also did the cooking - sometimes assisted, perhaps, by one of Kay's female servants - but she evidently did not live on the premises.) Everybody, students and pupils alike, rose at 5.30am, washed and dressed and made their beds during the fifteen minutes that followed, and then devoted the next hour to housework. At 6.45am, providing the weather was satisfactory, they marched outside and worked in the garden for an hour. Returning to the house, they would deposit their tools and wash and then attend at 8.00am for a non-denominational religious service and listen to announcements made by the superintendents. Breakfast was at 8.30am and standard lessons - on every day except Sunday - would commence an hour later.

The pupils were divided into two classes, but they would be united from 9.00 to 9.30am for religious instruction. They would then separate, the lessons taught between 9.30 and 11.00am being mechanics, arithmetic, mental arithmetic and etymology. They would be re-united from 11.00 until noon for instruction in either geography or music:. They would then return to the garden for an hour, where they would attend to the animals on a small farm which had gradually been built up - namely, two cows, three pigs, three goats and some poultry. 'It seemed important', Kay writes, 'that they should learn to tend animals with care and gentleness; that they should understand the habits and the mode of managing these particular animals, because the schoolmaster in a rural parish often has a common or forest-right of pasture for his cow, and a forest-run for his pig or goat, and might thus, with a little skill, be provided with the means of healthful occupation in his hours of leisure, and of providing for the comforts of his family.' [8] (These particular lessons may have been rather less than enthralling so far as William was concerned.)

Dinner would be at 1.15pm and the classes would be together at 2.00pm for an hour's lessons in drawing of some kind - mechanical on two of the days and maps on two more, with perspective, and use of the globes, being set aside for Thursdays. From 3.00 until 4.00pm the classes would separate, the lessons taught during the next two hours including algebra, grammar, natural history, and the memorisation of various tables. Saturdays afternoons, from 2.00 until 5.00pm, would be devoted to examinations. From 5.00 until 6.00pm they would again be working in the garden and attending to the needs of the animals - milking the cows being a crucial event - before being granted fifteen minutes' break in which to smarten up. Supper would be served at 6.15, and 7.00pm marked the commencement of an hour's drill and gymnastic exercises. From 8.00 until 9.00pm different activities would be pursued in the upper and lower classrooms, the upper being devoted to copying music or notes on geography or mechanical formulae, with the history of England being read aloud (the only occasion, it seems, on which that particular subject was allowed to intrude), while the lower was used for singing practice - it speedily became known, indeed, as the Singing Hall. There would be a brief evening service at 9.00pm and everyone would then retire to their slumbers.

The Sunday routine was understandably different. 'After divine service', runs Kay's account, 'one of the sermons of the day is written from memory. In the evening the compositions are read and commented upon, and the Catechism or some other portion of the formularies of the Church is repeated, with texts of Scripture illustrating it. Some of the elder students teach in the village Sunday-school.' [9] From time to time, however, everyone on the campus would be rounded up to participate in a strenuous long walk, ideally to a place of historical interest.

The same meals ('as frugal as possible') were eaten by staff and pupils alike in a large room, the masters sitting at a table in its centre and helping out with the carving when necessary. General conversation ('avoiding the extremes of levity or seriousness') was permitted and the atmosphere appears to have been quite a relaxed, congenial one.

So far as the *manner* of teaching was concerned, emphasis was placed upon not being harsh or over-strict with the pupils but on explaining things in a calm, patient and unhurried way. This was, perhaps, a doctrine of perfection, but it does seem to have been relatively successful. Dr Kay evidently endorsed Guizot's definition of the ideal schoolmaster - 'a man not ignorant of his rights, but thinking much more of his duties; showing to all a good example, and serving to all as a counsellor; not given to change his condition, but satisfied with his situation, because it gives him the power of doing good; and who has made up his mind to live and die in the service of primary instruction, which to him is the service of God and his fellow-creatures.' [10]

If William had joined the establishment by the end of January 1841 then he might well have attended a famous meeting at Exeter Hall on 1 February. This was the occasion when Hullah endeavoured to demonstrate, with the aid of several of the Battersea pupils, how - by a system developed by Guillaume Wilhem of Paris - the art of singing might be taught to the nation at large. His audience, with a large sprinkling of the great and the good among their number, were extremely impressed and classes began at the Hall on a regular basis.

The Battersea establishment was now becoming extremely well-known and attracting a steady stream of eminent visitors, including Prince Albert. On 16 February 1842 the Clerk to the Privy Council, Charles Greville, would accompany a small party which included Lord John Russell and the historian T.B. Macaulay. 'We put forward Macaulay to examine the boys in history and geography,' Greville records, 'and John asked them a few questions, and I still fewer. They answered in a way that would have put to shame most of the fine people's children. These schools are admirable'. [11] This visit took place a few weeks after William had left, but so far as 1841 was concerned two extracts from the diary of Mrs Caroline Davenport from Capesthorne, in Cheshire, provide vivid snapshots of the atmosphere:

[*Mon, 3rd May*] Set off in pouring rain to Battersea to see the school at Dr Kay's house. Found there [several well-known people].... The boys were explaining different principles of mechanics, and very well. The Bishop of Lichfield proposed they should explain the common pump. This they did very well, he asking them several questions and making them go back when they went too fast. A young Maltese, who is to keep a school at Malta, then did a grammatical lesson, and a nice little fellow of thirteen parsed and construed a sentence, all showing how thoroughly well they were grounded.... They were all very neatly dressed, looked very intelligent, and appeared very fond of Dr Kay and Mr Tufnell, and very happy. The most wonderful and beautiful part was the singing.

[*Thurs, 10th June*] At half-past eight in the morning Mr Davenport, Miss Shuttleworth, the Bishop of Norwich, I, and Arthur, went down to Battersea to hear first the Bible lesson at the village school, then to breakfast with the Edens, back to the village school for arithmetic, and writing, and singing. We then walked to Dr Kay's, and saw his garden and the boys at work.

And a subsequent undated entry is also of interest:

> [*Thurs.*] Mr Ottley and I lunched with Mrs and Miss Kay; Dr Kay not at home, but two very nice young men, brothers, who are at Cambridge. Mrs Kay is a charming old lady, so full of kind interest about the school. I saw the young man who is to come to us [to take charge of the school at Capesthorne], and of whom the ladies gave the highest possible character. Mr Hullah lunched there. We went afterwards to the village school, and stayed a long time, hearing McLeod's lecture on water, which was admirable. [12]

This makes it clear that some of the 'young gentlemen' had been earmarked for particular teaching posts weeks or even months in advance and that they were attending the Battersea establishment as a sort of finishing school, to be despatched to their new destinations as soon as the final sheen of Dr Kay's polish had been applied. On the other hand, wealthy patrons - with a certain vacancy to be filled - might simply have called in to see which of the students would be discharged from the production line in the very near future.

There are reasons for assuming, as indicated earlier, that William had been fast-tracked through the various grades that were in force at Battersea, his earlier experience and obvious intelligence having stood him in good stead. By mid-October he was clearly a master, for there survives (in that much-adapted *Student's Journal*) some jottings which display his book-keeping activities at that time. Dated 15 October, it shows him starting the day with £15. He then spent half-a-crown (two shillings and sixpence) on a dozen (exercise?) books, three shillings and fourpence on ten quires of paper, one shilling on a dozen pencils and four shillings on three mathematical books. It is assumed that these items were all distributed to the batch of pupils he was teaching at that time. For his own personal benefit, he then spent sixpence on a glass of Welsh pale ale - his membership of the United Abstinence Society had presumably lapsed by this time - five shillings on two flannels and three shillings in paying off the balance due on a pair of shoes. This expenditure totalled almost nineteen shillings and fourpence, leaving him with £14 in hand at the end of that day.

Of still greater interest is the text of a short speech which he declaimed, at some stage, to his fellow-students on the subject of geography. (It is probable that, perhaps on a weekly basis, each student in turn had to trigger off a debate on a subject chosen by one of the principals.) It is, admittedly, somewhat over-stated in places and perhaps falls midway in status between the level of a Victorian parlour game, in which the contestant has to talk non-stop but persuasively about a particular topic for several minutes, regardless of how much he really knows, and a spirited undergraduate declamation at the Oxford Union. He had evidently been instructed to convince his audience how essential it was that geography should be taught. The sweeping assertions pile up in an awesome progression, but the talk is well-designed and a satisfying peroration eventually reached. 'Geography', William declared,

is a branch of Knowledge which, far less adapted than most others for ambitious display, is more than most characterized by practical utility. It is less a showy accomplishment than a solid acquirement; it is not so much a thing for occasional exhibition, as a matter of every day's demand, and constantly recurring application. It may be truly said, indeed, that of all departments of secular study, this is at once the most universally and the most uniformly important for the various classes of men who are desirous of employing their lives in practical exertion, or of cultivating their minds by general knowledge.

The importance of geographical knowledge to both these classes of men is too obvious to require much illustration. To every system of practical accomplishment its value is direct. In every one of man's active pursuits - the greatest and the most trifling - the Knowledge of the earth which we inhabit is power and the want of it is weakness. A geographical miscalculation will more than any other ignorance involve a man in difficulties in the intercourse of ordinary life; a geographical miscalculation contributed more than all occasions else to overthrow the most extraordinary empire in the political history of man. To the lawyer the knowledge of Geography is necessary for throwing light on the constitution of politics, and the spirits of laws; to the physician as a basis for arrangement of his materials, and the comparison of climates; to the divine as a resource for the illustration of his belief, and a guide to the application of his doctrines; to the soldier, for the regulation of his movements, and the calculation of military chances; to the sailor, at once in the choice and in the conduct of his undertakings; to the merchant for the Knowledge of his commodities, and the [destinations?] of his traffic; to the agriculturalist, for the expansion of the primary laws of his science, and for suggesting the special arrangements of his practice; to the politician for the adequate intelligence of the statistics of his own country, the nations of foreign States and the balance of political powers, to the man of the world for its connexion to all that practical knowledge which is appropriate to the character of a cultivated gentleman. For, viewed as a branch of general Knowledge not less than as a necessary part of practical accomplishment, will the value of geographical science become manifest. It is not merely that Geography is itself a science, ample in extent, and rich in valuable and interesting material; but it persuades and mingles with almost all other Knowledge. Every real excellence, except God, is local, and hence every event of which we have any Knowledge has its locality. The relation of place is thus one of the most constant principles of association in every science and in every mind. And he by whom the facts of that relation are not in some degree truly understood, is destitute at once of the most necessary safeguards against delusion and one of the most important principles for the consolidation of systematic truth.

1Terra incognita has always been one of the favourite haunts of unlicensed fancies, and the prolific birthplace of popular delusions. The extension of general knowledge has always kept pace with that of geographical science. Thus, Haley [sic], the founder of mathematical geography, was the founder of Grecian philosophy. Thus, the discovery of America was one final element in the combination of causes which, three centuries ago, produced the revival of general Knowledge and the resurrection of the human mind. Thus, in these later ages of general illumination, has it become a national object to the most enlightened people of the earth, and a fond enterprise to her most adventurous children to lift the veil which has so long concealed the secrets of the Southern Ocean and those of the Frozen Pole. Geography turns our attention to objects in their own nature of the rarest interest to every reflecting mind, for what [more] should man have a direct curiosity to know than the form of his own dwelling-place, the arrangement of that great theatre on which the drama of his own wondrous history is acted. Geography is one of the bases of History; deprived of that, the latter becomes a blind, erratic, unattractive form. To the philosopher, the relations of terrestrial space, the influences of local circumstances, the phenomena of various regions, the universal connexion of beings and of events with space, supply the materials of the riches, the most interesting, and most important of all his speculations. To the man of devotion, there are no resources richer than the store of geographical information for unfolding to him the character of man, and the constant providence of Him who 'created not the world in vain', who 'formed the earth and man upon it.' As Cicero said of Greece, that at every step we tread upon a history, so of the whole terrestrial sphere, we may say that every glance we cast upon it rests upon something worthy of being known - some admonition to the living, or some memorial of the dead, some monument of the manifold nature of man, his greatness or his degradation - some token of the all-seeing providence of God, his presence, his wisdom, his goodness, or severity.

A study thus teeming with important information peculiar to itself, and this connected with all of practical science that is known to man, is, for this one reason, alone most important to be thoroughly understood, and one most difficult to be worthily expounded, most useful to learn aright, and arduous to teach. [13]

2The position of the Deity (at a time when Darwinian speculations were beginning to call certain fundamental matters into question) was confidently reconciled with whatever revelations might still come to light, while Cicero and Sir Edmund Halley were brought forward as useful buttresses and Napoleon had his knuckles rapped for not having done his homework so far as Russian winters were concerned. The allusion to discovering 'the secrets of the Southern Ocean and those of the frozen Pole' was a reference to a current exploration of those regions undertaken by James Clark Ross - demonstrating, in effect, that the speaker was fully up-to-date with current events. A lively debate, once he had resumed his seat, presumably took place.

Whatever the mechanics involved in William's ascent from the status of pupil-teacher, it is clear that by the late autumn a wealthy patron had put in a bid for his services as a fully-fledged schoolmaster. The precise date on which he left Battersea (mid-December, perhaps?) is unknown, but there has survived the draft of an emotional 'Goodbye' speech - much amended and often indecipherable - which he would have sought to commit to memory. It will have to serve as an approximation of what he actually said on the day. 'Situated as I am at present,' it begins,

> and considering the very favourable manner in which you received my name, and as we are now to part, it is, I suppose, appropriate ... your sympathy has so inclined me - that I avail myself of the present occasion to say a few words in acknowledgement.
>
> It is impossible for me to express what my feelings are.... It was more than I expected and deserved. I must, of course, attribute a good deal of this to the formality inseparable from occasions like the present, but still I do believe (and I think I have reason for believing) that much, if not all, of the kindness you have shown towards me this night was dictated by real feeling and not the mere offspring of the emotion of the

moment. My friend Bragg has said that parting is a painful thing and this indeed is the case - especially for those who have lived happily together for any length of time. In such a case no one can ever know how painful it is until he has experienced it himself.

I have now been with you for some time, and have in my impressions that during that period I endeavoured to pursue the 'even tenor of my way' [14] as peaceably and agreeably as I could. I am fully sensible of some faults I have to account for, and perhaps that they will all be buried in the past, and that we shall look and hope for better things for the future. I have of course experienced a degree of friendship and sympathy from all. For that is much in the nature of things in spiritual as well as material attractions and attractions between living as well as between inanimate bodies, and this must, of course, exist in greater force in some persons than in others; but notwithstanding this I hope and trust that I have earned the goodwill and esteem of all of you, and I hope also that I have contracted more than one friendship during my stay in Battersea which will terminate only with life itself, nay not even then but that when we have quitted the present stage of existence they will be renewed under happier auspices, and with greater strength and purity.

I have made these few general remarks concerning myself, and as I am but a poor, unpractised hand at public speaking, I would willingly end here if I could do so with propriety; but I feel it would be unpardonable of me to omit particular mention of Dr Kay, to whom I am so deeply indebted, as will my teaching [be].

He then recalled, in the passage which has been quoted at the outset of this chapter, his state of mind when writing originally to Dr Kay and how immensely grateful he had been that his appeal for admission had not fallen on deaf ears. 'With regard to my teachers,' the text continues,

> I can only express my gratitude to them for the advantages (great I was going to say) which I have received from their instructions. It would be presumptuous in me to bestow any praise, for they are above praise, but those praises which I cannot withhold are an expression of my admiration of their skill as teachers. The more I have become acquainted with them the more has this admiration of their abilities increased. I embrace this opportunity of thanking them also for the attention and uniform kindness I have received from them and I hope that if anything I have said, or done, at any time, has occasioned them any pain that they will accept the expression of my sincere regrets and I will only add my sincere prayer that they may long enjoy health and strength to direct the studies of the people of this Institution, and that they may continue to send [out] further teachers having a share of that skill and enthusiasm which they possess in such an eminent degree.
>
> I shall always regard the year I have spent in Battersea as the most important in my life, and this Institution as the means by which I was brought from a *miserably* useless life to one which I trust will be a happy one and not altogether destitute of usefulness to others. [15]

'It was more than I expected and deserved' he had planned to say at the outset, with the air of one spontaneously responding to tumultuous and totally unexpected applause. Yet it was not quite like that, for the fact that he had prepared this lengthy response beforehand indicates that a spot of artifice has come into play - the tumultuous applause was *precisely* what he had expected. And there was also that parenthetical remark - 'great I was going to say' - which was to be modestly uttered while being simultaneously discarded and disowned. For somebody who was avowedly 'but a poor, unpractised hand at public speaking' he seems, in short, to have mastered pretty well, and at an early age, some of the little tricks of the skilled orator.

The precepts of Thomas Gray notwithstanding, it is also worth noting the apologies he makes (twice over) for having said anything in the heat of the moment, on sundry occasions, that may have rankled with its recipient(s). He is determined to mend his ways and button his lip in future and hopes that those combative remarks will be forgotten. (Clearly, he was conscious of having been argumentative or provocative at times.) His final words, echoing those sentiments of Guizot, were presumably well-received by Dr Kay. The good doctor might also have reflected, with a wry smile, that William's evident resolve to exercise greater restraint in future had not come a moment too soon - for his new employer was an aristocratic and autocratic lady, somebody in whose bad books the doctor himself had periodically featured. The lady in question was Lady Byron.

6 - A BYRONIC INTERLUDE

CANTO 1 : EALING

On Saturday, 4 June 1842, with all the apparent assurance (one assumes) of a practised young man about town keen to impress a younger brother, William George dropped into a coffee house in the Strand and skimmed *The Athenaeum*'s review of the newly-published *Book of the Poets*, dismissing it half-contemptuously (the anonymous review, that is, not the book), as 'a rambling rhapsody'. [1] (It was mainly about Chaucer and its author, we now know, was Elizabeth Barrett.) *The Book*, published by Messrs. Scott, Webster & Geary, was a massive anthology in two substantial volumes. The first covered the pre-1800 period in 458 pages, while the second, running to 506, dealt with the 'modern poets of the nineteenth century', forty-three of whom (with the interesting exception of Tennyson) were indeed represented. We do not know whether William purchased these hefty tomes, but if he did then he would have seen that the splendidly ornamental title page of the second volume, with its twirls, whirls and flourishes, was surmounted by an oval-shaped picture of Lord Byron - the only face permitted to adorn that majestic portal. (His counterpart, on the corresponding page of its predecessor, was Chaucer.) Employed as he was by the disgruntled widow of someone who had now become a semi-legendary figure in the recent history of both Britain and Greece, the stuff of which national heroes (however unruly their private lives) are indubitably made, he would have hesitated to display that second volume to the pupils of Ealing Grove school - for there was always a possibility that its proprietress might suddenly enter the room and explode with rage.

And this despite the fact that he happened to be extremely fond of poetry and frequently wrote down snatches of verse that had caught his attention. His favourite poem, which he went to the trouble of copying out in full, heading it with the title of 'Woman' and retaining for evermore, ran as follows:

She was a Phantom of delight
When first she gleam'd upon my sight;
A lovely Apparition, sent
To be a moment's ornament:
Her eyes as stars of Twilight fair;
Like Twilight's, too, her dusky hair;
But all things else about her drawn
From May-time and the cheerful Dawn;
A dancing Shape, an Image gay,
To haunt, to startle, and way-lay.

I saw her upon nearer view,
A Spirit, yet a Woman too!
Her household motions light and free,
And steps of virgin liberty;
A countenance in which did meet
Sweet records, promises as sweet;
A Creature not too bright or good
For human nature's daily food;
For transient sorrows, simple wiles,
Praise, blame, love, kisses, tears, and smiles.

And now I see with eye serene
The very pulse of the machine;
A Being breathing thoughtful breath;
A Traveller betwixt life and death:
The reason firm, the temperate will,
Endurance, foresight, strength and skill;
A perfect Woman; nobly plann'd,

To warn, to comfort, and command;
And yet a Spirit still, and bright
With something of an angel light.

Clearly, this represented for William the culmination of his dreams, the ideal woman whom (in 1842) he had yet to encounter. The author of the poem was another William - Wordsworth, in fact, who had written it in 1804 in honour of his wife.[2] Lord Byron dismissed most of Wordsworth's poems as 'trash'[3], and he might have lingered, with an ironic smile, over this particular production, which formed a striking contrast to the poems which he himself penned (after 1815, at any rate) as descriptions of his own wife. Most pithy, perhaps, was one dashed off as an endorsement to the deed of separation which she had forced upon him:

A year ago, you swore, fond she!
'To love, to honour', and so forth:
Such was he vow you pledged to me,
And here's exactly what 'tis worth.[4]

In 1812, when *Childe Harold's Pilgrimage* was published, Byron became the greatest celebrity of his day. 'At twenty-four', Macaulay later reflected, 'he found himself on the highest pinnacle of literary fame, with Scott, Wordsworth, Southey, and a crowd of other distinguished writers beneath his feet. There is scarcely an instance in history of so sudden a rise to so dizzy an eminence.'[5] He was pursued by a host of adoring feminine admirers, foremost among whom was Lady Caroline Lamb. Exultant yet momentarily dazed, he lurched from one passionate affair to another. But his attention was caught, and curiosity aroused, by Lady Caroline's cousin, someone who was ostensibly - nay, ostentatiously - *not* in love with him It seemed most improbable that anything would come of this, for Anne Isabella Milbanke was a high-principled intellectual young lady, with an interest in mathematics, and (apparently) nurturing a romantic attachment elsewhere. She found Byron 'very interesting' [6] but clearly belonged to a far more exalted league than one to which his rakish lordship could aspire. 'I have no desire to be better acquainted with Miss Milbank [*sic*],' he told Lady Caroline; 'she is too good for a fallen spirit to know, and I should like her more if she were less perfect.' [7] But in April 1814, he confessed to Lady Melbourne that he did 'admire her as a very superior woman, a little encumbered with Virtue' [8] and eight months later they were married. It was a terrible mistake on both sides. Their union lasted for one year and three weeks. A daughter was born towards the end of that period, but convinced that it was not safe for her to remain under his roof Lady Byron left his London house as soon as it was possible to do so. She was certain, by this time, that he was not only mad but also very dangerous to know. She had belatedly come round, in short, to her cousin's way of thinking. And a little while later, with a spot of assistance from that same quarter, she reached the firm conclusion that he had also had an incestuous relationship with his half-sister, Augusta Leigh, and had perhaps fathered a child by her.

Secrets were divulged in strict confidence and dreadful rumours soon began to spread. 'The obloquy which Byron had to endure', Macaulay commented in 1830, 'was such as might well have shaken a more constant mind. The newspapers were filled with lampoons. The theatres shook with execrations. He was excluded from circles where he had lately been the observed of all observers.' [9] After penning a stinging rebuke to his wife, 'Fare Thee Well', Byron sailed off into exile in April 1816. For many months, he riled against her. Writing to Augusta in December 1816 he referred to 'that virtuous monster Miss Milbanke', who had almost driven him out of his senses', and described her in May 1817 as 'that misguided and artificial woman, who bears and disgraces my name'. [10] Yet, by degrees, his mortification faded, his humour and zest for life returned and he was primarily anxious, almost pathetically so, to obtain news of his daughter, Ada, and to learn what her behaviour and interests might be. A fresh life developed, magnificent and hilarious poems continued to pour out and to all intents and purposes he enjoyed what was, except in name, an immensely happy second marriage to Teresa Guiccioli.

At home, meanwhile, the climate of opinion was changing. The initial howl of contumely, to quote Macaulay for the very last time, gradually died away and 'those who had raised it began to ask each other, what, after all, was the matter about which they had been so clamorous, and wished to invite back the criminal whom they had just chased from them. His poetry became more popular than it had ever been; and his complaints were read with tears by thousands and tens of thousands who had never seen his face.' [11] And, to crown everything, he died in April 1824 at Missolonghi, drawn there by the cause of fighting for Greek independence. When his body was brought back to Britain two months later, and laboriously borne off to the ancestral mausoleum at Newstead Abbey, he was accorded what was almost a State funeral

Lady Byron, in the meantime, periodically allowed it to be known that she forgave her husband for his unspeakable treatment of her, donning a long-suffering face on such occasions. But she bridled with rage when she found other people suggesting that perhaps her *own* behaviour had at times been unreasonable and that there had been, not to make too fine a point of it, faults on both sides. On such occasions, she invariably briefed a squad of sympathisers to smite the doubters into the dust, while staying officially aloof from such activities. This apart, however, she endeavoured, with stern and dedicated countenance, to carve out a totally fresh life for herself and became deeply involved, by degrees, in a host of worthwhile, benevolent pursuits, causes and campaigns. She was the more easily enabled to do this by having become an immensely wealthy lady in her own right. Her mother's brother, Thomas Noel, the 2nd Viscount Wentworth, died in April 1815 without leaving any legitimate heirs and the family fortunes passed to the Milbankes, who were obliged, as a consequence, to change their surname to 'Noel'. They swiftly established themselves on the Wentworth estate at Kirkby Mallory in Leicestershire and when Anne's mother died in January 1822 she herself formally became Baroness Noel-Byron and inherited most of the family fortune. She signed her letters as 'A.I. Noel Byron' and the world at large continued to knew her simply as Lady Byron.

When living with her parents at Seaham, County Durham, Anne had been instrumental in establishing a small village school. The extent to which she could actively involve herself in its administration after 1814 would have been extremely limited, and in 1815 her parents moved from Seaham to Kirkby Mallory (some 150 miles away), but while seeking to manage it from afar she entrusted its day-to-day maintenance to the local vicar and his daughter. A letter which she wrote to him in November 1818 indicates that she continued to take a keen interest in how it was administered and to make available the necessary funds for that purpose. [12] She was deeply influenced at this time by learning of the experiences of Henry Pestalozzi (1746-1827), a Swiss educationalist who had endeavoured to establish a school for orphans and vagrant children at Unterwalden twenty years earlier. She was also absorbed, for a time, in the teachings of Robert Owen and the development of the Co-operative Movement, with its emphasis on basic communal activities. Of still greater interest, a little while later, were the achievements of Philipp Emanuel de Fellenberg, which had been publicised by Lord Brougham. A one-time protégé of Pestalozzi, until their views diverged, he had established an experimental school at Hofwyl in Switzerland which seemed to be doing great things. In the first instance, it had been designed to train local children in agricultural techniques, qualifying them to work on the land, but its curriculum had developed to take in such basic matters as reading, writing and arithmetic. Lady Byron visited the school in 1828 and was greatly impressed. Eleven years later, indeed, she published, anonymously, a short book entitled *What de Fellenberg has done for Education*, running to 105 pages and retailing for the modest sum of fourpence. (But not as anonymously as all that, for the *Westminster Review* - suitably primed - was able to reveal to its readers that this peon of praise came 'from the pen of Lady Byron'.) [13]

She had established a school for Kirkby Mallory children in 1818, locating it at the village of Newbold Verdon, two miles to the north. But after the death of her father, in March 1825, she was imbued with a strong desire to escape from that part of the world for an indefinite period. Entrusting management of both the estate and the school to other hands, she and her entourage of small daughter and servants embarked on what must have been a rather dreary grand tour of suburbia. By degrees, as she tired of one short-term location after another (and became partially disillusioned with the Co-operative Movement), she drifted nearer to west London. Following a three-year sojourn at Hanger Hill in Ealing, she took up residence in 1832 at a nearby country house at Fordhook, located on the boundary between Ealing and Acton, which had once belonged to Henry Fielding. Here, at any rate, was a location where she finally felt thoroughly at home, and (as a newly-installed grand lady, itching to do good works in the community) lost no time in making her presence felt. She resolved to set up yet another school for impoverished local children - both boys and girls - at Ealing Grove. Its administration, taking into account ideas generated by de Fellenberg (and also by Owen, who had founded a Rational School on similar lines) was the mission that would preoccupy her during the ten years that followed.

The precise date of the establishment of her 'Fellenbergian institute' (as she proudly described it) is not clear, but it is generally agreed that by 1834, following much careful preparation, it had definitely arrived on the scene. Lady Byron had decided that its pupils should be a mixture of boarders and day-school attendees, and an undated memorandum (1835 vintage?) states that 'at present' it consisted of 24 boarders and between 40 and 60 day scholars. It was to remain very much under her own tight control, for (as set out in another undated memorandum) she thought it undesirable for it to become a public institution. Her four basic reasons for resisting the intrusion of officialdom were:

1. That Religion must then assume a more formal and doctrinaire aspect for the satisfaction of the Church.

2. That there must be a more fixed plan, less susceptible of experimental variations, and imposing more restraint on the exercise of the Master's judgment.

3. That the numbers would be increased to an extent which I think incompatible with due attention to individual character.

4. That this School, being a private one and somewhat in advance, as to [times?] of the Government ones, would afford the latter the opportunity of profiting by the success or failure of different experiments. [14]

So, within a year or two of its establishment, the Ealing Grove school had become equipped with sixty or seventy pupils (most of their fees being waived in the first instance) and all of them were small boys. They were obliged to spend a minimum of three hours a day working in the garden, tending individual allotments, while 'indoor' tuition covered the 'three R's' plus geography and natural history. ('The manual labour', Lady Byron noted, somewhat acidly, 'will necessarily limit the intellectual instruction sufficiently, if care be taken that the boys acquire no more than they can understand.') [15] Religion was taught in a cautious and undogmatic fashion for Lady Byron was, in all but name, a Unitarian. There was no corporal punishment but standards of behaviour were recorded by credits and debits (taking the form of red and black badges) and punishment meant that certain privileges would be withheld.

An elderly retired actress called Joanna Baillie, a great admirer of Lady Byron, visited Ealing Grove and reported to a friend in great delight that she observed sixty 'boys of the common ranks ... who after doing their lessons of writing etc got up at the sound of a little bell, and ran eagerly each to his spade or mattock, and worked away at levelling ground and other country work as sturdily, and, in proportion, as effectively as men, but far happier. They work as carpenters too, and keep all the premises in order, and mend their own shoes and clothes. It seems to me an education well qualified to make them industrious and happy, and ready to turn their hands to anything - boys especially qualified for new settlers in our colonies; and the carpenters and gardeners of Acton and Ealing are mighty glad to have them for apprentices, a very good proof of the good effects of their schooling.' [16]

In the first instance, the school was manned primarily by volunteers, with daughter Ada among their number, under the direction of a properly qualified headmaster (a Mr Atlee succeeding an unsatisfactory Mr Craig in 1835), but some assistants proved more capable than others. By 1841 Lady Byron was reaching the conclusion that assistant staff should also be properly trained.

In the light of the foregoing, it will be evident that, so far as educational matters were concerned, she was vastly more knowledgeable than Dr Kay. It was a subject which had preoccupied her for more than twenty years. Dr Kay, in comparison, was a virtual newcomer to the scene, an enthusiastic amateur who, over a short space of time and with tremendous zest, had determinedly equipped himself with all the latest information and theories but whose practical experience of teaching the young, prior to 1840, had been limited. Relations between them were often somewhat tense but allowances were made on both sides and they endeavoured to co-operate. Lady Byron supplied the doctor with advice when it was sought and took a dutiful interest in the Battersea experiment. She sponsored one of the pupil-teachers (Mather Hirst, aged 15) [17] and, in need of a newly-qualified young teacher to serve under Mr Atlee, it was appropriate that, before looking further afield, she should turn to Dr Kay to see what his institution might have available.

It is deeply exasperating, for William's biographer, that there are no records to explain how his appointment to the Ealing Grove school came about. It must be surmised, however, that - anxious to impress Lady Byron with the very best that his training college had to offer - Dr Kay, with much pride, wheeled him forward as the star pupil. An interview (or interrogation?) would have followed. A preliminary exchange would presumably have taken place at Battersea, in Kay's presence, and the likelihood is that William was then invited to visit Ealing Grove to see for himself the premises where his potential services were required. One assumes that the visit was rounded off by another interview with Lady Byron in which the headmaster, Mr Atlee, would have participated.

Lady Byron was, at the time William first met her, not far short of her fiftieth birthday. Harriet Martineau, writing to Crabb Robinson in October 1842, reported that she had still not fully recovered from the traumatic experience of her marriage but that she endeavoured to put a brave face on things and was apparently capable of being 'bright and gay' when her health permitted. Unfortunately, however, people were put off by her 'excessive shyness' and also daunted by the 'apparent dryness' of her remarks once that initial shyness had been overcome. Carlyle referred to her in 1839 as 'a pale melancholy woman' while Benjamin Haydon, who had painted her portrait in 1840, thought her 'a double X icicle'. [18] In private life, whether ruling the roost in her domestic circle or zealously absorbed in running her schools, she was a lady of very strong convictions and autocratic manner, capable of laying about her with all the authority of the Queen of Hearts. The first headmaster of Ealing Grove, Mr E.T. Craig, had been dismissed for failing to adhere sufficiently closely to the doctrines promulgated by Fellenberg, despite having been sent to Hofwyl (at her ladyship's expense) on a special training course. His chief fault, apparently, was that he had failed to socialise sufficiently with the boys.

Charles Nelson Atlee, the second headmaster, had noted the reasons for his predecessor's downfall and proved much more amenable to pursuing the desired ethos of a family atmosphere. He was, moreover, a local lad, already well acquainted with many residents of the area, and ideally qualified to take over. Born in 1808 or 1809, so approximately twelve years older than William, he had lived in Ealing all his life and prior to 1835 had been a master at the nearby St Mary's National School. He appears to have been an admirable teacher and held in high regard by the local community.

Lady Byron and Mr Atlee were confronted by a neatly-attired, stocky, polite young man with a pale face, dark curly hair and a pleasant smile. He was thoughtful but spoke with firm assurance, in a voice which presumably retained some traces of a Welsh accent. He had evidently accumulated a reasonable amount of general knowledge and, to all intents and purposes, could bring a genuine degree of enthusiasm to bear on the task of teaching the young. He had been strongly recommended by Dr Kay and on this occasion, at any rate, the doctor's judgment would be held to have been fully justified, for her ladyship, with all her high standards, was satisfied with the new recruit's credentials and general bearing. He started work at Ealing Grove (so his *Journal* records) on the evening of Monday, 31 January 1842 and his starting salary would have been in the region of £75 to £80 per annum.

At which point, and before taking this narrative any further, it is necessary to say something more about that *Student's Journal*. It will be recalled that William had acquired this notebook three years earlier and that he had used it for its legitimate purpose as a diary for several weeks (3 June to 4 July) in the summer of 1839. Those diary entries occupy pages 2 to 10 of the *Journal*. Page 11 is blank but on pages 12 and 13 there are jottings about his income and expenditure in 1841. On page 14 the date on which his employment at Ealing Grove commenced is recorded, together with other significant dates in his early career. Then follows (for reasons to be explained shortly) a long list of book titles. Thereafter, in the form in which it now exists, most of the subsequent pages of the *Journal* are taken up (though not necessarily in strict chronological order) with meticulous entries about expenditure and income during the 1840s. On one occasion, however, William turned it upside down and, starting from the back, filled up pages 137 to 134 with three mini-articles. The first, copied from the reminiscences of Harriet Martineau, is a description of the saintly Dr Charles Follen (1796-1840), a German scholar living in Massachusetts who had been an ardent opponent of slavery. The second, entitled 'Fear & Love in Education', would appear (from its slightly amateurish style and sententious reflections) to have been written by William himself. The third consisted of thoughts on morality and religion taken primarily from the writings of Sir James Mackintosh. There are, in the *Journal* as it exists at present, no further diary entries - but one notes that 36 leaves (pages 37 to 108) have been torn out.

In *The Making of Lloyd George* W.R.P. George relates that in the summer of 1842 William decided to write down his thoughts and reflections 'in a notebook'. He began on Friday, 3 June (exactly three years after he had commenced his 1839 diary) and hoped to jot something down each day. In fact, the entries were made only on a spasmodic basis, usually on a Sunday. The last, says Dr George, was dated 31 July and the journal was not resumed until 1854. [19]

Dr George quoted extremely generous extracts from these entries in his book (pages 41 to 44) but did not make it clear whether William was setting down his thoughts in a totally fresh notebook or whether it was, once again, that reliable all-purpose *Student's Journal* which had been pressed into service. If the latter, then it would be reasonable to conclude that this fresh material appeared on the seventy-two missing pages (37 to 108) referred to above. The reason for speculating on this matter, at what might seem excessive length, is that the material which Dr George saw and used in 1976 seems to have disappeared. Until such time as it comes to light, assuming that it is still extant, we are dependent solely on those long extracts which he quoted in his book. These are certainly much better than nothing, but the insertion of dots at several points indicates that material has been omitted. When it has been possible, on other occasions, to check Dr George's transcriptions against actual documents, it has become apparent that he had a tendency to act in an editorial capacity when reproducing material written by his grandfather. There were silent abridgements, simplifications and adjustments. He was well-intentioned and may even have made small corrections as a sort of automatic reflex action, not regarding them in any way as distortions. He states, indeed, that he is quoting verbatim, but it must nevertheless be borne in mind that the entries which appear in his book are filtered and abridged versions of what William wrote originally. There is no way of knowing whether they represent (say) 75% or 50% of the authentic text. But, having said that, it must be instantly conceded that what Dr George does reproduces is quite startlingly frank in its nature and that one feels almost churlish in wishing that more such material could have been made available.

It is clear, from the extracts of the journal supplied by Dr George, that William was not abundantly happy at Ealing Grove school. The reasons for this will be examined in a moment, but it should be noted that there are no descriptions of the school as such and that it only impinges marginally on his ruminations. It is largely from sources elsewhere, therefore, that a picture of his working environment can be conjured up. The census for 1841 shows that there were thirty-eight boarders at that time, with ages ranging from 8 to 15, and one assumes that there were at least fifty day-boys still in regular attendance. Mr Atlee lived on the premises, with his wife and three children and maidservant, and so too did a surprising number of ancillary staff. John Cox and his wife were gardeners, James Carter (with wife and child) supplied general labour and (presumably) acted as caretaker, and a Mary

Malcock (with two teenagers) was a market gardener. For the gardening activities, it must be emphasised, loomed large in the school's curriculum and Lady Byron had evidently enlisted some professional guidance for the marketing of the pupils' produce. With ninety to a hundred children to be cared for at any one time, there must have been at least two full-time teachers to assist Mr Atlee. By the start of 1842 one of them was William and the other seems to have been a Mr Goodall. There may also still have been some help from unpaid volunteers.

William was doubtless based in lodgings fairly close to the school. We know nothing about them, but the fact that brother John was his guest for a few days in June suggests that he was not too cramped for space. From time to time, he would have joined the Atlee family for dinner, and there were occasional invitations to lunch at Fordhook House (which would impress his son eighty years later) [20], but we have no precise record of such events. He discharged his duties competently enough, it seems, for his employers evidently had no cause for complaint, but he himself did not rank his performance highly. 'I am far from being in a contented frame of mind just now,' he wrote in that final 31 July entry, which may have marked the end of the term. 'The principal cause of this dissatisfaction is my indifferent success in the school. I feel the want of more extensive and exact information than I possess at present, as well as more energy and activity in communicating it.... I must resolutely aim at a higher standard - to do more or nothing at all.... As a preliminary to this it is important that I should decide upon the subjects to be studied and form some plan for pursuing them. In the first place, I think that I am tolerably up in *Grammar*, so that I may feel easy about that. Geography also, I am sufficiently advanced to keep ahead with very slight preparations.' Some additional stock-taking was presumably intended to follow, but at this point the entry ends. [21]

At Battersea (and, indeed, earlier), he had been convinced that teaching was his vocation in life. In the company of his peers, and hailed as one of the outstanding pupils of 1841, he had been buoyed up with ambition. He had been positively exhilarated when he delivered his farewell speech. But at Ealing, functioning as a relatively small cog in Lady Byron's educational machine, his resolution sagged. Life suddenly became rather mundane. The discipline needed to keep him active, and searching for higher objectives, would now have to be self-imposed if it was to be imposed at all. But the drive was momentarily lacking. And was teaching, after all, really such a marvellous career as all that? 'I am still very unsettled in my mind as to my future plans and prospects,' he had written on 19 June. 'I cannot somehow make up my mind to be a schoolmaster for *life*. My present position does not altogether satisfy me. I want to occupy *higher ground* sometime or other. I want to increase the stock of my attainments but hardly know how to set about it.' The previous week he had reflected (drawing upon Thomas Gray once again) on how wonderful it would be to become a great writer, to 'bequeath to posterity a legacy of "thoughts that breathe and words that burn"', and on 3 July he resolved to write a little every day, 'if possible', and acquire literary skill by degrees. It would also enable him, by charting his own changing reflections, to become more familiar with himself and, ultimately, lead to a greater knowledge of other people's characters as well. But, sadly, this resolve would not be carried through. It was the second time he had failed, for on 6 June he had declared, almost in desperation, that it was essential that he write more often: 'I must *record something* - have something to show myself for the time that is past - so that I can say that I have lived and did something at a particular time past. In looking back upon my past life, I find it is all of such a dreary character.' [22]

He also despised himself for telling a lie - or, at any rate, for giving an extremely misleading impression. Mr Goodall told him, early in June, that he had just purchased a newly-published edition of Shakespeare (presumably the one which Charles Knight had brought out in eight magnificent volumes). William had seen and examined the new publication in a bookshop a few days earlier 'and this combined with a little vanity, or rather the shame of acknowledging that I had no copy of Shakespeare, induced me to give him to understand that I also had lately bought a copy of the very same edition. There is no use in mincing the matter, especially to myself, for if I did not tell a direct and actual falsehood, I certainly conveyed a false impression to his mind, in that I deceived him. Now this is a very pitiful and disgraceful affair.' Hanging his head in shame, but lacking a father-confessor, he devoted a further 187 words to berating himself over this 'very lamentable' incident. Self-flagellation (on paper, at any rate) was the only conceivable way of making amends. [23]

Another great worry at this time was the state of his health. Playing with the boys early in June, he had coughed up two or three specks of blood. This was the reason why, accompanied by John, he went to London on 4 June to seek advice from a certain Dr Elliotson. But the doctor was unavailable and it is not clear whether William sought advice from any other practitioner. From this point onwards, however, he began to brood about his health, and may have developed into something of a hypochondriac. His diary entry for 12 June refers to his 'indifferent' state of health and on 31 July he would attribute his current lack of energy primarily to the same cause. For he had been put 'to the necessity of setting a constant watch over myself, and of measuring all my actions and movements.' Once his health improved, so he assured himself in more optimistic moments, he would be able to leap into action again. [24]

There were very few (if any) people with whom he could converse freely and at length, complaining in his diary on 12 June that he lacked 'congenial society', and the short visit from his brother John (now aged sixteen) probably helped to cheer him up. (He noted, presumably with approval, that John had 'picked up a good many ideas about human life, morals and literature'.) Following the unsuccessful visit to Dr Elliotson, they had called on a friend called Thomas Rendall (a medical student, based at King's College, from whom advice and reassurance would have been sought). They eventually fetched up in the coffee house referred to at the outset of this chapter and then wandered along the Strand. They lingered over several book-stalls and looked in at a bookshop in King Street, Covent Garden - where, much to his delight, William was able to purchase 'a very pretty volume' containing all of Shakespeare's plays and poems for the sum of four shillings. [25] Even though it was not that aforementioned super-de-luxe edition, he would be able, once again, to hold his head high in the presence of Mr Goodall. (The part-works edition of the bard which William had been collecting in 1839, equipped with splendid illustrations, was also one for which Charles Knight had been responsible, so he was not totally unfamiliar with that particular editor's handiwork and erudition. He could have pleaded this to himself in semi-mitigation.)

The subject which dominated him over and above everything else, however, even though he could not bring himself to utter the word, was Sex. It seems, on the face of things, that not much had changed since 1839. Almost certainly, William was still a virgin. The ideal woman (as described by Wordsworth, at any rate) had not yet materialised and he felt desperately lonely. He gazed on women from afar - decent women, that is, as distinct from the occasional flirtatious, shameless floozy who may have crossed his path, inducing shudders rather than delight - and wrung his hands in despair at the apparent impossibility of finding someone who came even close to the poet's vision.

His mind dwelt much upon the urgent necessity of being married as soon as circumstances permitted. But - dreadful reflection! - might it not prove to be a miserable rather than a happy experience? On that visit to Rendall, on 4 June, he learnt that Rendall's brother James was having a wretched time with a 'very fickle and spiteful' wife - a case of having married in haste and repenting at leisure, it seemed. 'Truly', he reflected afterwards, 'the selection of a wife is a serious affair. How often may that poor fellow have to repent of his precipitancy! The more I think on the subject of matrimony the more important does it appear to me. Three or four years ago I would have required a week to come to a decision; but now, a year would hardly suffice. As a man advances in years he becomes more cautious; he then hesitates before taking any important step. If a youth of 18 or 20 falls in love, he would marry without a moment's hesitation, but the man of 25 or 30 stops and considers long and seriously before making such an important change in his condition. He does not look on matrimony simply as a legal means of gratifying his own passion, but he looks upon it as a very important change in his condition, and one which is intimately connected with his future happiness or misery.' [26]

Thus ruminated this very intense young man. He returned to the subject in his journal entry for 12 June. 'I have become possessed of late', he glumly recorded, 'by a strong desire to be married. This renders me discontented with my present situation - my mind is unsettled, and constantly wandering off to this favourite subject - *perhaps* more is the pity. I add this because I think it is a great blessing for anyone to be really and truly in love. I am convinced however that I shall remain unsettled until I have effected this dread change in my condition. I begin to feel the want of a home - to be surrounded by those to whom I feel that I am an object of interest. In short I want to be *loved*. That is an exquisite pleasure, second only to the pleasure of loving.... I know, I feel that I have a capacity for love - even now my pent-up affections are struggling to find vent.'

For George Speed, an eleven-year-old pupil at the school, had recently lost his father. William had conceived a great affection for the boy, secretly vowing that he 'would do anything in my power that would be likely to benefit him. I am almost ashamed to confess it to myself, but there was actually a secret pleasure mixed with the pain I felt on hearing of his father's death. I immediately found relief in the thought that it would now be very probably in *my* power to befriend him! There was a luxury in that thought.' [27]

There was bravery in such candour, moreover, for William was confronting his demons as honestly as he could, but this was dangerous ground and he speedily returned to his preoccupation with finding a satisfactory wife. There was, he decided, no point in marrying a person one did not love, for a husband and wife needed to confide in one another with total frankness. If there were no sympathy between them, then mutual disgust would develop. Yet there were, on the other hand, plenty of examples which showed that domestic unhappiness did not necessarily prevent one from accomplishing great things, such as writing a book   For confirmation of (and perhaps consolation for) this final reflection, he would later copy out a quotation from an unidentified writer: 'Everywhere but in novels, the marriage of convenience has proved an excellent institution; while what are generally called love-matches have been, are and ever will be prolific of misery. They spring from passion and terminate in early satiety. The romance disappears - the sentiment subsides - the woman remains!' [28]

With gloomy realism, William thus tended to discount the intermediate stage that might elapse between functioning as a single and solitary agent and being shackled, for better or worse, in a state of matrimony for evermore. The notion of simply enjoying life in a relaxed, unhurried, natural fashion while simultaneously extending the range of his social acquaintances, and perhaps encountering one particular young lady with interests in common with his own, evidently did not appeal. Perhaps he felt, with advancing maturity, that he had now passed beyond the ingenuous pastimes of his youth - musical evenings, amateur dramatics or walks in the country - and needed to concentrate on finding someone who was reasonably acceptable as quickly as possible. He was becoming a young man in a hurry, impatient to embark upon the next stage of his life without delay - even if marriage proved, in the event, unpalatable. Triumphant attainment of that *'higher ground'*, his ultimate but ill-defined objective, was what needed to be borne in mind!

William's financial accounts for 1842 are incomplete, some of them having been recorded on pages now missing from the *Journal*, but details of his expenditure for the period from mid-August to the end of November are extant (though sometimes hard to decipher). August was clearly a holiday month, with trips to Harrow and Kew Gardens, and sundry train, omnibus and boat fares to unknown destinations. [29] Much of his expenditure went on books - and not simply on such basic items as a Bible and Prayer Book (combined), text-books on grammar and the Rev. John Todd's *Student's Manual* (1840), designed to form and strengthen the intellectual and moral character and habits of students. There was, for example, a volume entitled *Sacred Geography*, Dr Johnson's *Lives of the Poets*, Jeremy Taylor's *Sermons* (first published in the mid-17th century) and various other titles (Lord's *Lectures*, for instance) which can no longer be clearly identified. He also acquired some German books and bought sundry journals. Expenditure on food and drink, plus snuff and cigars, was zealously noted down. Herschell's Biscuits, costing three shillings, were quite an expensive item, and may have been intended as a present to his hostess at a dinner-party. He attended a lecture at a Mechanics' Institute but no other outings are mentioned at this time. Unexpectedly, perhaps, is an entry for half-a-crown relating to the purchase and carriage of guinea pigs - intended for young George Speed, perhaps?

William left Ealing Grove school on 31 December 1842, having been there for precisely eleven months. His first spell of full-time employment thus came to an end. A new chapter in his life was about to begin, which his biographer must mark in appropriate fashion, but he remained a teacher - and he remained, moreover, the protégé of Lord Byron's widow.

CANTO 2: NEWBOLD

Lady Byron had moved to Esher in the summer of 1842. She was satisfied that, with Mr Atlee at the helm, she had left Ealing Grove school in competent hands - and it was formally transferred to him a little while later. At some stage, however, she also returned to the ancestral home at Kirkby Mallory and developed a renewed interest in the school at Newbold Verdon. Information about this school is extremely sparse and it is not clear how it had fared in her prolonged absence, but in some respects it may have served as a pilot scheme for her third scholastic venture. When developing, in 1834, some thoughts on how parents could be persuaded to send their children to Ealing Grove, 'and keep them there as long as possible', she described how parcels of land could be allotted to them, to develop as they thought fit, as an inducement. 'I need not dwell on the well-known moral effects of this plan,' she concluded - and added, as an afterthought, 'This has answered in Newbold Vernon in Leicestershire'. [30] In charge at Kirkby Mallory during the periods of her absence was Charles Noel, presumably a distant relative, who acted as overseer or steward of both the estate and the school. (One is tempted to draw a parallel with Malvolio and the Lady Olivia, but the census return for 1841 shows that Mr Noel, aged thirty-one, was a married gentleman with two children.)

There are a number of scenarios which might explain why Lady Byron transferred William to Newbold Verdon. It may have been that he did not get on too well with Mr Atlee, or it may have been that the Ealing Grove school had now become top-heavy with staff of an extremely good calibre - over-endowed, as it were, compared with a less satisfactory situation at Newbold. Or it may have been that the state of William's health was a cause of concern and it was thought that the Leicestershire air, and a less onerous routine, would do him good. It was possibly a combination of all these factors. (And, just conceivably, there was a fourth, to which we will shortly return.) Whatever the reason, William had a three-month break from teaching (a recuperation period, perhaps) for he did not start at Newbold until 1 April 1843. He apparently went from London to Tunbridge Wells, and thence to Bishop's Stortford and Cambridge, before returning to Trecoed for two months' holiday. (There is no way of knowing whether it was simply from curiosity, or for particular purposes, that he visited those towns.) It is just conceivable that, with some time to spare during his stay at Trecoed, William tried his hand at literary composition, with results to be considered later, but at the end of March he moved to the Midlands to take up residence in the small village of Newbold Verdon. Apart from another holiday break in the second half of August, he would remain there for almost exactly one year. Kirkby Mallory was two miles to the south, Leicester seven miles to the east and Market Bosworth (the nearest shopping centre) three miles to the west. Bosworth field, where the great battle had been fought, was thus in close proximity.

Daniel Defoe, visiting Leicestershire more than a century earlier, noted that the whole county seemed 'to be taken up in country business ... particularly in breeding and feeding cattle', with herds of sheep which could keep London supplied indefinitely. But he also noted that there was 'a considerable manufacture carry'd on here, and in several of the market towns round for weaving of stockings by frames; and one would scarce think it possible so small an article of trade could employ such multitudes of people as it does; for the whole county seems to be employ'd in it'. [31] Newbold Verdon, and its immediate vicinity, was one of the locations where this industry had flourished but by the 1840s it was in serious decline - so much so that in 1845 a public inquiry was held into the growing unemployment and destitution among frame-work knitters in that area. Two of their number, Thomas Ball and Thomas Priestnell, gave evidence which provided, in passing, a useful and graphic picture of how the Newbold school had been operating and the reputation it now enjoyed.

Q.   Is there any free-school there?

A.   Yes. They [the children] go to the free-school till they get six or seven years of age, and then they are eligible to go to Lady Byron's school by paying tuppence a week. I had two boys there; but one I took away when he was 15 years of age; and the other is still there; he is about 12 years of age. The parents of all the children who go there have the privilege of a bit of land, about 800 or 900 each, at about the same rent as the other. That is extra to the allotment ground [20 acres made freely available by Lady Byron] that I have spoken of.

Q.   What system is pursued at Lady Byron's school?

A.   There are some little bits of land for all the boys which they manage entirely themselves, 100 each; they set it with potatoes, or anything they think proper. They pay 6d a year for it. The parents find the seed, and the manure as well, whereby they are instructed. They teach them up as agriculturists; the master takes them out two or three hours a day, to work in the gardens.

Q.   What are they taught in the school?

A.   To read the scriptures, writing and arithmetic, and a good prayer is put up every day at noon, and they are taught to sing hymns.

Q.   You say that you have had one child there till he was 15 years of age; what did you put him to when you took him away?

A.   I am a carrier, and I take him to market twice a week, and I am in hopes of getting him apprenticed.

Q.   Do you find that the education he has received there is good?

A.   It is a great satisfaction to me, and think that it will help him on in the world. I should not by any means [now] think of putting him to be a frame-work knitter; if the trade were as it used to be, it would be the best thing that I could think of.

Q.   Have the parents the advantage of any of the produce of the allotments held by the children?

A.   Yes; I have derived as much as 10 shillings in the produce of one year, from my own boy's hundred.

Q.   Have you any opportunity of seeing whether the boys taught at Lady Byron's school are better conducted and turn out better than others?

A.   Decidedly so. Those attending the free-school have not had the advantage of being trained in the same regular and industrious habits, and consequently their conduct is not so good. There are two or three schoolmasters, and they take a great deal of pains with the boys. I would challenge my little boy against any boy in the country to read. [32]

The total number of pupils in attendance is not clear but that reference to a teaching staff of two or three masters suggests that it could not have been so very different from Ealing Grove, i.e., eighty to ninety, although in this instance they were probably all day-boys.

We do not know what William thought of the place (a village consisting of approximately 50 houses and 400 residents). We do not know what the people he was working with thought of him. In the total absence of any other records, we are solely dependent on his book-keeping entries for fragmentary details of his life at this time. It is a distorted view, but it is better than no view at all.

'Look after the pennies and the pounds will look after themselves' is an adage in which he believed wholeheartedly. He diligently recorded at this time the purpose for which every penny and every halfpenny with which he parted company had been spent. (It must be borne in mind, of course, that the price of goods and services have increased eighty-fold since 1842. There were twenty shillings to the pound in William's day, so in purchasing-terms a shilling from that period - made up of twelve pre-1971 pennies - would be roughly equivalent to £4 in present-day currency and a Victorian penny would be roughly equivalent to 33 'modern' pennies.)

His salary appears to have been paid in a rather casual manner, as and when it occurred to somebody to do so - or it may simply be that the erratic state of his book-keeping methods, whereby one year is sometimes mixed in with another, or incoming cash fails to be recorded, is to blame for this impression. Lady Byron and Mr Noel each paid him £10 on 13 June 1843 (but the entries appear on different pages, so this may be an inadvertent duplication). Mr Noel also paid him £2 in September, £4 in October and £5 in December. On this basis, his total salary for 1843 amounted to only £31. No payments at all are recorded so far as the first quarter of 1844 is concerned, unless they are encompassed by the entry made on Sunday, 31 March (six days after leaving Newbold) of 'cash in hand' totalling £21, two shillings and tenpence-halfpenny.

Expenditure was meanwhile recorded in unremitting (but often indecipherable) detail. On 13 June 1843 (that date again!) he pays a Mr Brown four shillings (for rent, perhaps). On 1 July he purchases a cravat and gloves and has a hair-cut, which suggests a special event is imminent. Security at his lodgings may have been lax, for three days later he purchases (for half-a-crown) three locks. On 10 July he pays a boy tuppence to go to Bosworth on an errand. Most of the entries (for newspapers, pamphlets, stamps, food and drink, washing, etc) are very mundane. Tobacco is a regular purchase and so too (but more occasionally) are cigars. Books continue to rank high among his acquisitions..

On Sunday, 11 August there was an outing to Bradgate Park, one of the beauty spots of Leicestershire, which cost him elevenpence. Four days later, his holiday commenced. He was in Birmingham on the 18th but, seemingly, in London for the greater part of the time - a visit which cost him, in all, five pounds and eighteen shillings. (Greenwich, visited on the 23rd, is the only locality specifically mentioned.) The most expensive single day came on 28 August, when a visit to the theatre cost him one shilling and sixpence, a copy of *The Wealth of Nations* was purchased for eight shillings, both breakfast and dinner cost fivepence and supper cost sixpence - in all, ten shillings and tenpence. He returned to Newbold on 5 September, presumably refreshed in body and spirit.

There are a considerable number of detailed entries for the last quarter of 1843, but not until the festive season arrived is anything slightly out of the normal routine noted. On 21 December he despatched a parcel to Wales, which cost him one shilling and sevenpence, on Christmas Eve he gave Mr Morton (the school's odd job man, one suspects) sixpence and on 26 December he purchased a pair of spectacles for his mother for the sum of nine shillings and despatched them to Trecoed (the postage costing another sixpence). On 27 December he paid one shilling, as the cost of listening to some singers, and two days later attended a tea party - again, his own financial contribution to the proceedings was one shilling.

He sometimes purchased chemicals, perhaps to conduct an experiment for the benefit of his pupils. Flasks, tinfoil, tissue paper and bladders, linked together as part of a bulk purchase on one occasion, are intriguing items. On 10 February 1844 another dinner was in the offing and in honour of the event he invested in a waist-piece and a new cravat, plus the inevitable hair-cut: a get-together at the Mechanics' Institute (price two shillings) apparently rounded off the day. On 3 March he paid sixpence for drinks at Kikby Mallory (the first and last time that particular location is mentioned), with carriage from Leicester (for himself or for books?) costing another sixpence. On 5 March, and again on 6 March, he spent threepence on sending a letter. These are the last expenditure items recorded for 1844 in the book-keeping entries of his *Student's Journal*. (They appear on page 117. Dr George assumed, not unreasonably, that the entries on pages 118 and 119, following on immediately and referring in the first instance to expenditure in February and March, also date from 1844 - and they encouraged him to attempt an outline reconstruction of William's subsequent activities in that year. [33] But those entries were made, in fact, five years later - by which time fresh blank pages in the *Journal* were in short supply - and relate solely to 1849.)

A recurring item in his expenditure was 'Carriage for books', purchased in Leicester and elsewhere, and by the beginning of 1844 his private library was extremely impressive in its range and scale. A list compiled a little while later identified forty-seven specific volumes. Some of them, such as *Sacred Geography* and Dr Johnson's *Lives of the Poets*, we have already encountered, but *The Wealth of Nations* is absent from that list. So too are Jeremy Taylor's *Sermons* and the Rev. John Todd's *Student's Manual*, although *The Sunday School Teacher* (1838) and the newly-published *Lectures to Children*, also by the prolific Rev. Todd, are included. Other volumes which it is possible to identify are Edmund Burke's essay on *The Sublime and Beautiful* (1757), John Herschel's *A preliminary discourse on the study of natural philosophy* (1831), *A Compendious German Grammar* (1833) by A.B. Bernays, the Rev. Samuel Wood's *A Grammar of Elocution* (1833), Augustus de Morgan's *First Notions of Logic* (1839), Lord Brougham's *A Letter on National Education to the Duke of Bedford* (1839), the works of 'Shakespere' and Thomas Campbell's *Poems*.

There were a host of standard textbooks, such as *Self-Instruction in Arithmetic*, a *Geography Primer*, an *Introduction to Science*, a guide to *Minerals and Metals*, some *Song Exercises*, a *History of Cotton*, *Lessons in Mechanics* and somebody's thoughts on *The Art of Reading*. Other titles are *Customs' Report* and a *Common Place Book* in two parts. Religion was catered for by a *Prayer Book* and 'Shelby's' *Bible*. He had a *Welsh Dictionary* plus a book on Irish Grammar and, seemingly, a companion volume which dealt with Irish arithmetic. There were works on ornithology and astronomy. There were part-works which he was collecting, one of them entitled *Entertaining Knowledge*. Other items, such as Hopkin's *Expedition*, Trufino's *Life*, Reed's *Grammar*, Barnes's *Grammar*, Leuliom's *Exercises* and Hall's *Algebra*, sound extremely erudite but are likely to mean little or nothing to the present-day reader. A biography of Napoleon comes as comparatively light relief. In all, therefore, when allowance is made for the aforementioned absentees, William must have possessed at least fifty books.

But there seems to have been precious little fun in his life.   One wonders whether he still found time (or even deigned) to read works of fiction.   It will be recalled that in 1839 he had earnestly copied out extracts from *Ernest Maltravers*, which had made a deep impression on him, and relevant to remember Trollope's misgivings about the effect which the dauntless heroes depicted in Bulwer Lytton's novels, excelling in knowledge and resourcefulness, might have on a very young man - 'They would be apt to make him think he could be every thing at once' and lead to him consuming his nights in the deepest of studies.   It must certainly have been the case that much midnight oil was burnt in William's room, just as it had been in the days when he was an apprentice to Dr Millard.

But something very strange happened on Monday, 25 March 1844.   William abandoned all his books and all his clothes, other than those in which he stood up, and fled at top speed from his lodgings at Newbold Verdon.   The one thing that he most definitely did *not* leave behind in his flight, for which we must be thankful, was his precious *Student's Journal*.   (The abandoned apparel consisted of two pairs of trousers, two pairs of drawers, one shirt, three pairs of hose and socks, one cap and one pair of gloves - not to mention a clock and two umbrellas, or 'brollies'.)   So far as one can gather, he never went near Newbold again.   Dr George, noting this sudden departure, thought it an 'extraordinary' event but could offer no explanation. [34]   But his knowledge of the exceptional character of the two establishments where his grandfather had been working was scant.   Forty years later, and slightly better informed on these matters, it is possible to hazard a cautious guess.

When Lord Byron vanished into self-imposed exile in the spring of 1816 he left behind not only a wife but also a four-month-old daughter, Augusta Ada, on whom he had barely clapped eyes after the day of her birth. Her upbringing had been singular and severe. Lady Byron had been determined that she should know little or nothing about her father, during the time in which she was growing up, and it was not until she reached the age of twenty and had been married for five months that she was allowed to see a life-size portrait of him (previously concealed behind a curtain) for the very first time. Lady Byron had done her utmost to ensure that, by this stage of her life, Ada (as she was exclusively known) would be deeply embroiled in scientific and mathematical interests to the virtual exclusion of everything else, including poetry. To a large extent, her strategy had been successful - but emotionally her daughter was left in a somewhat fraught, unbalanced state.

Ada evidently taught arithmetic at Ealing Grove for a while and in July 1835 (partly to escape from her mother, perhaps) she married William King, who was created the earl of Lovelace in 1838, and moved to her husband's estate at Ockham Park in Surrey, where another school was established. Henceforth she would be known as Ada, Countess of Lovelace, and as such her name would be linked with that of Charles Babbage for evermore in the eyes of Posterity, for she became intensely interested in his analytical machine - primarily, it seems, as a sure-fire means of backing winners at the race-track.

Her marriage was an unhappy one. She was bored with the three children who resulted from it and contemptuous of her husband, despite his earnest endeavours to please. She was, in fact, slightly mad. Her biographer, Benjamin Woolley, has described her 'as flirtatious, outspoken and often shocking; she consorted with people at the margins of society as well as those at the heart of it; she rebelled against the impositions of her gentility and gender'. [35]

There were various people in the public eye who attracted her attention and unstinting admiration. One of these was Dr John Elliotson, who was renowned as an eminent physician for most of his career and moved in literary as well as medical circles, being a close friend of Dickens, Thackeray and Wilkie Collins. He was very much a high-flyer. But his over-enthusiastic advocacy of mesmerism, and revelations by *The Lancet* of the very dubious techniques he employed at public demonstrations of its alleged efficacy, obliged him to resign his University College Hospital post in 1838. He continued his professional career, his home at Bedford Square becoming the base-camp for his activities, and despite being discredited he retained a small but influential army of admirers during the remaining thirty years of his life.

Now William, it will be recalled, had coughed up two or three specks of blood in May 1842. One would have expected him to visit a general practitioner in the Ealing area to seek advice and treatment but he had gone, instead, direct to Dr Elliotson - almost to the top of the tree, as it were. Somebody had obviously urged him to do so - somebody who was taking a keen interest in his career and welfare. It might, conceivably, have been Lady Byron herself, but it is perhaps rather more likely to have been her daughter - who, paying a short visit to her mother at Fordhook House or dropping in at Ealing Grove, could well have been attracted by this handsome, dark-haired, serious and unworldly young man, six years her junior, and resolved to further his education in her own inimitable fashion.

Ada had 'form' when it came to unorthodox pupil-teacher relationships. Some ten years earlier she had had a passionate affair with a young man engaged to instruct her in shorthand, who was sacked when their relationship was discovered. It was only the swift intervention of the young tutor's family, when - alarmingly distraught - she arrived out of the blue at his home one day, that prevented an elopement from taking place. It is just possible, therefore, that Lady Byron, noting the interest that her daughter was taking in the young teacher, thought it might be prudent to transfer him to Newbold Verdon and out of harm's way.

Something cataclysmic undoubtedly happened to William on 25 March 1844. It is conceivable that Ada, revisiting her childhood home at Kirkby Mallory, sought him out, renewed their acquaintance and made it emphatically clear that a much closer relationship was desired - and that William, horrified and frightened by such a revelation, lost no time in making tracks for the nearest exit. It was a situation which he was not remotely equipped to handle.   But it must be emphasised that all of this is surmise. There is no record of Ada's movements during the first quarter of 1844 nor, it seems, any papers in existence which shed any light on the events of this time. Whether the belongings which William left behind were ever sent on to him must remain largely a matter for conjecture but there is a tiny sequel, to be narrated shortly, which suggests that they probably were.

As a footnote to the foregoing, it is interesting to note that one of the items in William's library at that time was a book which he referred to, in his *Student's Journal*, as '*Intr to Comp:*'. One would like to think that the full title of this volume was *An Introduction to Computers* (or *Computing*) and that it was a gift from somebody who, in the present context, could be fairly easily identified. Or, at any rate, a book which could indicate a shared interest. *Voila*, we have a smoking gun - a definite connection between Lord Byron's daughter and Lloyd George's father has been established!   In an ideal world this might have been the case.   But it seems that the word 'computer', as subsequently applied to machines of the type which Babbage was developing, did not come into general use for another thirty years or so. Whatever '*Comp:*' represents, it is unlikely to be 'computers' or 'computing' - unless the author of this mysterious volume, which has so far eluded discovery, was radically ahead of his (or her) time.

7 - AN HONORARY 'SCOUSER'

It must be assumed that in the first instance, after fleeing from Newbold Verdon, William was left with no option but to go straight home to Trecoed and take stock of the situation. He glumly listed in his *Student's Journal* all the items that he had left behind him and recorded on Sunday, 31 March 1844, at the end of the financial year, that his 'cash in hand' amounted to £21, two shillings and tenpence halfpenny [£21.14 in modern currency] - a sum which had dropped to £13 and four shillings [£13.20] by 30 May. Those are the very last entries he made in the *Journal* for 1844 (in the form in which it has come down to us, at any rate) and there are none at all for 1845. So what did he do next?

The springboard for his first professional appointment had been the Battersea teachers' training college. It may just be, with the termination of that appointment, that he turned to Dr Kay for advice, but that gentleman no longer existed - or not, at any rate, in the form that William had previously known him. Himself somewhat smitten, not so long before, with the charms of Ada, Countess of Lovelace, to the extent of writing her several coy and rather curious letters, he had finally achieved a long-desired eminence and respectability in June 1842 by marrying Janet Shuttleworth, a wealthy Lancashire heiress. But there was an important condition. He was obliged, as part of the marriage settlement, and by special royal licence, to change his name. Henceforth he would be known as Sir James Kay-Shuttleworth. He acquired in one fell swoop not only a wife but also a baronetcy - plus a stately home, in the form of Gawthorpe Hall. He would remain Permanent Secretary to the Education Office until 1849 but his links with the Battersea complex had come to an end. There could be, therefore, no help from this quarter.

To find a possible answer to our question, we need to leap forward almost eighty years. It will be remembered that William's youngest son (William No. 5) planned to write a full-scale biography of his father in that fateful year 1922, when the great name George was on virtually everyone's lips and the time seemed propitious for an account of his immediate ancestry. But a certain vote at a certain club brought six years' ascendancy to an end and the name of George would be, for a generation or so, sullied and eclipsed. The project was therefore abandoned. In the course of gathering material, however, the would-be biographer had consulted Anne Williams and jotted down on 6 November 1922 a list of the places where William was definitely known to have lived after leaving Lady Byron's employment - i.e., for the final two decades of his life. These, to the best of her knowledge, were Talgarth, Wakefield, Liverpool, Pwllhelli, Rawtenstall (a synonym for Newchurch misspelt, forgivably, as 'Rottenstall'), Manchester and Bulford. (Haverfordwest, while featuring in a subsequent paragraph, was not mentioned in the list and Wakefield ought to have come between Liverpool and Pwllheli, but it is otherwise reliable.) [1]

The reference to Talgarth a small market town in Breconshire with a population slightly less than 1,400, is unexpected. This is the only mention of it encountered by the present writer but Anne obviously believed that it was William's next port of call after he left Newbold Verdon (and after he had recuperated for a short time at Trecoed). Statistics compiled in 1847, for inclusion in the Government 'Blue Books' of that year, showed that 183 children attended its two day-schools. The Commissioner concerned, Jelinger C. Symons, visited both of them. He was not greatly impressed by the Church school, where the headmaster (a crippled ex-carpenter) seemed inadequate and the children not very bright but thought that the British School, almost adjoining it, was a model of its kind. Presumably the latter was where William would have worked, but for how long (and, indeed, if at all) it is impossible to say.

In mid-July 1846 the book-keeping entries resume, for with a grand entry all to itself, occupying in solitary splendour the topmost part of what is otherwise a blank sheet (page 124 of the *Journal*), there are recorded the expenditure details of a journey from Wales on the 15th and 16th of that month. William had a meal at a nearby restaurant before boarding the train for his overnight trip - 'Gave J. Saunders for dinner 1/4' runs the first line, although the total carried across to the final column is one shilling and eightpence. Could fourpence have been added *en route* as a tip? Then, on the next line, come biscuits (tuppence), drink (sixpence) and a book (half-a-crown), totalling three shillings and tuppence. But he forgets to record the cost of his railway ticket. For the next stage, he leaves the train and continues by steamer (fifteen shillings for himself and three for his luggage) and, after disembarking, continues by cart (another half-a-crown) making a sub-total of one pound and sixpence and a grand total of one pound, five shillings and fourpence. At the end of his trip he treats himself, as a separate item of expenditure, to a well-deserved pint of brandy (three shillings) and one must conclude, sadly, that his membership of the United Abstinence Society had well and truly lapsed.

The destination is unstated in the *Journal*, but in view of the fact that water had to be crossed, and bearing in mind the well-established belief (which, as we will shortly discover, is only partially correct) that William worked in Liverpool for at least six years [2], until the end of 1852, it is reasonable to conclude that the train from Wales had taken him to Birkenhead, where he boarded a steamer to cross the Mersey on the final stage of his journey.

For he had been appointed headmaster of a school in the centre of the city at a salary of £80 per annum. This is the point in time at which his book-keeping entries resume but it is possible, of course, that he had already been based in Liverpool for many months and was simply returning there after a short break. His expenditure records are of interest because they suggest that he was, during that summer, in the throes of setting up some kind of a bachelor establishment. He may have been in lodgings for a while, and the purchase on 21 July of a cask of beer (fifteen shillings) and another pint of brandy strongly implies that celebrations were in the offing - in which case, there were clearly fellow-Liverpudlians with whom he was already on affable terms. Could he now have been promoted from the post of ordinary teacher to that of head teacher? His subsequent purchases included a baking tin, two tubs and three table-spoons. On 5 August he bought a bedstead (twenty-one shillings) and a paillasse, or straw mattress (three shillings) plus work-stands (seven shillings and sixpence). There were a host of other items, but he was vexed to discover on 8 August, when trying to balance his accounts, that he was seven shillings adrift - 'Very disp. at the mistake.' (That unrecorded railway ticket might have been responsible.) On 12 September he purchased a water closet for nine shillings. Probably for security purposes (and also, perhaps, for company) he acquired a dog.

William's thoughts about Liverpool are unknown, but the fact that he stayed there so long shows that the atmosphere - a tremendous contrast to that of the villages or suburban towns he had known previously - was not uncongenial to him. Liverpool was now Britain's premier port and fresh and massive docks were under construction on both sides of the Mersey throughout the 1840s. Its population had increased at a formidable pace, almost doubling between 1821 and 1841 (from 149,400 to 286,500) and soaring to 376,000 by 1851.

Much of the increase in the 1840s was due to the influx of people from Ireland, where the terrible potato famine raged unabated, although many of those settlers were short-term and emigrated to America as soon as they could. The Liverpool to Manchester railway had been established in 1830 and Lime Street station had opened in 1836. Zoological Gardens were opened in 1833 and the Grand National was officially run at Aintree for the first time in 1839 (although there had been predecessors which also claimed that distinction). Princes Park in Toxteth, designed in part by Joseph Paxton, had opened in 1842. There had been, since the 18th century, several theatres in the town. The Liverpool Philharmonic Society was formed in 1840, for the purpose of organising concerts of classical music, and its own purpose-designed Philharmonic Hall arrived on the scene in 1849. It was, in theory, a thriving, exciting city with undeniable cultural aspirations. There was big business and big money in Liverpool - but there was also much poverty.

For a notion of what he might have made of the place we must turn to the diary of a relatively kindred spirit, namely that of Nathaniel Hawthorne. William left Liverpool in January 1853 and Hawthorne arrived six months later to take up the post of American Consul. In the first instance, he did not find the city prepossessing. The fog and the coal smoke did not appeal and he considered the Mersey a rather dreary river which, even in the best of weathers, bore the colour of a mud-puddle. The vast number of vessels which used it attracted his attention - 'There are a great many steamers plying up and down the river, to various landings in the vicinity, and a good many steam tugs; also, many boats ... [and] here and there a yacht or pleasure boat.' But most of the ships were 'ensconced in the docks; where their masts make an intricate forest for miles up and down the Liverpool shore. The small black steamers, whizzing industriously along, and many of them crowded with passengers, make up the chief life of the scene.'

The dense crowds in the main thoroughfares affronted Hawthorne and he noticed that many of the poorer people were barefoot. The fact that women carried baskets on their heads, with great dexterity, he found fascinating, but he was appalled by the numbers of beggars - who also infested the steamers for much of the year, sometimes playing musical instruments which were painfully out of tune. The splendour of a dinner at the town hall impressed him, with the footmen attired in fabulous uniforms, but he did not form a high opinion of his fellow-guests ('elderly John Bulls ... without refinement') and the buildings of the city, apart from the town hall itself, seemed largely nondescript. (The best, it should be added in parenthesis, were yet to come.) What did appeal to him, however, was wandering around 'the dark and dingy streets, inhabited by the poorer classes. The scenes there are very picturesque in their way; at every two or three steps, a gin-shop ... women nursing their babies at dirty bosoms; men haggard, drunken, care-worn, hopeless, but with a kind of patience, as if this were the rule of their life; groups stand or sit talking together, around the door-steps, or in the descent of a cellar.... They appear to wash their clothes occasionally; for I have seen them hanging out to dry in the street.' When he ventured beyond the central part of the city, out into the suburbs, he found areas that were more agreeable. 'I rather think', he confessed, 'the middling classes - meaning shopkeepers, and other respectabilities of that level - are better lodged here than in America; and what I did not expect, the houses are a great deal newer than in our new country.' Scattered among these modern villas, moreover, there were old stone cottages which were basically ugly but which became picturesque thanks to the shrubbery clustering about them. The surrounding

Lancashire countryside, savoured when he went still farther afield, also met with his approval. [3]

Hawthorne and his family stayed at Mrs Blodget's capacious boarding-house in Duke Street, which catered exclusively for Americans. He was a keen walker and probably explored the surrounding area with some interest. Having strolled to the western end of Duke Street and crossed the slanting main road (Hanover Street) he would have been confronted with two alternative but parallel routes for continuing in a northerly direction. The choice lay between Paradise Street slightly to his left and Manesty's Lane slightly to his right, the distance between them being no more than a few yards. But if, prior to 1849, a northward bound walker were in a whimsical frame of mind, the choice could be regarded as crucial - as the acid test for separating Liverpool's saints from Liverpool's sinners. For the comparatively wide Paradise Street, with its large octagon-shaped Unitarian chapel and reassuring hint of an ultimately blissful destination, clearly beckoned to the pure in heart. But the much narrower Manesty's Lane had very unpalatable connotations, for it commemorated the existence of an eighteenth century entrepreneur called Joseph Manesty - a Liverpool merchant who had owned a fleet of slave ships and made his fortune from the notorious 'triangular' trade linking Liverpool to Africa and the West Indies. (A lurid biography by William Maginn, published in 1814, relentlessly kept his memory alive.) The city fathers were embarrassed but hesitated to change the name - for Manesty had, after all, contributed to their prosperity and done more than anyone else to establish Liverpool as Britain's chief port. (Bristol's involvement in the slave trade had, by contrast, paled into comparative insignificance.) And, moreover, ameliorative measures could be taken. Manesty's palatial villa had long ago been demolished and the arrival, by degrees, of shops and warehouses helped to make the Lane seem respectable. So too did the establishment of a small school linked to that aforementioned Unitarian chapel (located immediately behind it). And Mr Tate, it should be mentioned in passing, would have a refining influence. But the name of Manesty would remain on record as an awkward reminder of the city's darker side - a blemish that would never be quite eradicated, not even in the twenty-first century.

In 1784 a town meeting had reached the conclusion that more Sunday schools needed to be provided for the children of Liverpool. A considerable number were speedily established without too much difficulty, since they could be accommodated within existing church and chapel buildings, but their arrival on the scene, and the paucity of knowledge revealed among the pupils attending them, led to the inevitable realisation that there should also be a far greater number of day schools for the children of the poor - elementary schools, or charity schools as they were usually known. A short distance from Manesty's Lane was located one of the city's oldest, a Blue Coat establishment dating from 1722, but such facilities were, literally, thin on the ground. Some of the churches and chapels which had already established Sunday schools now took the initiative in establishing day schools as well, once the funds required for the buildings and for the salaries of the staff needed to maintain them had been raised from their congregations. Others schools evolved as a result of charitable bequests. The school in Manesty's Lane, sponsored by and adjoining the chapel in Paradise Street, came into existence in 1792 together with a handful of others. It had 119 pupils by 1812 (70 boys and 49 girls) with 46 attending the Sunday school. By 1825, with a Mr and Mrs Mason in charge, the number of day-pupils had increased to 160 (80 boys and 80 girls) with 24 Sunday school attendees. By 1846 the number of day-pupils had swollen to approximately 200 (the sexes being roughly balanced) and there was very little space to spare in the buildings which housed them. At which point it must be made clear that Manesty's Lane school was the establishment over which William, assisted by a Mr Gallagher and a Miss Martha Goffey, now presided. (Miss Goffey's nephew, who would survive until May 1915, would play a significant role in his life, and would also have a hand in helping to shape the destinies of William's two sons.) [4]

The Paradise Street Unitarian Chapel had itself not been constructed until 1791 and the probability is that the day-school had been designed at the same time by the same unknown architect rather than being tacked on as an afterthought. The octagon-shaped chapel was really quite a handsome building, but it did not greatly appeal to the minister entrusted with its sole administration from 1835 onwards. The minister in question, who set his heart on replacing it eventually by something even more spectacular, was a certain James Martineau - a very well-known author, philosopher and zealous Unitarian divine who, at the age of thirty, was busily engaged in carving out a distinguished and sometimes controversial reputation for himself. In 1840 he took up the position of Professor of Mental and Moral Philosophy and Logic at Manchester College but remained in control at Paradise Street.

Equally well-known, though in a somewhat different and rather more colourful fashion, was his sister Harriet. Dr George tells us that William had been for many years a reader of periodicals such as the *London Literary Gazette* and the *National Review* to which they both contributed. [5] The source for his assertion is not immediately apparent but William's *Student's Journal* certainly contains, as we have noted already, an extract from Harriet's description of Dr Follen. She was a large, cheerful lady but unfortunately stone deaf, so that one had to shout down her ear-trumpet if a conversation was to be attempted. Dr George conjectures that it would have been a stimulating experience for William to have been friends with both brother and sister, but there is no evidence to suggest that in the first instance he spent a vast amount of time in the company of James or, indeed, that he ever came into close contact (if any) with Harriet. He was not himself a Unitarian, but took a tolerant, ecumenical view when it came to matters of religion. Manesty's Lane school, despite being set up and supported by the Paradise Street congregation, was open to the children of parents of all denomination and they were admitted and instructed free of charge. William's closest and most constant link with the chapel seems to have been the venerable Thomas Bolton, a well-known Liverpool merchant (and ex-mayor), a prominent member of the congregation who acted as its treasurer, but he would obviously have had no objection to Dr Martineau's request that he assist with providing instruction at the Sunday school.

Apart from teaching in his school during the weekdays, and in the chapel on Sundays, William also supplemented his income by taking evening classes (presumably for adults) but these appear to have come to an end after 1846. It may be that he found they were intruding too much into his spare time and leaving him exhausted.

We do not know how long William's bachelor establishment lasted - and he may, of course, have moved from place to place, taking his modest items of furniture with him. The amount he spent on 'lodgings' fluctuated in a curious fashion. The word is not mentioned in his book-keeping records for 1846 but appears frequently in those for 1847 - and the amount is never the same twice over, hovering on a weekly basis between seven and nine shillings. His expenditure records for 1848 are not extant, and - for reasons which will become abundantly clear in a moment - the word does not appear at all in those for 1849.

In February 1847 he was apparently unwell, for a doctor's bill of thirteen shillings and sixpence needed to be settled, and there is a hint that he embarked on a short walking holiday to recuperate. He purchased a walking stick and, seemingly, a map of Essex (two items which each cost sixpence) but it is not clear how far afield he went. Regular exercise may have been recommended, but there is only one specific reference to a country walk. Apart from basic household provisions such as milk, bread, eggs, meat, vegetables, tea, coffee, sugar and mustard, etc., we find ale and tobacco (and the occasional cigar) featuring regularly in his expenditure records. He continued to buy books (the latest edition of John Wade's *British History, chronologically arranged* is one that can be specifically identified) as well as newspapers and magazines such as *Chamber's Journal* and *Punch*. (Other newspapers and journals might have been studied at a public library, for there is a reference to tuppence-halfpenny - admission fee, presumably - in respect of a News-room.) He went to the theatre and to concerts from time to time, plus the occasional magic lantern show, and seems to have been reasonably well-off.

It is perhaps worth recording, for it was an episode which attracted attention at the time, that the school came under attack on 7 December 1847. A very small boy, possibly a disgruntled pupil, threw a stone and smashed one of its windows. Emboldened by this initial success, he then went up to the building and smashed a second pane of glass with his foot. At this point officialdom intervened. 'On being detected', reported the *Liverpool Mercury*, 'he was secured and taken to bridewell, but this appeared to have been a task of no ordinary difficulty, as it was stated that three police officers were barely adequate to accomplish it. The prisoner kicked most unmercifully, and in one instance the organ of destructiveness was brought so prominently into play, that he

bit a person in the arm who came to assist in his capture.'
(Could the injured party have been the school's headmaster?)
Brought up in court the following morning, with his head
barely reaching the front of the dock, the culprit was found
guilty of breaking windows and ordered to either pay ten
shillings or to go to prison for fourteen days. It is not known
which option he selected. [6]

As it happens, the school's days were already numbered
by this time: it may be that the small boy simply saw himself as
an advance representative of the demolition squad which
would, in all probability, be approaching eight months hence.

'The Unitarian sect in Liverpool', Nathaniel Hawthorne would
note in March 1854, 'have, as a body, great wealth and
respectability.' [7] Their leading member had great clout as well,
for in 1845 Dr Martineau persuaded his co-religionists that
they should build themselves a towering and splendid Gothic
chapel in Hope Street, designed to awe and dazzle passers-by
and to out-class all their rivals. (Humility, it seems, was not
one of their virtues.) Mr Bolton would helpfully add, a little
while later, that Paradise Street ('a place of business and
bustle', as the *Mercury* described it) was no longer an
appropriate show-case for their minister's remarkable abilities.
[8] Moving to a more select area, on the other hand, would
display his talents to maximum advantage. And lo, it came to
pass just as the great man had decreed. A site was purchased,
tenders were sought, details agreed, contracts signed, and there
dawned on Tuesday, 9 May 1848 the moment when works
officially commenced. 'The day being remarkably fine,' the
Mercury reported, 'there was a numerous attendance of ladies
and gentlemen, for the accommodation of whom two large
platforms were erected. The children connected to the
Manesty-lane Schools were on the ground, and took up their

position round the place where the foundation stone was deposited.' Amidst thunderous cheers, the stone was formally laid by Mr Bolton. Speeches were delivered and the children sang a specially-composed hymn. [9] Work proceeded apace and seventeen months later a huge new chapel adorned with a magnificent spire, barely distinguishable from a fully-fledged cathedral, opened for business in Hope Street. The *Mercury* hailed it as a 'noble and beautiful edifice'. Those venturing inside, as a modern commentator has observed, found it 'steeped in medieval gloom, with stained glass windows, a side pulpit and high altar, stone figures and elaborately carved dark wood pews.... in sharp contrast to the light and airy, square or octagonal chapels of [Joseph] Priestley's rational dissent.' [10]

In the normal course of events, one would have expected the Paradise Street chapel to remain in use until its successor was ready. But the course of events on this occasion was highly abnormal. Dr Martineau preached a final sermon at Paradise Street on 16 July 1848, at the end of which the premises were locked up. They would never again be used for religious purposes. By special dispensation, and accompanied by his family, Dr Martineau then set off on a tour of Germany which would last for more than a year, not returning to England until September 1849. Pending the completion of the Hope Street edifice, the worshippers at Paradise Street, deprived of both their minister and their chapel, had been instructed to go to Unitarian chapels elsewhere. (Dr J.H. Thom and other Liverpool-based divines no doubt welcomed them with open arms.)

From the outset, the intention was that both a new chapel and a new school should be erected in Hope Street. In the first instance, however, the site purchased (costing approximately £5,000) was only large enough to accommodate the new chapel. But the managers wished to put both the Paradise Street building and the Manesty's Lane building on the market, as a single package, without delay. It must be assumed, therefore, that the school closed down at much the same time as the redundant chapel. The good news was that three wealthy members of the congregation were in the throes of clubbing together and purchasing for £1,000 a site immediately behind the Hope Street chapel which would be ideal for a new school. The bad news was that it would be three years before the new buildings could materialise. Arrangements were evidently made for some of the children to be educated at makeshift premises in Seel Street, but those premises could scarcely accommodate the whole 200. Nor, while the period of interregnum lasted, were three members of staff needed on a full-time basis. In effect, William's school had melted away, just as Dr Martineau's chapel had melted away. He was out of a job. But the congregation were anxious to retain his services and it was evidently decided that William, like the minister, should be allowed to take Sabbatical leave (on full salary, one gathers) until such time as the building works were complete. Such an arrangement seems extraordinarily generous and a tribute, in any case, to the recognised quality of his abilities. There is no clue as to whether Miss Goffey and Mr Gallagher benefited in a similar fashion.

The chapel was snapped up an enterprising gentleman called Joseph Heath, who transformed it in 1850 into the Royal Colosseum Theatre and Music Hall. (It did a roaring trade until 1878, when the roof fell in.) Less clear is what (if anything) happened to Manesty's Lane school, for an establishment of that name was still functioning as late as the 1930s. It might have been the original building, taken over by a different group of people, or it might have been a totally new building erected on the same site. It is one of those things that we simply do not know.

Nor do we know when William's period of prolonged leave commenced, for his expenditure records for 1848 have disappeared. But we *do* have such records for almost the whole of 1849, and they make intriguing reading. They recommence in February 1849, and it soon becomes apparent that he is *not* in Liverpool and nowhere near the place. For the first and last time in his life he is, to all intents and purposes, a gentleman of leisure - and one with ample funds at his command.

Place-names are mentioned but the earliest of them do not make a great deal of sense. 'Dorford', 'Orford Gate' and 'Durford Gate', so far as William's writing can be deciphered, are locations which it is impossible to pinpoint with any degree of confidence - and may, in any case, be variations of the same word. But towards the end of February he arrives in Thorney, a village eight miles east of Peterborough, and lingers there for a couple of days. He then goes to Peterborough itself and again stays for at least two days: there are bed, breakfast and servants to be paid for. Strangely, there are no entries for almost a month, but on Monday, 26 March he is at the mysterious Durford Gate, catching a train to Leicester (a familiar city), where he stays overnight before returning to Thorney. On the 28th he moves from Thorney to Peterborough and thence to London. On 3 April he treats himself to an expensive new watch (£8) and also to a hat-case (five shillings) and then sets off for Wales via Bristol, reaching Tenby on Good Friday (6 April) and Haverfordwest on the Saturday. He stays at Haverfordwest for a couple of days and makes several purchases - clothes for himself, a 'Bonnet for Mary' (probably his mother) and a card and a book for John, whose birthday evidently fell at this time - in April 1847 William had sent him a coat. (He also had to buy a replacement hand for that expensive new watch.) He then arrived at Trecoed and remained there, seemingly, until the end of the month. Early in

May he was again on his travels and retracing his steps - Tenby, Bristol, London - and taking a cab from Paddington to reach his old stamping-ground of Battersea. There is no mention of lodgings so he presumably stayed with a friend for what seems to have been slightly more than three months. A great many books were bought during this period, which will be considered shortly - although a volume entitled *The Physiology of Digestion* (1836), by Andrew Combe, is in a different category from the others. Taken in conjunction with the purchase of sundry medicines, plus an Engel thermometer, it indicates that William was still worried about his health

On 14 August he set off on his travels again. From central London, he took a train to Blisworth Junction and a bus to Northampton, where he purchased a black silk scarf. From here he paid a third brief visit to Thorney, staying at the Duke's Head inn. This is the last statement that can be made with any real certainty, for from this point onwards William's expenditure records start to fade away. He maintained them in desultory fashion for a little while longer, recording the purchase of a greatcoat in November (£3), but they eventually dwindle to a couple of random entries for each month and stop completely after February 1850 (when sixpence in respect of a sacrament and two shillings in respect of a raffle are the very last items featured). William was reasonably well off by this time - on 2 April 1850 he would send £40 to Trecoed, as a contribution to household expenses - and must have decided that there was really no purpose in keeping such records on a regular basis, especially since he no longer bothered to total them up. A couple of isolated payments are jotted down on isolated pages, such as that gift to Trecoed, but his book-keeping routine - once maintained so zealously - was now totally abandoned.

The likelihood is that he returned to Liverpool after leaving Thorney (timing his return to more or less coincide with that of Dr Martineau). A postal order for one shilling sent to Battersea on 24 August, and one for four shillings and sixpence sent to 'Chesterton' on 7 September, were presumably in settlement of outstanding debts. A decidedly unexpected item is the sum of almost five shillings, spent on the 'carriage of books to Newbald [*sic*]', on 28 August. One can only speculate that, back in his rooms, he had been sorting out his much-cherished library - for small sums were also spent on the 'mending' of books at this time - and that, if his own original collection had been forwarded to him from Newbold at some stage after March 1844, he had now belatedly discovered that there were volumes in it which did not actually belong to him and was conscientiously returning them to their rightful owner. (This is a rather tortuous explanation, but it must be ruefully acknowledged that William was sometimes a rather tortuous person.)

The fact that he visited Thorney on three separate occasions in 1849 provides matter for speculation. Could there have been a particular young lady living there with whom he was anxious to keep in touch? Or could there have been some other reason? As it happens, 1849 was a rather special year in the history of this fenland village. The 7th Duke of Bedford had decided to modernise Thorney by transforming it into a 'model village', equipped with proper water and sewage facilities, some additional cottages, a school and shops. The architect entrusted with bringing these improvements into effect was Samuel Sanders Teulon, who began work in 1849. He was also extremely interested in what was becoming known as 'the Gothic revival' and may just possibly have visited Liverpool to observe the Hope Street developments, where he could have made William's acquaintance, but this is a very tenuous possibility. In the absence of any other information, therefore, there is a faint but improbable chance that William simply wanted to keep an eye on the changes at Thorney as a means of satisfying his own curiosity.

But there does exist the merest fragment of some additional information. This takes the form of a small scrap of paper thrust into the *Student's Journal*, approximately 4 by 2.5 inches, dated '23rd June 1849'. It records a dozen or so minuscule items of expenditure, largely in terms of pence and halfpence, but it is impossible to make much sense of the abbreviated entries. The word 'Sessional' and the name 'McCulloch' appear and there is, twice over, the word 'Prophecies'. Also in duplicate are (seemingly) the words 'Talk & duty'. The scrap of paper does contain, however, one complete sentence, *not* entered as an item of expenditure, and the heart leaps up at finding that it is positively intelligible. This reads 'Book sent as specimens to Thorney'. And looking again at those entries in the *Journal*, one finds on 30 May the entry 'Thorn. Post 2/11' and on 23 June the words 'Chap: Book 2/8'. The name 'McCulloch', with expenditure of tuppence-halfpenny solemnly recorded against it, also features in that second entry.

These jottings, for what they are worth, do suggest that it was at this time (with an extended break from teaching duties), rather than earlier, that William made a determined effort to try his hand at literary composition. It would have been a case of now or never! It will be recalled that, according to the slightly muddled but nevertheless intriguing assertions of W.D. Phillips eighty years later, he was 'acquainted with' the publisher John Murray (someone with whom Lady Byron had connections). As a kindly patron of budding talent, it is possible that she had agreed that her name could be cited for introductory purposes at such time as William was ready to submit samples of his handiwork for professional scrutiny. Was Mr McCulloch qualified to pronounce judgment? At which point, and with a sample ready to hand, this would seem an opportune moment to peruse the little composition which William inserted at the back of his *Journal* in the early 1840s. Entitled 'Fear and Love in Education', it runs as follows:

> I saw two extreme contrasting cases, in near neighbourhood, of girls brought up, the one in the spirit of love, the other in that of fear. These two girls are the best teachers of moral philosophy that ever fell in my way. In point of birth, organisation, means of education, they were about equal. Both were made to be beautiful and intelligent. The one is pallid, indolent (with the repudiation of learning), tasteless, timid and triste, manifesting nothing but occasionally an intense selfishness, and a prudery beyond belief. The education of this girl has been the study of her anxious parents from the day of her birth: but they have omitted to let her know and feel that anybody loved her.
>
> The other the darling of a large family, meeting love from all eyes, and hearing tenderness, in every voice, is beautiful as a Hebe, and so free and joyous, that her presence is like sunshine in a rainy day. She knows that she is beautiful and accomplished; but she is, as far as eye can see, absolutely devoid of vanity. She has been apprised, over and over again, that people think her a genius: she silently contradicts this, and settles with herself that she can acquire anything, but originate nothing. She studies with her whole being, as if she were coming out next year in a learned proposition. She dances at balls as if no[thing] lay beyond. She flits hither and thither, in rain and sunshine, walking, riding, or driving on little errands of kindness; and bears the smallest interests of her friends in mind in the heights of her mirth and the depths of her studies. At dull evening parties she can sit under the

lamp (little knowing how beautiful she looks) quietly amusing herself with prints and not wanting notice: and she can speak out what she thinks and feels to a circle of admirers, as simply and earnestly as she would to her own mother. I have seen people shake their heads, and fear lest she should be spoiled; but my own conviction is that this young creature is unspoilable. She has had all the praise and admiration she can have: no watchfulness of parents can keep them from her. She does not want praise and admiration. She has other interests and other desires; and my belief is that if she were left alone tomorrow, the last of her family, she would be as safe, busy, and in due time happy, as she is now under their tender guardianship. She is the most complete example I ever witnessed of a being growing up in the light and worth and perfect freedom of love; and she has left me very little toleration for authority, in education more than in anything else.

It is readable enough, though perhaps rather highly-strung. One is not persuaded that this is a truly detached observer jotting down his casual thoughts, nor is one is necessarily overwhelmed by the quality of the prose, but it is not totally amateurish. It carries a certain force, and a publisher's reader might hesitate before rejecting material of this standard out of hand. (And the present writer may, in any case, be totally mistaken in attributing the piece to William's own pen - it could have been dashed off by Washington Irving, or somebody of that ilk, with William simply copying it out because it took his fancy.)

Whatever dreams he may have cherished at one time of producing a great literary work, and without knowing how hard he may have striven to make his mark, it has to be recorded that no trace of a book written by this particular William

George has ever come to light. There is a slender chance, of course, that he may have adopted a pseudonym, but this takes us deep into the realms of improbable conjecture. It is pointless to pursue such speculation. But he would have been gratified to know that his son and his grandson, each of them bearing the name 'William', would manage to fulfil those dreams - and, in the process, succeed in keeping memories of himself alive.

William had to pay a substantial price for his period of prolonged freedom - although it might be considered, in the circumstances, a perfectly reasonable one. Dr Martineau, though obviously well disposed towards the day-school maintained by his Paradise Street chapel, and enthusiastic about its new premises, was first and foremost a minister of religion. In a speech delivered on 22 December 1851, at a gathering to celebrate the completion of the schools which would be replacing the Manesty Lane establishment, he proclaimed the paramount importance of Sunday school in the life of children and hoped, in effect, that the new buildings would be as well-used on a Sunday as they were during the week. The spiritual as well as the physical needs of young people needed to be met. 'In the erection of the new church', so the *Liverpool Mercury* reported him as saying, 'no provision was made for the reception of the children on the Sabbath; and if the result should be that those boys and girls who otherwise would attend went to no place of worship, got no instruction at all, and were left to the questionable care of their parents - if such should be the result, it would be deplored. But if they found it possible to employ that room [at the new schools] by the introduction of Sunday services, and a system could be adopted which would reach the hearts and meet the spiritual wants of the children, and they could have those services conducted by Sunday school teachers, that would be an influence far more valuable than any which attendance at the church could produce. He considered Sunday school teaching of the highest value, and he knew from his own experience the benefits that would arise even to those who devoted themselves to the work. It was in a Sunday school that he first received those impressions which induced him to devote himself to the ministry. He was satisfied young men were little acquainted with the advantages to be derived from Sunday school teaching; and there was no instruction, nor any training conferred by Sunday school labours. As regarded the arrangements for Sunday schools, he thought they ought to collect all the children of the day- schools not otherwise provided for and whose parents were willing they should rather come there than to any other Sunday school. He considered that in general Sunday school teaching was of too slight a character, and that teachers did not prepare themselves sufficiently for the work. This was a great object. Every teacher ought to qualify himself by reading the Scriptures, and the study of those subjects which he was called upon to teach. Without that little permanent good could be accomplished. He called upon the young men belonging to the congregation to come forward and devote themselves to the work, by which means the advantages of their spacious and commodious schools would be more largely extended. Increased support, in the shape of pecuniary assistance, would also be required, when it was recollected that they had now room in the schools for 420 children, more than double the number they had formerly the means of educating.' [11]

It must be assumed that sentiments very similar to the foregoing had been forcibly delivered to William in the summer of 1848, before Dr Martineau set off on his German travels. As the putative headmaster of the new day-school, William was strongly exhorted to think of himself as the headmaster of the new Sunday school as well - and for the latter, indeed, to take precedence in his thoughts. Teaching the three R's was all very well and good, and a highly commendable activity, but teaching the word of the Lord was of still greater importance - and the young men who came forward as Sunday school teachers would themselves need to be trained and instructed in how best to go about their missions. While being granted a prolonged Sabbatical, therefore, William would need to prepare for the task that lay ahead by undertaking an intensive course of study.

William had purchased, as we have noted, a considerable number of religious books in the past. The works of Jeremy Taylor, the Rev. John Todd and the Rev. Samuel Wood were some with which he was familiar by this time, not to mention *Sacred Geography*, and in June 1847 he had purchased some tracts written by Joseph Barker (a well-known contemporary and sometimes controversial preacher). But his expenditure records for 1849 show that he was now purchasing such books with enhanced intensity: in effect, he had embarked on a self-regulated training course. Those works which can be identified from the brief references made to them are *A System of Education for the Young* (1840) by Samuel Wilderspin, *Help to the Reading of the Bible* (1838) by the Rev. Benjamin Elliott Nicholls, *Sermons* by the Rev. John Travers Robinson (1833), and *Conversations with Children on the Gospels,* a two-volume treatise by Amos Bronson Alcott published in Boston in the mid-1830s. The newly-published *Collection of Sacred Music for the Use of Schools* by James Tilleard was an inevitable addition to the collection. Others for which no supplementary information can be found are *Steps to National Theology*, *Explaining the Catechism, Saint's Tales* and sundry tracts and prophecies - plus items simply referred to as 'books'. Some light relief from this severe course of study was afforded by the Lambs' *Tales from Shakespeare* and two books of poetry.

A book published in 1849 which went unmentioned in his *Journal* was *The Philosophy of Religion* by J.D. Morell. It attracted a considerable amount of favourable attention and William must surely have added it to his library at some stage. John Daniel Morell was four years older than himself. The son of a Congregational minister, he had studied theology at Glasgow and Bonn and had himself served as a Congregational minister for three years at Gosport before deciding that he was, perhaps, too much of a rationalist and free-thinker to fit comfortably into an orthodox religious hierarchy. His detailed assessment of current European philosophy, published in 1846, greatly impressed Lord Lansdowne, who (aware that he was looking for a new position) invited him to become a school inspector. Morell took up this post in 1848 (holding it, indeed, for almost thirty years) and would write several short books about English grammar during the 1850s. He specialised, it seems, in keeping an eye on the Nonconformist schools, a task which he would share with Matthew Arnold from 1851 onwards, and a few years later he would come into direct contact with William. Impressed by the young Welshman's abilities, he would eventually play a crucial role in shaping the character of his career. According to du Parcq (who may, of course, simply have been echoing Rees), the two men became close friends. [12]

William may have been back in Liverpool in time to see the new chapel formally opened on 16 October 1849. More than two years would elapse, however, before the new school buildings would be ready for use and he must obviously have been carrying out some *ad hoc* duties for Dr Martineau in the meantime. He may have taught at the provisional school in Seel Street and he may have been contacting the parents of potential pupils and seeking out young men in the Hope Street congregation who might be recruited and trained as Sunday school teachers. In the absence of records, one can only speculate. On 10 January 1850 he paid a Mrs Creer one pound and six shillings for the rent of rooms (covering four weeks, presumably) but the census return for March 1851 shows him as a lodger ('a teacher, aged 33') at No. 6 Devonport Street, Toxteth Park. His landlord was Robert Leigh, a joiner with a wife and five children, and a fellow-lodger was Charles Taffe, another teacher, several years his senior.

Three new school buildings, fronting on to what were then Caledonia and Sugden Streets (and not to be confused with the rival Hope Street school, a short distance away, operated by the BFSS), were formally opened on 22 December 1851. Able to accommodate, as Dr Martineau proudly proclaimed, 420 pupils - 160 boys, 160 girls and 100 infants - their arrival on the scene was something of an event. The architect, Mr Raffles Brown, could be justly proud of his handiwork. The school-rooms were spacious and airy. An imposing tower formed part of the design and there was a house for the master - into which, presumably, William now moved. It was located under one end of the boys' school-room and consisted of a kitchen, scullery and bedroom in a half-sunk basement and a parlour and two bedrooms above them. 'The parlour windows', the *Mercury* excitedly informed its readers, 'have an excellent view of the east end of the church, usually considered the most interesting view of that edifice.' [13]

It must have been a moment of crowning glory for the new headmaster to be taking charge of such an establishment. And yet, exactly a year later, he resigned his post. This may have been for health reasons and that he was exhausted, both mentally and physically, from the long period of preparation and the strain of the responsibilities that he had been shouldering. More probably, there were periods of severe self-doubt over his role as Recruiting Officer for Dr Martineau's Sunday schools and it could well be that he feared being drawn too deeply, much against his will, into the web of the Unitarian hierarchy. W.R.P. George quotes an undated note that he saw in William's notebook when he examined it in 1976 (but which, sadly, is there no longer). He did not understand what it referred to, but he was unaware of his grandfather's dilemma during his final years in Liverpool. The note, evidently written during 1852, reads:

> Perhaps, however, it's all for the best - my present false position so uncomfortable that I can hesitate no longer - shall speedily be *forced into a decision*. (**On that point**.) [14]

For it must be reiterated, once and for all, that William did *not* consider himself a Unitarian. But he must surely have felt, from his intense involvement in establishing and overseeing the Sunday schools at Dr Martineau's new chapel, that he was masquerading as one. Their relationship had now become far too close for comfort.

Whatever the precise reason, his second stint as a headmaster came to an end in December 1852. But the managers of the school decided that his departure should most definitely not go unmarked. His love of books and of serious reading was evidently very well-known, for he was formally presented on 26 January 1853 with a complete set of *The Penny Cyclopaedia*, published by the Society for the Diffusion of Useful Knowledge and running to fourteen splendidly bound volumes, each composed of about a thousand pages. (It was the Victorian equivalent of Wikipedia.) They were accompanied by an oak bookcase in which to keep them, plus a copy of *Webster's Dictionary* on the inside cover of which were inscribed the words 'Presented to Mr William George by the teachers and conductors of the children's service of Hope Street Church Sunday Schools as a token of respect and esteem on the occasion of his leaving Liverpool, Christmas 1852'. [15] It was, undeniably, a huge and heartfelt tribute to the conscientious services William had rendered, and indicated beyond a shadow of doubt that his abilities had been fully appreciated. And delight of delight, to round things off with a spot of panache - the icing on the top of a very rich fruit cake, as it were - there was a signed portrait of Dr Martineau himself, which (like the fifteen hefty books) would be retained by William and his descendants for evermore.

Somebody who had been roped in to assist with the arrangements for the presentation was Thomas Goffey, a lad of seventeen who was the nephew of Martha Goffey, one of William's two assistants. His father was a sea captain and his aunt evidently kept an eye on him during her brother's protracted absences. Thomas may have been a pupil or pupil-teacher at Manesty's Lane before being articled as an attorney's clerk Intriguingly, there still exists one of the invitation letters which he sent out. Dated 19 January, it is addressed to a 'Miss L. Cox' but since it was preserved in William's papers one wonders whether it ever reached the lady in question. [16] The intention had obviously been that he should pass it on to her. Was she aware of the event anyway, thereby rendering a written invitation unnecessary, or did he deliberately withhold it? Had their relationship come to an abrupt end? These too are matters that will never be resolved. The records show that a Miss Caroline L. Cox, aged 24, the daughter of a wealthy broker, was living at No. 89 Dingle Hill, Park Road, Toxteth Park in 1851, but whether this was the young lady for whom the invitation was intended will have to remain a matter for speculation.

As must be the question of what William did next.

8 - HAVERFORDWEST REVISITED

It must be assumed that, after he left Liverpool, William went home to Trecoed and that a period of recuperation and relaxation followed. His immediate future was far from clear and the notion of abandoning teaching altogether, and pursuing a completely different kind of career (providing that it was not farming), came under close consideration. W.R.P. George tells us that there was 'an undated scrap of paper between the leaves of his notebook' (i.e., the *Student's Journal*) which ran as follows:

> Have today felt a strong reaction against an inclination for farming - because I haven't sufficient means. I should be obliged to submit to a very humble life and many privations - because I should find the life a very dull one - and because farming unfavourable to intellectual pursuits.
>
> A Stationer's shop at H'West - publish an almanac (Welsh) - send it to fairs and markets - also a monthly mag. price 2s. - 'The Cambrian Chronicle' of facts and opinions.... OR Bookseller's shop in Fishguard. Write down all that occurs to me about further course ... Think of Liverpool - Liberty and independence of such a life. [1]

The present writer has been unable to find such a scrap of paper. He did discover, however, *another* scrap of paper thrust into the *Journal*, which runs as follows:

> A period: printed by Perkins - cheap - v. little profit - or bookseller's shop in FGuard - Canvassers all over the country - attend all fairs - a selection of Eng. periodicals & cheap, simple books - also a selection of

Welsh - what to consist of etc - write down <u>all</u> that
occurs to me about future course
- think of LPool -
Liberty & independence of such a life.
July 5 Keep the period: constantly in view, & prepare
for it - ½ hr <u>daily</u> corresp!.- write to Noncom:

The second paragraph quoted by Dr George incorporates, of
course, some of the phraseology which appears in this second
set of jottings. It is just conceivable that William *did* write the
same thing twice over, but far more probable that Dr George
came across two or even three separate scraps of paper and
merged them into a composite document, abridging and editing
the texts as he thought fit so that the finished production would
make sense to his twentieth century readers.

It is clear, at any rate, that the Sabbatical period of
freedom which William had enjoyed during his employment in
Liverpool was, in retrospect, a golden age and one that greatly
appealed to him. The sheer drudgery of teaching was
something to which he did not wish to return in a hurry -
freedom and independence, such as he had known in 1849,
were the goals to be aimed for!

And yet, in the event, these soap-bubble dreams came
to nought. We have no idea where he was or what did in 1853,
but in the spring of 1854 he returned (with reluctance, it must
be assumed) to the world of education. Advertisements of
varying length, inserted in local newspapers, proclaimed that
on Monday, 3 April Mr William George would open an
English School for Scientific and Commercial Education in
Upper Market Street, Haverfordwest, the terms being one
guinea per quarter. They explained that Mr George was a
Trained and Certified Teacher and had 'enjoyed superior
advantages of studying the most improved Modern Systems of
Education.' 'Great attention', the longer version added, 'will

be paid to the study of the English language, a knowledge of which is now indispensable to the successful pursuit of every business and profession in this country. Much useful general knowledge will be imparted by conversational lectures, suited to the capacities of the pupils, and illustrated by diagrams and experiments.' Religious teaching was touched upon by implication, since a quotation from Dr Fellenberg featured prominently - 'I call that Education which embraces the culture of the whole man, with all his faculties - subjecting his senses, his understanding and his passions to reason, to conscience and to the evangelical laws of the Christian revelation.' [2]

The origins of this school are obscure. There was living accommodation for its proprietor, but it is not clear whether William was running it single-handed or whether he had engaged any assistants. Another mystery is how he had managed to accumulate the funds needed to establish himself in a large building equipped with all the necessary furniture. George family legend had it that a very wealthy widow called Brown assisted him and (in one version) that he was obliged to marry her as part of the bargain. As suggested at the outset of this book, two different episodes appear to have been conflated. The information about the wealthy widow would have been imparted to Elizabeth Lloyd, William's second wife, whom he married in 1859, and she may have mentioned it to her brother, Richard Lloyd. It was passed down by word of mouth to the following generation, and then to the one after that, and became a little garbled in the descent. If we consider the name 'Brown', as pronounced with a Welsh accent, we are not too far away from the name 'Brunn' or 'Burun' - and 'Burun' was apparently the original 11th century family name of the Byron family. (When he started writing his epic poem in 1811, Byron named its hero 'Childe Burun' initially but after a while prudently changed it to 'Childe Harold'.) One is momentarily reminded, moreover, of a snatch of dialogue that occurs in an M.R. James story - 'They say it was a lady of title that married twice over, and her first husband went by the name of Brown, or it might have been Bryan.'[3]

There are strong grounds for supposing, in short, that it was Lady Byron who advanced William the necessary funds which enabled him to get started with his very own school - and the Fellenberg quotation may well have been inserted for the gratification of his mentor. It is clear that Elizabeth Lloyd was not well-educated and doubtful whether the name 'Byron', as borne by a famous poet, would have meant anything to her. The fact that a wealthy widow-lady bearing the surname Brown, Brunn, Burun or Byron had once helped her husband was enough information in itself to digest, and not of overwhelming importance. It would not have been until many years later that she would have needed to recall it, perhaps in response to questions from her children. In the process, the name was perhaps remembered somewhat imperfectly and so the legend of the mysterious 'Mrs Brown', a fabulously rich widow who came to William's rescue rather like a Fairy Godmother, passed into family history.

William now resumed making entries in his *Student's Journal*, but the relevant pages have disappeared so we are dependent, once again, on transcripts made by Dr George in 1976. This means that the texts which will be quoted in this chapter are not necessarily 100% accurate. On Wednesday, 5 April he records that he had opened the school two days earlier but had been disappointed by the small number of pupils who had presented themselves. 'Much annoyed at having missed my way as to the preliminaries - would have been much safer and avoided the appearance of failure if I had remained in the country until I had a sufficient number to begin with. Another mistake was to fix a uniform charge of a guinea a quarter. Better to divide the school into three sections - to take all who offer - charge 20 shillings a quarter for the 1st, 15 shillings for the 2nd and 10 shillings for the 3rd. This will perhaps produce an average of 15 shillings.' [4]

The emphasis in his advertisement on the English language, 'knowledge of which is now indispensable to the successful pursuit of every business and profession in this country', may have been a mistake. It was a tacit acknowledgement of the impact made by the notorious 'Blue Books' of 1847 - the report of the Government's Commissioners of Enquiry into the State of Education in Wales, which had roundly condemned the widespread use of the native language in the Principality's schools as misguided, futile and (ultimately) harmful. Hackles had risen when the report was published and some of the local residents might have been alienated by William's endorsement of the Commissioners' conclusion. But 'English School' was shortly afterwards amended to read 'Commercial School' - and then, finally, to 'Commercial Academy' - and the number of pupils gradually increased. [5] W.D. Phillips, in *Old Haverfordwest*, listed a considerable number of subsequent local worthies who attended it in their youth. [6] One of them was seven-year old Edwin John, son of the town clerk, who records that William 'was a severe disciplinarian - rather passionate, sometimes having recourse to the old-fashioned punishment of caning.' [7]

Dipping into William's miscellaneous papers, one encounters a curious medley of items. (Many of them probably dated from the early 1840s, but the fact that he retained them shows that he still found them useful.) A small notebook has the heading 'Geography of Palestine', which is then crossed out, followed by notes (in pencil) on slate, gold, silver, mercury or quicksilver, iron, lead, tin, zinc, chalk and clay, which are followed in turn by some simple sums. On a separate sheet, there are some notes on how the brain works which may have served as the basis for homilies and sermons. [8] He had copied out scraps of poetry and extracts from various articles and speeches that he came across. Inserted in his *Journal* is a detailed account of the physical appearance of Prince Albert, taken from the *Birmingham Journal* and probably referring to his first visit to that city in November 1843. Similarly, a description of the Duke of Sussex, a son of King George III, is copied out from a speech delivered by Lord Ashley on 7 December 1843. Extracts are taken from a book by somebody called N. Arnold (a distant relative of Thomas or Matthew, perhaps?) called *Life and Common Sense.*

The feeling that he himself should set down on paper something - indeed, *anything* - of a creative nature still asserted itself from time to time. 'Very desirable', he records, 'to write much more frequently remarks which are suggested in private reading. Should not be too particular what to write about - it is constant practice that gives facility, no matter what the subject.'[9] Carlyle's collection of Oliver Cromwell's speeches and letters, published in 1845, evidently formed part of his reading and he commented with great admiration on the stunning power of the great man's oratory: 'A deeply political, practical and precise intention animated all his words, pierced through their confusion, pervaded all their windings; and he impelled his auditors with resistless force towards the object which he wished to attain, by exciting in their minds, at every step, the impression which it was his object to produce.'[10] Assuming that it has not been polished up by Dr George, this was quite an impressive description, indicating a distinct improvement in William's literary style. And it betrays, perhaps, a lurking fascination with world leaders who possessed the gift of the gab. (Cromwell, it should be remembered, had a dash of Welsh ancestry in his genes, and may have been capable of soaring into a state of inspired ecstasy not far removed from the *hwyl*.)

The railway, reaching Haverfordwest at the end of 1853, had brought with it many visitors. Among them, it seems, were a Miss Legge and her companion Miss Huntley. We do not know the precise relationship between these two ladies or why they had come to Wales or where it was that they stayed - whether at one of the large houses in the area or at a hotel. The Legge family as such was quite well-established among the gentry, though never overwhelmingly prominent, and it may be that Miss Legge was the employer and Miss Selina Huntley the paid companion. Or it may, of course, have been the other way round. Or they may simply have been friends.

Nothing is known of this particular Miss Legge. But we do know a reasonable amount about Selina Huntley. She had been born on 18 August 1819, the daughter of Thomas Day Huntley (named after a famous children's author) and his wife Elizabeth, and was baptised at St James, Westminster on 12 September. Her father was an engraver and they lived in Bond Street. She had two elder brothers (Thomas Johnson and William, born in 1812 and 1814 respectively) and two younger ones (George and Samuel, who arrived in 1826 and 1828). Her father died in December 1832 at the age of fifty and was buried in the parish of St George's, Hanover Square. Elizabeth (nineteen years younger than her husband) was pregnant at the time and gave birth to another daughter (Ann) in 1833. (There was evidently a third daughter as well, but it has proved impossible to discover anything about her.) Elizabeth continued the engraving business, assisted in the first instance by William and later by George and Thomas Johnson. (The latter had evidently been named after a Harry Johnson, who was a close family friend.) [11]

The census taken in 1841, when Selina was 21 (although the return gives her age as 20), shows her working as a milliner in the illustrious setting of St James's Palace, Pall Mall, together with ten others. One of them (aged 30) may have been in charge of the rest and the youngest was aged 15. Selina could well have been there for four or five years. (The novelist George Augustus Sala, reminiscing in 1895, recalled his 'dear mother' telling him 'that in William IV's time, when the Sailor King and Queen Adelaide held a Drawing Room at St. James's ...a certain number of privileged London milliners and dressmakers used to be allowed to stand behind the Yeomen of the Guard, lining the stairs, and take note of the fashions of the ladies' dresses' Quite possibly, these were the Palace's own contingent of milliners and dressmakers endeavouring to ensure that they kept abreast of the latest fashions.)

In the census return for 1851 we find that Selina is living at No. 70 Welbeck Street (a northward continuation of Bond Street) and is the head of the household. She is a dressmaker and in partnership with Eliza Amos, aged 28. They have a servant called Jane Nixon (aged 21) and a lodger called James Murray (aged 36). Knocking four years off her age, Selina claims to be 27. Her mother, living nearby at No. 74 New Bond Street with two of her sons, is still an engraver and painter.

But a few years later, accompanied by Miss Legge (possibly one of her dressmaking clients), Selina arrived in Haverfordwest. At social gatherings in that relatively small community she encountered William and was greatly attracted by him. What transpired between them can only be surmised, but the upshot was that they became engaged, presumably during the winter of 1854/55, and agreed to wed during the school's Easter holiday.

At which point, it must be explained that Selina was suffering from phthisis pulmonalis (otherwise known as consumption or tuberculosis) and that this had been diagnosed two years earlier, in 1853. From the outset, therefore, William knew he was becoming engaged to a woman who had only a short time to live. In the deciphered words of his son's shorthand account, jotted down in 1922. 'Miss Huntley [was] a chronic invalid who was madly in love with him. He married her to save her life!' [13] William clearly liked her but it does indeed seem to have been the case that he was acting primarily from compassionate motives.

Selina had evidently set her heart on being married in the fashionable church of St George's, Hanover Square (where, as noted above, the funeral service for her father had been held). For the purpose of reading the banns on three consecutive Sundays, however, she would need to be resident in the parish for several weeks. She moved back to her mother's Bond Street house, perhaps early in March, and William accompanied her - although it may be, of course, that until the Easter holiday actually commenced, he simply put in the odd token appearance at weekends - 'showing the flag' in Hanover Square, as it were. Easter Day fell on 8 April and they were married the following Thursday (the 11th). Both of them were recorded as being of 'full age' and as residing in Bond Street. The wedding, performed by the Rev. A. Alston, was witnessed by Elizabeth Huntley and Harry Johnson.

They returned to Upper Market Street but their happiness was destined to be short-lived, for Selina's illness grew steadily worse. She was, seemingly, of a cheerful disposition but she must have been lying down and coughing for much of the time, growing steadily weaker, and William's energy was now divided between running his school and tending his sick wife. William's niece, a girl of eighteen called Martha James (the daughter of his sister Gwenllian) came to Upper Market Street from Trecoed to look after this newly-acquired aunt and was with her when she died, on 4 December 1855. Selina was buried in the churchyard of St Thomas's four days later. Inserting a notice of her death in *The Cambrian*, which was published on the eve of the funeral,

169

William paid tribute to an 'amiable and beloved wife'. Edwin John would remember her as 'a sweet lady whom the boys liked very much'. [14]

For reasons touched upon in the Introduction to this book, her death probably changed the history of the world.

9 - A POSTING TO PWLLHELI

It is impossible to say how close their marriage had been. Even so, for the space of eight months, William had shared his life with somebody else for the very first time, and the gap created when Selina disappeared from the scene must have been enormous. His loneliness, which had previously been endured for so long that it had become a state of normality, would now have been accentuated a hundredfold and the thought of remaining in residence at Upper Market Street for any further length of time would have been depressingly bleak. Perhaps, indeed, unendurable. The details of his precise movements during the opening months of 1856, after returning to Haverfordwest in the wake of the family's annual Christmas get-together at Trecoed, are unknown. But it can be surmised that, with many sharp and painful memories still fresh in his mind, he had now seen more than enough of the place and that, three or four months later, he either sold the school to a new proprietor or else closed it down and terminated his lease. [1]

What we do know is that, before the year was out, he was teaching at Wakefield. (And was presumably still a headmaster, since - as we shall see in a moment - he would bridle at the notion that he should accept second position at a school elsewhere.) His address, in what appears to be the only one of his letters that survives from this period (and, indeed, the very first letter of all to survive), is given as 'St John's'. [2] This cannot be a reference to the city's Anglican church. where a school was not established until 1861, and may be denoting a Baptist church of that name. Or it may simply indicate the particular locality in which he was living.

Wakefield, a thriving and prominent market town based on the River Calder with a population of more than 17,000 residents, was the leading conurbation of Yorkshire's West Riding. Located within striking distance of both Leeds and

Barnsley, and endowed with a well-known fictional vicar, it could have been quite an agreeable part of the world in which to settle down. But there were a good many local industries and the tang of the air was evidently unpalatable to William, for he cautiously allowed it to be known, among his contacts in the teaching profession, that he had no desire to stay there any longer than necessary.

Towards the end of the year, one of those contacts, the Rev. William Roberts, a Baptist Minister active in South Wales on behalf of the British and Foreign Schools Society, sounded him on how long it might be before he was free to transfer to an alternative locality. What kind of salary did he have in mind and would, say, a position as second-in-command at a school in Blaenau, a small town in Monmouthshire, be of any interest? William returned to Trecoed for another Christmas and did not respond until 21 January 1857. 'I thought it better', he explained, 'to defer my reply till after my return hither, as I might then be able to say when I should be likely to be at liberty. The time is not fixed however; and I do not intend to say anything more on the subject to the Committee before I have another school in view. If I heard soon perhaps I might be released at Easter. With respect to the salary, I should not be disposed to take much less than £60 a year. I understood that as much, and sometimes even more, is given to masters of lower schools (which I should prefer). I know that the master of the National School in the small town of Haverfordwest had £60 a year, a house & garden, with coal & candles. However, one of my chief considerations in desiring to move is my health; and a good school in a healthy locality would be a more important object than an extreme salary. The situation of Second Master at the Blaina [*sic*] school would not meet my views.'[3]

William's mother and his step-father, Benjamin Williams, paid him a visit while he was at Wakefield. This could have been purely for the pleasure of his company, of course, but it may also have related to the ultimate stewardship of Trecoed. The lease for the farm had been in Mary George's name during the first twelve years of their marriage but it was transferred to Benjamin, for a period of twenty-one years, in August 1842. [4] There was a strong possibility that Mary would pre-decease her husband, since she was a good many years his senior, and there would have been a family discussion as to how the farm should be disposed of in due course. One can only assume that William would have assured them that farming, as a full-time career, still did not appeal to him and it would doubtless have been agreed that, until future notice, he could still regard Trecoed as his home and that there would always be a room for him there. As a consolation prize, as it were, it was agreed that a small cottage which belonged to Mary should be passed to him after her death so that he would thereafter receive the tenants' rent for it.

Solace was probably sought in the purchase of books, for William continued to be a compulsive reader and clearly found it impossible to pass a bookshop without venturing in to see what it had to offer. In addition to those volumes which have been noted earlier, Dr George tells us that his library contained George Fox's *Journal*, Gilbert Burnet's *History of the Reformation*, Hallam's *Constitutional History*, Arthur Penryhn Stanley's *Life and Correspondence* of Thomas Arnold (two volumes, 1844), *The Schoolmaster: Essays on Practical Education, selected from the works of Ascham, Milton, Locke and Butler* (two volumes, 1836) and the *Report of the Commissioners into the State of Education in Wales* (two volumes, 1847), the notorious 'Blue Books' already referred to. 'It is evident', Dr George concluded, 'that William George's interest in books was far wider than that of the average British schoolmaster of his generation. He had built up his library by devoting a substantial proportion of his small income towards it and the transport of his library from one home to another during his frequent moves was an additional strain on his slender financial resources.' (Dr George also mentions several other books which he claims William had purchased, but his descriptions are a little confused and one of the items listed - J.R. Green's *A Short History of the English People* - would not appear until 1874.) [5]

One wonders, in passing, whether, in addition to tackling these hefty tomes, William ever sought light relief in reading fiction. Did he, for example, peruse the works of contemporary novelists such as Dickens, Thackeray, George Eliot, Charles Reade or Trollope? There is no way of knowing. It would also be helpful to know what his thoughts on contemporary politics might have been. His niece declares that he 'was well up in affairs of State and current events, and especially well versed in politics', a firm assertion which, by default, will have to suffice. [6]

He may still have been at Wakefield in April 1858 when he sent his mother a photograph of himself. 'If you admire it,' he remarked, 'you can hang it up by my other portrait which you have at Trecoed... To me the face appears to wear an expression of great earnestness, as if I were occupied by some business of pressing importance.... Well, I am trying to joke a little and perhaps it is best for me to do so, though I assure you I am far from well. Yesterday was a beautiful day. I went for a walk but though I did not walk very far, I felt quite tired on the way back and the friends who were with me had to give me some help. I must look for a small school in the country as soon as my time is up here.' [7]

He was, seemingly, coming to think of himself as a permanent invalid, but his dream of 'a small school in the country' eventually materialised - or, at any rate, something equally as good - for that summer he found himself taking up residence in Caernarvonshire in North Wales. For he had been invited to become headmaster of the newly-built Troed-yr-Allt British school at Pwllheli, situated on the southern coast of the Lleyn Peninsula overlooking Tremadog Bay - or, if it be preferred, the northernmost end of Cardigan Bay. (In theory, on a very clear day and with an astonishingly good telescope capable of scanning seventy miles, it might have been possible to glimpse Strumble Head and Fishguard at the southernmost end.)

Pwllheli, like Wakefield, was a market town, but the environment was totally different from the one William had known in Yorkshire. It was fresh, bracing and pure delight - its name meant, literally, 'salt water basin'. With a beach some four miles long, it was an ideal health resort for valetudinarians of all ages. The only drawback was that most of its 2,500 residents were Welsh-speaking and William would have to work hard to recapture a smattering, at least, of his native tongue. (It was in 1858 that he wrote that apologetic letter to a Welsh Baptist minister, based in Pembrokeshire, which has already been partially quoted: 'I wished to say a few words to you in Welsh - but I am sorry that I cannot do so, although Welsh is my mother tongue - and I knew very little English until I was nine years of age - but I have used English almost ever since. The English language has done with me what the English people have done with our country - taken possession of the richest and largest part of it. No sooner do I use two or three Welsh words than their bolder English brethren thrust forward and the poor timid Taffies shrink back to hide themselves and I cannot, in spite of the utmost effort, find them again in time.') [8]

The school's foundation stone had been lain in the spring of 1856 and it had taken approximately a year to build. For reasons that need not detain us too long, there had been controversy over both its location and character. Throughout the 18th century a school at Troed-yr-Allt had been located on that spot. Known as the free grammar school, it had functioned, in theory, under Anglican auspices. But it had been an intermittent, fragmentary outpost of the National Society, faltering on an uncertain path and perilously short of funds for most of its existence. Its last headmaster moved on to other things in 1841 and the deserted building fell into disrepair. Small schools elsewhere in the town provided rudimentary education for a limited number of children, and a National school opened at at Penlleiniau (at its other end) in 1843, but the situation was not satisfactory. [9] In 1851 the site's accredited owner handed it over to the BFSS. It would be argued later by disgruntled members of the National Society that he had not really had the authority to do so and that some dexterous sleight-of-hand had been employed. They were also much affronted by the fact that the Privy Council, with the support of the Charity Commissioners, readily provided £500 for the old building to be demolished so that a new state-of-the-art British School (subscribed for by a great many of the local residents) could be erected in its place. But the protesters were out-numbered and out-gunned, for the advocates of the new school were headed by the formidable figure of Hugh Owen, Chief Clerk of the Poor Law Commission and a famous educationalist. He had sounded a clarion call in 1843 by issuing an open letter to the Welsh people urging them to think in terms of establishing a British school in every parish of their land for the benefit of Nonconformists. They would be staffed by properly-qualified teachers, fully conversant with English but also equipped with at least a rudimentary knowledge of the Welsh language as a means of embracing all-comers. Owen, as it happened, would be primarily responsible for establishing a Teachers' Training College at Bangor in 1856 which - for he had much in common with Dr Kay, although they were not closely acquainted - owed something to the Battersea establishment.

Great was Hugh Owen's renown, in short, and he was supported in the town by a dissenting Minister, the Rev. Thomas Phillips, and (until his death in 1855) by a well-known local shipbuilder called William Jones. In a bid to win over its entrenched opponents by emphasising an element of continuity, the promoters started referring to it as the Pwllheli Free School and pointed out (a) that more than half of its eleven trustees were churchmen and (b) that it would not actually accept funds from the British Society, although the Society's precepts would undoubtedly be followed. The big, bad wolf, it seems, was genuinely anxious to convince its critics that it really was a lamb at heart..

The new school was ready for use by the spring of 1857. 'On the ground floor', the town's historian has recorded, 'was the boys' schoolroom, spacious enough to take up to 400 children, and on the floor above, with a separate entrance, was the girls' schoolroom with the same dimension. Each schoolroom had a separate classroom and adjoining the building was the master's house.' [10] As yet, however, although a mistress had been found to take charge of the girls (being obliged to find her own house, it seems), a master had yet to materialise. The *Caernarvon & Denbigh Herald* (in common, presumably, with journals elsewhere) published on 25 April a notice from the Clerk to the Committee, Mr Breese, to the effect that they were about to appoint a master who would be required to teach the Classics, French, Mathematics and Navigation and who would either be equipped already with 'a Government certificate of competency' or else be prepared to take one. The salary would depend upon the successful applicant's qualifications. Controversy continued, however, and on 27 June, the *Herald* published an appeal from a despairing Morell (reproduced as Appendix III) urging the local residents to forget their differences 'and unite in forming a vigorous school for the town, where a good secular education

177

shall be supplemented by religious instruction, based upon the only Word of Life.'

There had not been an instant rush of applicants for the post of headmaster. Eventually, however, a Mr J. Mackintosh from Scotland came forward, at which there was a great sigh of relief, and the school became fully operational at the end of July with an initial intake of some 200 pupils. But another crisis gradually developed. Mr Mackintosh, however well qualified he may have been academically, was hopeless at maintaining discipline. By the summer of 1858 the situation was evidently dire - could there have been riots or rebellions? - and the boys' school had to be temporarily closed down. This was a true emergency! Mr Mackintosh was requested to pack his bags and depart. The need for a capable successor was urgent in the extreme and it may have been Morell who was instrumental in persuading William to step forward and volunteer his services. (One hopes that he was able to negotiate some reasonably satisfactory terms in the process.) As noted already, it is possible that he had worked in a British School at Talgarth fourteen years earlier, but his general experience and proven capability would have been more than enough to satisfy the desperate managers. In effect, he had been 'head-hunted' for his latest position and there would have been no more than a token glance at his credentials.

For all practical purposes, William functioned in the first instance as a one-man fire brigade. But normality was restored in double-quick time, much to the relief of the managers. Du Parcq claims that William, while 'averse from corporal punishment' - a statement which would have greatly surprised Edwin John - 'had the indefinable gifts which make a disciplinarian, and he brought order out of chaos.' [11] A loud, commanding voice, allied with firmness of demeanour, probably achieved much but the cane could well have been in evidence, if only as something to brandish at moments of extreme tension. (A teacher-trainer in the mid-twentieth century, recalling some of his own experiences, would vividly describe how, at the start of lessons at a new school which had an alarming reputation for unruliness, he would enter the classroom with a thick cudgel under his arm and - without a word of explanation - quietly lay it down at the front of his desk before proceeding with the lesson. The pupils, it seems, took the hint and were as good as gold.)

Du Parcq was drawing, in the main, on the account written by Henry Rees in 1909. It will be recalled that Rees (who, incidentally, had *not* claimed that William was averse to corporal punishment) had described him as 'a man of average height but ... strongly built with broad shoulders and a thin, pale face; a high, wide forehead; [and] large, lively eyes', a description which was quoted, in effect, by both du Parq and William's descendants. 'He was', Rees had continued, 'an excellent musician and it is said that he was the first to teach the principles of the tonic sol-fa in the town'. His early brief association with John Hullah may have stood him in good stead, but elsewhere it has been suggested that Eleazer Roberts, a native of Pwllheli (but a resident of Liverpool) was primarily responsible for the introduction of the tonic sol-fa method into Wales.

'He was also,' says Rees, 'a regular and committed teacher of a class of young men at the old Pentrepoeth [Baptist] Chapel Sunday School and some of his pupils remain to this day who hold his memory in high respect. They bear witness to the fact that he was a robust and principled thinker whose debating and reasoning skills were without equal.' It is possible that a note on the subject of 'happiness', which he appears to have written at about this time, formed the basis of the peroration to one of his Sunday school sermons: 'We may be confined to close and narrow homes, shut up in cities and cut off from the sweet face of nature and the pure breath of

179

heaven; to regulate our diet may not be in our power; exhausted by sedentary toil, exercise may seem almost forbidden to us, and baths a luxury hardly to be thought of, but happiness may be ours: for it lies in doing good.' [12]

It will be recalled that Navigation was one of the subjects which the headmaster was required to teach, and the following short page of notes suggest that William made a valiant attempt to gen up on the subject - although he was speedily deflected into a sermon, which may not quite have been what the school's managers originally had in mind:

> Course: to men with compass of ship - needle *designed* to point always to the pole - but many disturbing influences - attracted by other & nearer objects - hence requires to be very carefully adjusted for even then very liable to get out of order. In an iron ship for instance the attraction of the surrounding area makes it extremely difficult to adjust the compass correctly.
>
> While free from these disturbing influences it serves as a true & safe guide to the mariner on his voyage, but sometimes goes out of restraint when ship far away on a reckless ocean; & then the captain can only find his way by observing the heavenly bodies.
>
> So it is with the conscience - were it entirely free to act as God at the first designed it to act, it would always direct us in the path of duty - always be a safe guide on our voyage through life. But alas it is not so - the disturbing influence of sin & ignorance often turn it from its true course [so] that it is no longer to be trusted. But happily we too have a heavenly guide to direct us in our perplexity & to correct the aberrations of conscience. [13]

William gradually became acquainted with the local residents, who were 'very kind' and made the young widower extremely welcome. He reported to his mother in mid-September 1858 that, in particular, a Mrs Jones and her son, 'who are considered among the first people in Pwllheli', had made a great fuss of him. They had invited him 'to sit in their pew every Sunday and they invited me to supper last Sunday. There I met Mr Williams' - almost certainly, Robert Williams of Aberdovey. This gentleman was collecting for the mission of the Welsh in London and William reminded him that 'we had met before at the house of Mr Nicholas Fishguard. As soon as he knew I came from that neighbourhood, he asked me about many people I knew there. He asked did I know Mrs Williams of Trecoed - *pobl dda, caredig iawn* [good, kind people] - When I told him "Mrs Williams is my mother", he jumped out of his chair. When he left he gave me a warm blessing. My dear mother, I need not tell you how pleased I was to hear him say that you were one of the best women in Pembrokeshire before that good company.'

He told her, in the same letter, about a recent meeting of the Methodist Association in Pwllheli and a most eloquent preacher referred to by some as 'The Great Gun' whose discourse had apparently made a great impression on him. 'He followed his text', William declared, 'and in his style of oratory there were occasional passages of fervid eloquence. However, he never seemed to struggle with the weight of great thoughts. All his gold seemed to lie in glittering grains on the surface; one watched in vain for an occasional monster nugget dug up fresh from the depths below. There was real gold however. Often as I have heard the love of Christ as manifested in His suffering, I have seldom heard it described with greater effect.' [14] It is possible that the preacher in question was Henry Rees, now in his sixty-first year, a towering figure who had delivered a sermon at the Penmount Chapel on the morning of 10 September. But there were, it must be added, other preachers at the three-day gathering (such as John Hughes, Joseph Thomas and David Saunders) who ran him close. [15] (Mr Williams, who had served as a curtain-raiser for Henry Rees on the evening of the 8th, commanded much respect but was not among the ranks of the most exalted.) *Not* present on this occasion, but doubtless spoken of, was the young Humphrey Jones, newly returned from America, who in company with David Morgan would be launching 'the great Welsh revival' the following year. [16]

William had a multi-faceted identity when it came to religion. It seems that much depended upon the personality of the individual to whom he was talking at any one time. To his mother, who was especially pious (and, later, to Richard Lloyd), he would relate details of sermons and preachers because he knew that such information would be received with gratification and relish. To a fellow-teacher, however, who had expressed religious doubts, his expressions were rather more mundane - or, at any rate, very cautious. 'I hardly know what to advise', he wrote, 'as to the course you should pursue in the school - your opinion of the value of the Bible as a religious text-book appears to be lower than mine now is. I was at one time prejudiced against it by the writings of the Socialists and controversies etc, with which I have now little sympathy indeed. I have lately been in the habit of writing down a little of the Book itself, and am getting back into the old opinion that as a source of instruction on the spiritual nature and destiny of man, there is no book in the world to be compared to it. I have very little doubt that this will be your opinion too, when you have gone through your allotted share of the discipline of sorrow and humiliation.'

These were worthy sentiments but perhaps somewhat less exalted in tone than might have been expected from one who had served as a recruiting officer for Dr Martineau's Sunday school, and who, only a few years earlier, had immersed himself in a vast number of books and tracts on the teaching of religion. (The date of this letter is unknown, unfortunately: it was quoted by W.R.P. George in 1976 but is seemingly no longer extant.) [17]

An extract from another letter quoted by Dr George (undated, once again, but probably written in 1857 or 1858) carried, however, what appear to be his definitive sentiments on one of the most sensitive subjects of all. (It shows, at any rate, that he had come to terms with the death of Selina.) 'When we think', he mused, 'how short a time we have to live in this world, it is a wonder we should allow it to engross all our thoughts and affections as we do. We cling to it as if it were our greatest good and shrink from the thought of leaving it. No doubt this strong love of life has been planted in us for a wise end. The world seems to be intended as a sort of apprenticeship to teach us how to live in another world. How little do most of us learn of our heavenly calling - But this love of life is only for this world. We must overcome the fear of death; unless we do so, we cannot meet death calmly. Yet many religious people cannot bear to think of death.' [18] It was, certainly, a subject which he himself would brood upon during the next few years.

The foregoing letter had been addressed to Captain William Williams, the fiancée of his niece Anne James. Born in 1838, she was the daughter of his sister Gwenllian Mary George (who preferred to be known by her second Christian name). Eight years older than William, Mary had married Levi James, a prosperous Pembrokeshire farmer, in 1834 and had several children. She was frequently in poor health, however. 'I was glad to have a better account of her lately', William had told the Captain, '... but her constitution like mine is not made to last long. But whose life is long? Some people live a few years longer than others, but after all, what is the longest life compared to eternity? A mere drop in the great ocean.' [19] William's gloomy forecast was fulfilled when Mary died on 16

December 1858 - and he would doubtless have reflected that, if his own life-span was to be the same length as his sister's, then he himself could probably expect to meet his Maker in 1866 or thereabouts. If he was going to get married, and start a family, then he needed to get a move on!

Information about the subsequent success of the Pwllheli school, and the number of pupils who attended, is sparse. One can only assume that, after the ructions of 1858, it proceeded without serious difficulty and that the headmaster and the headmistress had at least one assistant a-piece. D.G. Lloyd Hughes has suggested that the true complement of pupils during William's period as headmaster did not greatly exceed the number of 350, despite the ample space that had originally been provided by the school's optimistic designers. 'By the winter of 1863', he writes, 'the number was down to a little over 200. The deterioration in attendance no doubt reflected some of the difficulties of the committee of management. There is evidence that the boys' school in particular had to be closed [again] for some weeks (probably after the departure of William George in 1860) because of the failure to appoint a successor. By 1870, however, the school seems to have flourished if the evidence of a good inspection report is anything to go by.' [20] The census for 1871 shows that John T. Evans and his wife Ellen were headmaster and headmistress by that time and were living in the house adjoining it, together with the wife's younger sister (a pupil at the school) and a servant.

But in the autumn of 1858 that house was occupied by just one person - a young widower from Wakefield. And one who was clearly, as sage local observers would have agreed, in need of practical assistance. They might even have taken the view that he was in urgent need of a second wife. There is a story to the effect that he found her living next door in a house called *Y Castell*, in the service of a Miss Evans, but - for the reasons set out in Appendix IV - the evidence for this claim crumbles away the moment one touches it. The precise time and place at which William George met Elizabeth ('Betsy') Lloyd will almost certainly remain unknown, and narrative purposes could be served adequately enough by recording that they were married at the parish church of Denio by William Richards, curate of Llanor, on Wednesday, 16 November 1859, approximately fifteen months after William's arrival in the town. The groom was almost forty and the bride was thirty-one. But perhaps we can be a little more venturesome in our speculation.

Betsy Lloyd has entered this story sideways, as it were, and we have still to become properly acquainted with her, but it is worth lingering a moment longer to consider how it was that her path should have crossed William's in the first place. The details of the marriage certificate offer a possible clue, for the ceremony was witnessed not only by the bride's brother, Richard Lloyd (somebody else to whom the reader has not yet been introduced), but also by a Jane Jones.

One's first thought is that Jane Jones could well have been the lady who, with her son, had made William so welcome when he arrived in Pwllheli, insisting that he join them in their family pew and come to meals in their house. That particular lady was, indeed, none other than the widow of William Jones, the shipbuilder and ship-owner who had joined Hugh Owen and the Reverend Phillips in campaigning for the establishment of the new school in the first place. And her son Griffith, who had stepped very capably into his father's shoes and managed to sustain the family business as a flourishing concern, had been rewarded by a grateful community with the post of alderman. Their house, Brynhyfryd, was a majestic mansion standing in an acre of its own grounds, almost akin to a local palace, and commanding a splendid view of the bay. It had been specially built for William Jones in the early 1840s. Mother and son were indubitably, as William had observed, 'among the first people in Pwllheli'. They would have been equally anxious to ensure that the new school, so closely identified with their name, would have as secure a future as the shipbuilding business. The original headmaster, Mr Mackintosh, had disappeared from the scene after a disastrous few months and it was imperative that the school should not lose the services of his successor after an equally short period. Everything possible should be done to make him feel at home. Taking him under a motherly wing for a time, Mrs Jones was clearly much exercised about William's creature comforts.

The most pressing problem of all was, obviously, how the new arrival was to cope by himself in a large house. Mr Mackintosh might, for all we know, have been accompanied by a Mrs Mackintosh and perhaps even by a Mackintosh servant, but William was a first person singular with no such accoutrements. The house needed to be kept clean and there needed to be regular meals on the headmaster's table. Clothes needed to be washed and socks needed to be darned. Bedding needed to be changed. Fires needed to be lit in the winter and windows needed to be opened in the summer. Somebody who could act competently on his behalf and relieve him of all anxiety about such chores was obviously required.

That initial theory about the widow of William Jones being the lady who acted as a witness at the wedding receives something of a jolt when, on probing a little further, one finds that her name was actually *Anne*. But there is a supplementary link in the chain, for one of the two servants employed at Brynhyfryd at this time was called Jane Jones. [21] It is not beyond the bounds of possibility that mistress and servant conferred on the subject of Mr George's future domestic arrangements and that Jane warmly recommended her friend

Betsy Lloyd for the post of housekeeper. Betsy, several years older than Jane, was somebody who had been in domestic service since the age of 13 or 14 and who would be more than competent in carrying out the many duties which looking after a medium-sized house entailed.

It may be, for all we know, that Betsy attended the same Baptist chapel as both the Jones household and William, which would have been an in-built advantage or strong mark in her favour. But however the introduction was affected, the likelihood is that Mrs Jones and Jane Jones, acting in concert, were responsible for bringing Betsy Lloyd to William's attention, with Jane having played the crucial part in this exercise. It is not inconceivable, assuming that local susceptibilities would not have been irremediably shocked, that Betsy took up residence in the headmaster's house as full-time housekeeper. (The marriage certificate, completed on her behalf by either William or Richard, shows that she was living in Penlan Street at the time of her wedding. This is a street which was no more than fifteen minutes' walk away from the school but we have no idea whether she lived there for a year, a month, a week or merely a day.)

Matrimony is a serious business and not to be entered into lightly. In earlier years, as we have seen, William had pondered long and hard on the subject of finding himself a wife – he wanted, ideally, a soul-mate, somebody who was his intellectual equal. He had penned many anguished notes on the subject, seeking enlightenment on the best course to follow. It was an intellectual approach to an emotional subject. The background to his marriage to Selina Huntley is not altogether clear but she was evidently an intelligent, resourceful woman, apparently skilled in business techniques, and it would have been possible to exchange views with her on the great issues of the day as well as more commonplace matters. If the fancy took her she might even have dipped, now and then, into her husband's great library of books. Betsy, however, was a much humbler and probably a much quieter person. She was also illiterate and there was no question of her being able to read any of William's books. Her general knowledge must have been limited in the extreme. On the face of things, they were totally incompatible.

William was a shy, formal man who did not make new friends easily and it is probable that Betsy was also rather shy. Their initial relationship of master and servant could have developed into cautious amicability and after a few months William might well have reflected that, notwithstanding all his previous ponderous notes and assertions on the subject of matrimony, he could do worse than form a permanent union with Betsy. We have no idea what she looked like as a young woman, the only surviving photograph of her showing an elderly lady in a mob-cap with a tentative smile on her lips. At the age of 30, she might well have been extremely good-looking. And the reassurance of quiet homeliness and security, of which William had been starved for many years, could have been one of her major attractions. The probability is that he became so closely acquainted with her that he felt relaxed and happy in her company and, finally, was emboldened to propose. Familiarity breeds romance.

It must be emphasised that everything set forth in the five preceding paragraphs is pure conjecture. Until such time as fresh information comes to light, it is offered as a reasonable hypothesis without claiming to be anything more than that. But the name of Jane Jones definitely appears on that marriage certificate. There was a very special reason why she had been invited to the wedding (attendance at which, in Victorian times, was restricted to the chosen few) and it is suggested, with a fair degree of confidence, that for the performance of certain crucial services, which might almost come under the heading match-making, she clearly deserves to be remembered in the annals of Lloyd George family history.

10 - RECUPERATING IN LLANYSTUMDWY

William announced to his mother that he had been 'lucky enough to win one of earth's best and fairest daughters' whom he felt sure would be welcomed into the family with open arms. [1] It would have been eminently appropriate for Betsy to have accompanied him on his usual visit to Trecoed for the Christmas festivities in order to meet Mrs Williams, but it is not known whether this actually happened. With the bride's family, on the other hand, William would by this time have become thoroughly acquainted and the force of circumstances would shortly dictate that their acquaintanceship would become even closer than first anticipated. That immediate family, living in the village of Llanystumdwy (a village with just over a thousand residents, approximately five miles east of Pwllheli) consisted of her mother, her brother and her nephew.

Elizabeth had been born in Llanystumdwy on 1 October 1828, the second child and daughter of David and Rebecca Lloyd. [2] David, himself born in 1800, had in 1824 married Rebecca Samuel of Pwllheli, a girl four years his junior. He brought her back to live in a relatively large cottage in Llanystumdwy called Highgate which had a workshop attached, for David was the master-shoemaker in the village and had at least two employees assisting him in the production of home-made boots. He was also distinguished in another respect, for he was the ordained but unpaid minister of Capel Ucha Baptist church at Penymaes, Criccieth, a small town and seaside resort located two miles to the east. But he died in 1839 and Rebecca was obliged to become head of the household, taking over the shoemaking business and doing everything she could to ensure that it remained a thriving concern. Their son Richard, born in 1834, would eventually be absorbed into the family business (probably not being allowed much choice in the matter) but Rebecca stayed firmly in overall control and continued, throughout the 1840s and 1850s, to employ two men. The census for 1841, taken on 6 June, shows that the Highgate household on that date consisted simply of Rebecca (allegedly 41), Elizabeth (12) and Richard (6). The Lloyds' first daughter, Ellin (born in 1825) was a live-in servant on a nearby farm by that time.

Neither of the two girls, unlike their more fortunate brother, received much of an education and at the age of 13 or 14 Elizabeth would have followed her sister into service. The census for 1851 shows that she was a housemaid at Trallwyn Hall, four miles north of Pwllheli. This was the home of a landed proprietor called John Lloyd who was a magistrate and Deputy-Lieutenant, farming an estate of 190 acres. Family tradition (as distinct from hard evidence) claims that Betsy was also in service at several other places during the seven years that followed.

Ellin, in the meantime, had developed a close friendship with a labourer called William Jones, who worked on his father's 40-acre farm, Caerdyni, located to the east of Criccieth and almost three miles from Llanystumdwy. Events followed a familiar course and Ellin became pregnant. They were married in Criccieth parish church on 7 October 1846 and she gave birth to a boy at Highgate on 30 January 1847 whom they named David Lloyd. The child was weak and sickly and both cash and spare time were in short supply so far as the parents were concerned. They were not in a position to look after him properly and Ellin may have wanted to resume employment, whether as a farm or house servant, without delay. (She had been working at Eifion House, to the west of Criccieth, at the time of her marriage.) It was evidently decided that Rebecca would look after her grandson on a full-time basis, bringing him up with Richard's assistance, and that Ellin would join her husband at Caerdyni. She gave birth to five more children during the twelve years which followed but there was never

191

any question of David coming to join them. John Jones, William's father (aged 73 in 1851), evidently died during the 1850s. His wife, another Ellin, lived on for many more years but for all practical purposes William was head of the family and owner of the farm by the end of that decade.

One more development that needs to be noted is that Richard also followed in his father's footsteps in another important respect, for in March 1859 he succeeded him as minister at the Baptist church in Criccieth. By that time those particular Baptists had become a little more extreme, or (of it be preferred) perhaps rather more narrow-minded, in their views. They had adopted the doctrines preached by Alexander Campbell from the other side of the Atlantic, being very much a minority movement with an abundance of rules and prescriptive ordinances, but proud to be relatively few in number and taking for themselves the name of Disciples in Christ. Richard gradually developed into a first-rate preacher, though of gently persuasive rather than over-zealous tendencies, steering clear of the full-blooded 'hell-fire and damnation' school. He became ever more deeply immersed in complex Biblical studies during his moments of leisure, and it will be seen that to some extent he and William proved to be kindred spirits - especially so when it came to exchanging clerical gossip, and the latest news on how rival preachers might be faring.

The Lloyds, while not over-endowed with worldly goods (a source of rejoicing, from the preacher's viewpoint), evidently prided themselves on an illustrious ancestry. Early biographers of the future Prime Minister excitedly drew attention to the fact that the family in Llanystumdwy were offshoots of the Lloyds of Llwynderus who included such figures as Sir Gruffyd Lloyd, a doughty warrior, and Richard Lloyd, a pioneering astronomer, among their number. This may be the case, but the fame of these individuals does not seem to have penetrated into the twenty-first century and (at the risk of being smitten into the dust for such heresy) one is inclined to suggest that their status is mythical rather than factual. (Google knows them not, in short.)

At the start of 1860, William and Betsy would have been living in the house attached to the school. The disgruntled reader may feel that, even now, very little has actually been said about Betsy, a charge that must be readily acknowledged. The truth of the matter is, however, that there is very little to say, for she was a quiet, unobtrusive lady who went about her business efficiently but whose remarks - except on one particularly joyous occasion [3] - have gone largely unrecorded. (An extremely well-phrased letter to Thomas Goffey, which Dr George claims she drafted in the summer of 1864, is exciting at first glance but the elegant turn of phrase suggests that it had been written on her behalf by Richard - though doubtless expressing her thoughts and perhaps even, at certain points, at her dictation.) Du Parcq, acting on information supplied by Anne Williams, described her as 'a woman of medium height. Her complexion was fair, her hair very dark, her eyes brown, the expression of her thoughtful features one of great charm. The sound judgment and high principles with which her friends rightly credited her made her an ideal companion for the man she now married.' Her second son remembered her as 'rather a small woman, but with a good figure' and 'a very soft sweet voice': she had a sense of humour but was basically serious and could sometimes be quite firm. Somebody else recalled her calm face and 'slow distinguished speech', concluding that she was 'a gentlewoman in every gesture.' The most that could be remembered by Dr R.D. Evans, casting his mind back to the 1870s, was that she was 'delicate in health' and unable to attend the Criccieth chapel on a regular basis; she is said to have suffered from asthma in her later years. [4]

She was also delicate in health for much of 1860, for it would have been evident by March that she was pregnant. William was doubtless elated by the news and seemed in good spirits as winter gave way to spring, although only one scrap of paper containing his jottings has survived from this period. 'The inquisitiveness of the Welsh is powerful,' he wrote on 7 June. 'If a stranger asks them the way to a place they want to know his business there & where he comes from. This propensity supplied me with some fun once.' Tantalisingly, he did not record what the fun had been. These sentences were written in ink and then came a pencilled addition three weeks later - 'Pwllheli, June 30th 1860. Three years since last entry. Rose at half past 5 & went for a walk of 3 miles - enjoyed very much.' [5]

It could be argued that his marriage was the making of him. He could well have acquired a fresh layer of self-confidence and been able to confront the parents of his pupils with greater assurance, having a healthy and attractive wife of his own and content in the knowledge that they too would soon be starting a family. He could now speak to them on an equal footing. It may be from this time onwards that there dates that reputation he had for making an impact in the pulpit, whether it be at an adult Sunday school in Pwllheli or as a guest-speaker at Capel Ucha, of being 'invincible in argument and debate' - quick-witted and zestful. He was speaking with a newly-acquired authority and conviction, and one must recall the words of that old gentleman from Pembrokeshire - 'When he was on his feet, the whole place was buzzing.' At the age of forty, and perhaps influenced by the Welsh Revival (a short-lived phenomenon which apparently made itself felt throughout the Principality), William George was reaching full maturity.

But there were some serious setbacks to be overcome, even now, and he would be hard-pressed to maintain his buoyancy. For it soon became apparent that, probably because of over-work, William's physical health had taken a turn for the worse and that he would have to resign his headship of the British School. He was suffering from prolonged exhaustion. The news would have been received with dismay by pupils and parents alike, for he was clearly held in high esteem, and the managers of the school would have been devastated. There exists amongst his papers the text of a sermon which he apparently delivered as a farewell talk to his pupils. Its sentiments are heartfelt but simple and rather repetitive: he urges his listeners to relinquish selfishness and to follow in the footsteps of Christ by doing good in the world, gratifying God by assisting their fellow-men.

Surrendering his headship (at the end of July or early in August) meant that William also surrendered the house which had accompanied the post. With Betsy's time drawing near there was really no question as to where they could go next: she needed to be near her mother and Highgate thus became their only possible destination. Conditions would now have been slightly cramped (one wonders, in particular, where the great library of books was stored) and William would have been acutely aware of the difference - and also of his loss of status. Rebecca Lloyd was the head of the household, as she had been for more than twenty years, and in effect ruled the domestic roost as effectively as she did the shoemaking business: she doubtless made her second son-in-law extremely welcome, but relations may sometimes have been a little difficult. 'Life in the small three-up and two-down cottage must have been exceedingly cramped,' Dr George has written. 'Water had to be fetched daily and carried in buckets from the village pump; the earth closet, at the far end of the garden, was an unpleasant necessity, and ... the village highway running immediately in front of the house would ... have been covered from time to time with the dirt of animals driven by the drovers towards the near rail-head.' [6]

William evidently did his best to make himself useful: he would willingly have carried the water and one thing that we do know for sure is that he planted beans and potatoes in the garden. He was not short of cash and would have made (one assumes) regular contributions to the household expenses. The continuing purchase of books apart - and Morell's newly-published *Fichte's Contributions to Moral Philosophy* may have been a welcome solace at this time - he was not remotely a spendthrift and had always endeavoured to make good use of the funds at his disposal. A couple of items which have surfaced among his papers indicate his efforts in this direction. One scrap of paper, for example, which may have been the basis for a speech, suggests that he was at one stage the manager or secretary of some kind of thrift or investment club:

> To collect & rec: as communicated on all the debts & interest - to keep the books [& see after all debts *deleted*] - if debts not paid as as soon as due to see after them - *every penny* over the books must be accounted for - emph: that each have has [*sic*] his department clearly defined - what requirts. - of act made a matter of distinct understanding by previous agreements - Responsible for ⅓ of the losses. [7]

The other item is a letter dated 4 October 1858 from a business correspondent - a stockbroker, presumably - whose name is indecipherable and which was sent from 22 Clarendon Rooms. These were almost certainly the Clarendon Rooms located in South John Street, Liverpool, which was a well-known financial centre. Acknowledging a letter which William had sent them on 21 September, exploring the feasibility of cashing in certain shares without delay, it continues:

William George total. - I send you a report by this Post in which you will perceive that the year terminated in June last. If you wish to withdraw two shares, you had better give notice at once, and let me know how you intend receiving it.

2nd - Harrington [Building Society]. We have not commenced balloting in this Society yet, we expect in the course of a Month, or two, to do so, but you can have a quarter paid on each of your shares, at any time, e.g., you can receive £30 on account of each share now, and commence to pay at the rate of five per Cent per Annum, on the amount of cash received - Would not this be better than to withdraw from the 'Alliance Perpetual'? [8]

William clearly considered building societies a good investment, for retained in his papers, in addition to Annual Reports of the aforementioned Alliance Perpetual and Harrington Societies, were some for the Nestor, Minerva, Roch and Hercules Societies. He invested in all six. The Liverpool connection, identified above, would have been taken up during William's period of employment in that city, but he would return there from time to time and he had also kept in reasonably close touch with Thomas Goffey. The pupil-teacher who had organised his farewell presentation in 1852 was by now, at the age of 25, an articled solicitor and managing clerk and a year or two later would become a fully-fledged solicitor based at No. 5 Church Alley, Liverpool. He supplied William with legal advice, it seems, and may also have advised him on financial matters. (He would claim, in 1864, that William had been his 'dearest friend'.) [9]

Betsy gave birth to a son on Saturday, 15 September. In accordance with what had obviously been a pre-arranged decision, the parents instantly named him 'David' after both William's and Betsy's fathers, and 'Lloyd' in honour of his mother's family. But the tiny mite survived for only twelve hours. Despite the obvious spiritual consolations close at hand, the Sunday that followed at Highgate must have been a terrible time for the young couple. On the Monday William trudged to Criccieth to notify Richard Jones, the local Registrar, of both the birth and the death of David Lloyd George. The cause of death was defined as 'Suffocatio' - presumably denoting shortage of breath - and it was noted that the event had not been certified. The child was buried at Capel Ucha and Richard would have carried out the service. (The burial ground no longer exists and William's two subsequent sons never knew of their predecessor's brief existence.) [10]

The visit to the Registrar had been made on the 17th. Exactly a week later, on 24 September, William's mother died. The vivid account by his niece of what then happened, recorded in the first chapter, cannot be bettered:

> Through some neglect he did not receive the news of his mother's death until it was almost too late for him to arrive at he funeral. He arrived at Trecoed just as the funeral cortège was leaving the house, and, the nearest station being sixteen miles away, the poor fellow had to walk all the way to his old home, after a long tedious journey, because no conveyance had been sent to meet him, although there were plenty of horses on the farm, and a trap as well. As soon as he arrived, he joined the procession, which meant another mile to walk, as the mother's coffin was carried to the cemetery [at Jordanston] by the tenants and servants at their express wish, to pay her a last token of respect.

He would have stayed at least one night at Trecoed to recuperate and would then have made his way back to that other house of mourning at Llanystumdwy. In the space of ten days William had lost both his mother and his son and he and Betsy must have been deeply depressed at this time. He decided that, as soon as he was stronger, he must seek fresh employment as a teacher and in 1861 presumably alerted his contacts in the profession that he would be glad of a not-too-onerous post. There was no question, it seems, of his returning to the school at Pwllheli, where the duties had undoubtedly been heavy - and his continuing problems with the Welsh language might also have been an important factor. He was still at Highgate on 7 April 1861 when a fresh census was taken. Rebecca (58), still a shoemaker employing two men, featured as head of the household, followed by Richard Lloyd (26) and her fourteen-year-old grandson, David Lloyd Jones, described as a scholar. Her son-in-law, aged 39, came fourth in the pecking order, his official status being that of a British schoolmaster, and daughter Elizabeth (32), wife of the aforementioned schoolmaster, came last.

William was easy-going with regard to distinguishing between religious sects - clearly, he believed that all the roads led to the same destination - and while not necessarily claiming to be a fully-fledged Disciple of Christ in the Campbellite sense he would have acquiesced cheerfully enough in accompanying Richard, and the rest of the family, to the services at Capel Ucha. He evidently preached there from time to time and after the service was over it is probable that, on most occasions, he accompanied his wife, mother-in-law and David to Caerdyni, a mile further on, for lunch with the Jones family. (Richard normally lunched separately with his co-elder at Shop-yr-Eifion in Cricieth High Street, in preparation for the afternoon service.)

Two deaths in quick succession had been a severe blow but William was developing a new resilience and after the immediate grief would have viewed these matters in proportion. The infant mortality rate was, sadly, still extremely high while his mother had enjoyed a good life and very nearly reached the age of eighty. His relations with Trecoed (where his niece Anne was now acting as housekeeper) remained unaffected. With Benjamin Williams, he had always got along quite well and certainly harboured no acquisitive desires so far as the farm was concerned - but regretted that his brother John, now farming 170 acres in Kilshare, Fishguard, was unlikely to take over the tenancy when Benjamin died. He himself had 'inherited' the cottage left him by his mother, the rent from which would marginally augment his income, but there had been no legal agreement making it formally his.

On 30 July 1861 William was present, possibly in the capacity of Best Man, at Benjamin's marriage to a widow called Amy John. His presence was probably designed to help dispel any lingering family tensions. Afterwards, however, there was an unfortunate episode at the wedding breakfast. Each of the guests was served with a meal in which a lamb or pork chop featured as the culinary *piece-de-resistance*. The bride was suddenly called out of the room. As she did not return for some time, and everyone else had meanwhile finished their meals, Benjamin decided that it was a pity that her chop should be wasted and transferred it to his own plate - simultaneously depositing the bone of his first chop on to William's plate, which was empty apart from the remains of William's own chop. The bride returned to the room, saw that her plate was now empty and spotted that there were *two* chop bones on William's plate. She drew a natural but incorrect conclusion and flew into an uncontrollable rage with him, becoming hysterical in the process. [11] Benjamin presumably managed to calm his bride down eventually and to make it emphatically clear that he alone was responsible for the disappearance of her chop. One trusts that she then apologised to the blameless William, who must have been mightily relieved when the grim repast came to an end.

11 - MARKING TIME IN NEWCHURCH AND MANCHESTER

It was about now (i.e., in July 1861), so far as these matters can be accurately judged, that William and Betsy left Llanystumdwy, taking David with them. The boy served, in a sense, as a substitute son, and assuming responsibility for him was an extremely practical way of repaying Rebecca and Richard for their hospitality. William was fond of the boy and had spent much of his spare time at Highgate supplementing the lessons David received at his local school. He was clearly an intelligent youth and it was hoped that he could be trained up to become a pupil-teacher and, in effect, follow in William's footsteps. The main problem, however, was the very delicate state of his health, and a careful eye would need to be kept on him. (However hard he must have tried to banish them, one suspects that William would sometimes have been troubled by recollections of Selina's illness.)

Their destination was Newchurch in Lancashire - not the relatively well-known village in the Forest of Pendle, but a smaller one eleven miles to the south known as Newchurch-in-Rossendale. It now barely existed in its own right, having been absorbed for all intents and purposes into the town of Rawtenstall (by which name Anne Williams would remember it in 1922). It had a population of more than 20,000. Located on a hill in the Forest of Rossendale, it had been known as Kirk in medieval times: it was the erection of a new church (St Nicholas) in 1511 which brought about the change of name. Combined with four much smaller nearby villages, it also became a chapelry in the astonishingly-extensive parish of Whalley. In Clough-Fold, one of those adjoining villages, there was a long-established Baptist chapel, recently enlarged, which William would attend. It competed for custom with chapels for Wesleyans, Primitive Methodists and Unitarians, and these too he would probably visit. There were several stately homes in the area, plus a newly-built rectory. A *Gazetteer*, glancing briefly at the local industrial scene, tersely informs us that 'coal, freestone, and slate abound; stone is quarried; and the cotton and woollen manufactures are largely carried on.' [1]

While, at first glance, something of a mundane industrial backwater, and nothing like that 'small school in the country' which William had once hoped to discover, Newchurch was serviceable enough as a temporary base-camp. It was a relatively quiet part of the world and Crabtree Buildings in Waterfoot (another of those nearby villages), where they now rented rooms, had better sanitation than they had known at Llanystumdwy. In addition to young David, they were joined a little while later by Anne James, William's niece, whose presence (apart from being agreeable in itself) would be serving a crucial purpose at this point in time because Betsy was pregnant again. Their first child having failed to survive at Highgate, there was every reason to escape from the glum forebodings which would otherwise have arisen had they stayed there and to do everything possible to avoid possible mishaps on this second occasion.

There was a railway station close at hand, with speedy connections to Burnley in the north and Manchester in the south, and from the latter it was easy enough to reach Liverpool if William wanted to meet up with Goffey or any other of his Hope Street friends. The mail to and from *this* Newchurch was handled at Manchester, which explains why - although Manchester was sixteen miles away - he headed one of his few surviving letters 'Newchurch, nr Manchester' and another (absent-mindedly) as 'Manchester' alone, although he eventually adopted the routine of simply writing 'Newchurch'. He kept in close touch with Richard (who rarely went far afield) and, being more used to travelling than his brother-in-law, was able to carry out little errands on his behalf. 'I am glad you think of learning a little Greek,' he writes soon after settling down in Newchurch, 'I'll inquire about the lexicon when I go to L'pool or Manchester. I thought you would be pleased with the N. Testament: I have sent for another copy & hope you will soon point out a few passages with your remarks. Oh how I wish I had a little more time that I might pay some attention to such subjects & correspond with you reasonably upon them. Well I hope it will be the case soon.' [2] He also passed on to Richard his copies of a weekly edition of *The Times*.

Gawthorpe Hall, where Sir James Kay-Shuttleworth was beginning to endure a sad, strange and lonely existence, with his wife having fled abroad to escape his company, was only nine miles away. But whether William was aware of this, and whether he ever tried to make contact with his first mentor, is not known. It was a school inspector called Mr Davis, not Kay-Shuttleworth, who had been responsible for finding him the Newchurch post - and William made no secret of the fact that, although his latest school could be endured for the time being, he would escape from it without hesitation if anyone knew of a more promising billet elsewhere.

It is unlikely that William and Richard ever met again after the Georges left Llanystumdwy, and only nine of the weekly letters which they exchanged during the subsequent two years (all from William's side) have survived but they convey a pleasant impression of the good-natured friendliness that prevailed between the two men. Religious matters were usually covered with a fairly light touch, and sometimes (as will be seen from what follows) amount to little more than pure gossip, glee and speculation. 'We have received *Yr Herald Cymraeg* which interests us very much,' writes William in an undated letter. 'What in all the world is the meaning of Ll.

Rees advertising that he keeps a "Temperance" at Carnarvon? Has he joined them to live? Has he been appointed minister there?' On 10 June 1862 he acknowledges receipt of the sermon written by Dr Rose forwarded by Richard - there has so far only been time for a brief glance, but 'I liked the taste of it.' In October of that year he is intrigued at some upheavals taking place at the college established by Hugh Owen - 'What can be the reason that they are making such a *clean sweep* of the masters at Bangor?' he asks. 'I think I have heard that the state of the college has not been very satisfactory; perhaps the present masters are not qualified for their work. I hope the next set won't be all Methodists - that will be "one" great improvement.' [3]

Apart from postal communication, a Mr W. Williams (a bagman or commercial traveller, perhaps?) acted as a regular link between them. 'Could you send me Barnes's *Notes on the Testament* with Mr Williams?' asks William at the end of the foregoing letter. 'When is he coming? We have neither of us been to Chapel this morning, but I think of going to the Mursett this evening.' On 17 November 1862, knowing that Richard would be interested to learn of the shortcomings of rival preachers, William craftily worked himself up into a critical mood:

I went last evening to hear Mansell & was not pleased at all. His text was, 'There shall no sign be given to them but the sign of the prophet Jonah' & the subject such as a type of Christ. He gave Jonah a very bad character which I dare say he deserves. He is very fond of *alliteration* - his composition is studded quite thick with it from beginning to end. Last night I was seated in too conspicuous a place to take notes - I only remember a few examples: the s*t*a*b*le of *B*ethlehem, the *n*urseling of *N*azareth - the Cross could not *massacre* *his mercy.* What do you think of the taste of that phrase? Or the following when comparing the sacrifice of Jonah with that of Christ, amongst other things, he said, 'In the one case only a man was seized [by a whale], in the other *a Deity was damned*!' I think that is going too far for the rhetorical licence of the pulpit. Again, 'His arm is not yet *stiff* with beckoning; nor his voice *hoarse* with inviting sinners to return.' [4]

On 12 January 1863 there was a bumper bundle of such gossip, commencing with what was basically family information - for the gentleman referred to, in somewhat contemptuous tones, was distantly related to William - and eventually ending on an adroit note of flattery:

I understand that [the Rev. Henry] Davies, Llangloffan, bequeathed most of his money to Pontypool Academy, to the Bible Society & to Llangloffan. I think he had the name of being sicker than he really was because he was so covetous. He was very much *am y byd* & his farm was at a low rent, but he did not make nearly so much by it as many could have made. His land was not of good quality & he could not find it in his heart to part with his money even to make profitable improvements. I should think he disposed of his money very wisely: he had no children & his sister's children (my cousins) have enough of their own. By disposing of his property as he did it may be hoped that the world will be a gainer by his death - even if his life was not of much benefit to it. [5]

The enclosed slips about *y browd* H.C. Howells I cut from a *Seren Cymru* I saw at Trecoed. You see it gives the rev. gentleman a bit of a puff. The secret of it is that Hugh is trying for a place in the South. Lewis

Jones' wife told me that he had written to her husband about Brynhyfrid (his old church) & that he had been previously trying for another place the name of which I have forgotten. What can be the matter? Is it that they have got tired of Hugh, or that Hugh is looking for higher pay?

I hope the simultaneous removal of so many baptist ministers to the North is a sign that light is beginning to break in upon the methodistical darkness in which multitudes of your neighbours have been so long groping their way. I went to hear Breyn Grant on Sunday Evening but did not go to hear his lecture - I had had quite enough of him in his sermon. He is not at all to my taste. I found your description of him to be quite correct & remember very little of his sermon now. His text was Acts XVIII 32 & 34. He told us that congregations in the present day are made up of the same three classes, those who mock, those who postpone the consideration of religion & those few who believe. That was very well, but he went further to divide the congregation before him into three classes. He said 'We will suppose that the mockers are in the back gallery (where I happd. to sit) - those who put off to another day in the side galleries - & those who receive the word on the ground floor.' I did not think that a good text, perhaps I should view the matter differently if I happened to be amongst the elect on the floor. It occurs to me now that I forgot to say how much we both admired your eloquent eulogies on the Bible in the letter before Xmas. [6]

On 6 February 1863 he acknowledged receipt of a particularly interesting letter from Richard. This had forwarded a report from an unknown lady concerning some very serious ructions at Carmarthen's Presbyterian College. Her account of what 'Dr Nic' had been getting up to, William confirmed, was as new to him as it had been to Richard.

'Dr Nic' was Dr Thomas Nicholas. It may be recalled that he was William's cousin, although despite their close blood-ties the two men appear to have been only slightly acquainted. (William's mother Mary, and Thomas's mother Phoebe, were sisters.) Nicholas was three years older than William. What he did after leaving that Liverpool grammar school is unknown, but it is clear that he rapidly developed an interest in both Biblical studies and antiquarianism. In 1841 he began a course of studies at the Lancashire Independent College, based in Manchester, which had a formative impact upon him. [7] He then travelled abroad, first to France and then to Germany. Emulating the example of Ernest Maltravers, as it were, he became a student at Göttingen University, which - greatly impressed by his abilities - bestowed upon him both an MA and a PhD for his works on Biblical criticism. 'His vocation in life', in the words of Iwan Morgan, 'was originally intended to have been in the ministry among the English Independents, and numerous notes of his sermons ... prove that he must have been an exceptionally able preacher both in English and in Welsh. In 1847 he became pastor at the Old Chapel; Stroud, Gloucestershire, and about seven years later he settled at Eignbrook, Hereford.' [8] In 1856 he was appointed Professor of Biblical Literature and Mental and Moral Science at the Presbyterian College, Carmarthen, where Dr David Lloyd, an old-style Unitarian minister thirteen years older than himself (and previously the college's tutor in classics) had been appointed the Principal in 1853. (Lloyd, it should be noted, was a severe critic of Martineau, who he considered was - in partnership with two or three others - actively distorting the original tenets of Unitarianism.)

Nicholas was much respected by his contemporaries, it seems, for his scholarship and industry, and was evidently embarking on what would indeed prove to be a distinguished career. He was also, however, quite a pugnacious personality and an active campaigner for educational reform. He never shied away from controversy. In 1860 he came volubly to the defence of a fellow-professor of Biblical studies who had been, so he declared, unfairly dismissed from his post at the Lancashire Independent College, and in the autumn of 1862 he began writing a series of letters to *The Cambria Daily Leader* which urged that two fresh colleges be established in Wales, one in the north and the other in the south, to serve as the basis for a University for Wales. Lloyd evidently disagreed with his colleague's views, but what brought matters to a head was that Nicholas thereupon delivered a speech, or address, to his students, seeking their support for his campaign. They gave it wholeheartedly and Lloyd thereupon sent a letter to *The Leader* making clear that he deplored his colleague's behaviour in disrupting the quiet atmosphere of the college by introducing contentious issues and stirring up acrimonious passions. After such a public rebuke it seemed highly improbable that Nicholas would be able to remain in his post.

'I certainly think', William continued, 'that Dr Lloyd acted unwisely in writing to the newspaper to expose his colleague's proceedings, but I also think it very probable that he had received great provocation. It was injudicious & selfish of Nicholas to encourage the students to make such a fuss about his address. Poor, ignorant lads, their opinion was not worth much, certainly not enough to compensate him for losing the friendship of his fellow-tutor. It is probable however that there was "ill-feeling" between them previously, and that this affair of the address greatly exacerbated it. I shall be curious to know the end of the matter. I should think it will be a loss to Tom to lose the place & when he is not at all likely to get another so good. I have heard that he is a "dry" preacher. There is no doubt that he is a man of good ability & that his acquirements are far above them & the generality of ministers.'[9]

Nicholas, to round off the story, did indeed resign from the college. He moved to London, where William Williams, a Welsh MP representing a Lambeth constituency, had enthusiastically borne the cost of republishing his letters as a booklet entitled *Middle and High Schools and a University for Wales*. They attracted considerable attention and Nicholas would now devote himself whole-heartedly (until he eventually fell out with his fellow-campaigners) to the task of bringing such a University into existence. [10] (Dr Lloyd, his spirits perhaps weakened by the dispute, would die before the end of the year.)

Noteworthy, perhaps, is William's detached attitude towards his cousin's activities. He took a mild interest in them but was not himself inclined to campaign for a Welsh University - or, indeed, for much else. By this stage of his life he was primarily an amused observer of the contemporary scene and his letter of 6 February 1863 now moved on to other matters.

We both greatly enjoyed the account of the state of things at Penmount. The Seceders have been outwitted very cleverly. Of course there can be no two opinions as to the two who have done it. They are no match for Pugh. 'When rogues fall out honest men may get their own', & the disgraceful proceedings of these Penmount Methodists will, I hope, open the eyes of many to see the real character and natural tendency of their system and thus to promote the interests of true religion.

This quarrel improves the chances of Lewis Jones. I am glad to hear that he continues to get on so well there. [11]

Rather irritably, William reproached Richard on one occasion for not putting enough stamps on a small package he had sent: 'You put just one stamp too little upon the book, for which I had to pay 2d. I believe there is no odd number of stamps ... after a penny. The postman ought to know. But never mind.' [12] (Clearly, he was still bearing the ancient adage in mind.)

The subject of health loomed large in several of the letters. 'We are all pretty well,' William wrote on 31 August 1861. 'David is expecting a letter from you.' A postscript on the first page added 'We were very glad that you are all well - Mother it seems is not so much troubled with her headaches as she used to be. It seems that the potatoes beans etc that I planted are doing her good.' [13] A little while later (the letter is undated, but perhaps written in October) David suffered some gastric problems. He was sick once or twice, and William took him to the doctor's surgery for what was evidently a second visit. He sent Richard a cautiously hopeful account of what transpired the moment they got home:

I believe David continues to improve a little - he eats a little better than he did but he still throws up a little of his food. I took him today to the doctor to see if he could give him something else to settle his stomach. He examined him again carefully - more carefully than he did the time before, and he told me after David had gone out that his constitution is rather delicate; that he will require great care to be taken of him while he is growing or else he will go into consumption, but that he cannot find that there is any disease in him yet. He did not give any medicine but said that the best way to bring his stomach right is with proper diet - recommended us to get cod liver oil to give him. We procured a bottle this afternoon & he has taken the first dose. His aunt is uneasy to see him mend rather slowly, but it is the nature of a stomach disorder to mend rather slowly at first - I trust that in another week he will get on much more rapidly. The weather has been very unfavourable till now - today it's beautiful.

David would like for W. Williams to bring cloths for a Monkey jacket & a waistcoat; also a cap. I suppose WW knows the size of his head - the cap C. Williams gave him fits very well. We think it would be best to have his clothes made up here. His clothes are gone rather shabby & he would like to have the new clothes before he makes his appearance at Llanystumdwy. The stuff for trousers which he brought with him is not yet made up. [14]

More reports on David's health will follow, but this particular episode (of which we glimpse merely the tail-end) seems to have been the only one which gave cause for concern at this time. Betsy's own health will also be touched upon shortly and the state of William's own health seems to have been variable. He found Newchurch 'cold & rather damp' [15] but acknowledged that its air was quite pure. He ends his letters to Richard with a variety of farewells. 'Accept our united love' appears quite frequently and the unexpected 'Yours faithfully' is counter-balanced by 'Yours ever truly' and 'Yours affectionately'. Rebecca wrote less frequently than Richard and would be jovially reminded, from time to time, that her daughter was very keen to hear from her. 'Betsy hopes to have a letter from mother soon,' he writes on one occasion. 'She thinks there must be a good stock of local gossip on hand by this time.' [16]   But Rebecca, a strict Baptist, evidently felt that spreading tittle-tattle on the Sabbath was contrary to the precept of keeping it Holy and chose her moments for doing so carefully. 'Betsy is quite surprised', William comments, semi-reproachfully, 'that mother should so strictly adhere the "law of Moses". She has been expecting a letter from her for some days.' [17]

It must be assumed that William's contract with the managers of the new school (the location of which has not yet been identified) was only for twelve months. He was once again the headmaster and his second-in-command was a young man called James Mellor. David, together with two or three other lads, was a pupil-teacher.   William was not over-enamoured with his new post and anxious to find something better.   Even so, and bearing in mind that there was now David's position as well as his own to be borne in mind, he needed to proceed with great caution. Richard, towards the end of August, reported with some excitement that a friend called John Davies had advised him that there was likely to be a vacancy at a school called Cafa Mawr in the near future. Richard thought this sounded an ideal position from William's viewpoint and urged him to express an interest by writing to John Prichard of Llangollen, one of the most pre-eminent Baptist ministers of the day, who was involved in the school's management.   He must have been rather disappointed to receive a reply dated 31 August which took the view that they must act far more circumspectly:

If I am to think of Cafa Mawr at all it is desirable that I should know something about it soon. Mr Davis the inspector who recommended me to this school wrote to me about three weeks ago to say that he would be coming this way soon & that we could then have a talk about removing to another school. And then if he tells

213

me of a comfortable place a hundred miles further I shall not have a sufficient reason for refusing it unless I have some other place in view.

I don't like to write to Prichard Llangollen until I know a little more about the place, because he would take offence if he had recommended me & I did not accept it after all. My writing to him would in reality be making an application through him for the place. Couldn't you say to J. Davies that you & we wish very much to be living nearer each other & having heard of the Cafa School you would like to know when it will be ready, & you might perhaps say that I have a certificates testimonial from the inspector etc & that I am known to J. Prichard Llangollen who visited my school at Pwllheli.

I say this only in the way of suggestion: no doubt you can lay the matter before your friend in a better way than I can tell you. All I wish is that it should not appear that I am moving in the matter at present. [18]

It was, of course, the old story of a bird in the hand being worth two in the bush and William was not really prepared to burn his boats at Newchurch (to mix metaphors with a vengeance) until he was quite sure that he had a safe berth to go to. (And his adroit manoeuvring behind the scenes, as epitomised by that final sentence, would prove to be an inheritable trait.) Clearly, nothing at all came of the notion of moving to Cafa Mawr but it is a great pity that he hesitated to renew his slight acquaintance with Prichard, who was a very influential figure (and author of several basic books which would surely have featured in William's library). This might have led, just conceivably, to his inclusion on the modest teaching staff of the North Wales Baptist College established at

Llangollen in August 1862 (known initially as 'St Bartholomew's College'), over which Prichard would preside as Principal for three years: it could well have been an ideal appointment.

With no better prospects presenting themselves, as the next couple of months went by, we find William reverting to a much earlier state of indecision, wondering whether it would not be a wiser idea to abandon school-mastering altogether and devote the rest of his life to farming in his native Pembrokeshire. This may have been the result of a visit which his step-father evidently made to Newchurch on 18 November [19] - a highly unusual event - bearing the news, perhaps, that two farms close to Trecoed had come on to the market, or were in need of new tenants, and that one of them might suit William's needs. (Benjamin still felt uneasy, it seems, at retaining the old family home and was perhaps seeking to ease his conscience.) Whatever the source of the information, William approached somebody else living in the area (name unknown) and asked for an independent assessment. The response he received, as the following letter of thanks to his unknown correspondent makes clear, was not remotely encouraging:

> Excuse me for not writing sooner to thank you for your kind letter, I took your advice to have nothing to do with either of those farms. I hope however that a better chance will occur before long, & if in the 'old neighbourhood' all the better. I do not think I shall be able to hold out much longer at schoolkeeping. The bad air of a schoolroom, the wear & tear of teaching, & the somewhat harassing nature of the work require a stronger constitution than mine to withstand them. I have always been rather delicate, as you are aware, but I have lately had some warnings which *cannot* be long neglected with safety.... We have very bad times here

at present, & it is likely to be still worse. Of course the chief cause, as you are aware, is this unfortunate American quarrel, I can hardly call it a war, for there has been but little fighting, but only a great deal of noise and bluster. [20]

He was referring to the onset of the American civil war, which was having a serious effect on the Lancashire cotton trade. The parents of his pupils, and the individual 'directors' of his school, would have been feeling the pinch. He wrote, moreover, as a parent in his own right, for on 8 November (ten days before Benjamin's visit) Betsy had given birth to a daughter who was proving to be as bonny a child as they could have wished. They named her Mary Ellen - 'Mary' in memory of both William's mother and sister and 'Ellen' after Betsy's sister (i.e., David's mother). Rather surprisingly, perhaps, it was Betsy who made the journey to nearby Haslingden to register the birth on 23 November (a Saturday), and she was obliged - when it came to signing her name - to make a large cross, which the Registrar, John H. Law, confirmed was 'the mark of Elizabeth George'. One assumes that she was accompanied by Anne, who remained in Newchurch until early December, and that William himself was indisposed and unable to leave Crabtree Buildings. 'The weather is very cold here', he had told his Pembrokeshire correspondent, '& the ground has been covered with snow for some days. This neighbourhood is not unhealthy for those who are sound & strong but it is too cold & damp for those who are delicate.' He clearly included himself, as well as David, in the ranks of the latter.

On this occasion at any rate, only a fortnight after giving birth, Betsy's constitution was rather more robust than his own, but she too was seriously ill a year or so later. William told her, after she had recovered, 'I was walking about without knowing what to do.' He added that, if she had died, 'I was determined to leave the place at once - I couldn't think to stop on a day here.' [22] (In all probability, this was precisely what he had done after Selina died.)

The death of Lady Byron in May 1860 (eight years after her daughter) would have been noted with regret, while that of Prince Albert in December 1861, apparently from typhoid, would have given him glum pause for thought. He admired Victoria's Consort, who had been born at roughly the same time as himself, and the event was yet another reminder of time's winged chariot drawing steadily nearer.

David presumably returned to Llanystumdwy for Christmas, leaving William and Betsy (unless they visited Trecoed) to enjoy some time on their own, happily crooning over the new arrival. The next few months are a blank but spring brought some sunnier weather and a relatively sunnier mood for William when he updated Richard on 10 June 1862:

I am sorry we missed writing on Saturday as usual - I was unusually busy & consequently more than usually tired towards the end of last week, & as things are going on here pretty much as usual I postponed writing for a day or two; wanting the 'spirit' to move me.

I am glad to tell you we are all pretty well. David, I may say, is quite well, in good spirits, & as strong as ever. I daresay that the approach of the holidays, & of the visit to Llanystumdwy, have something to do with his good spirits. The time for his departure is not yet fixed, but probably it will be near the end of next week.... As he is now quite well, I do not like to test him so much as before the holidays: the other teachers might think that I am favouring him because he is connected with me. Besides we think that a month's more of idleness will be quite enough for his

217

good. It is time for him to gird on his armour to begin the 'battle of life' in down-right earnest...

David wants to go through Liverpool to go on by the steamers to Carnarvon — what do mother & you say to that? [23]

Their ward was, clearly, becoming quite ambitious in his plans, and developing some independence!

In November 1861, as noted above, Elizabeth had been unable to sign her name. It comes as a slight surprise, therefore, to find William reporting to Richard, eleven months later, that Betsy 'will write to her mother as soon as ever she can' - which suggests that, during these months, he had at last taken in hand the problem of her illiteracy and had taught her to read and write. One assumes that he had previously been reading Rebecca's letters to her aloud, and sending messages to Llanystumdwy on her behalf, but it may be that the desire to do these things for herself had acted as the necessary incentive for Betsy.

Making some quiet enquiries in the profession as to what positions might become vacant at the end of the summer term, William found that there were three or four which might fit the bill. But Providence, in the form (it must be assumed) of J.D. Morell, once again intervened. Knowing that William was unhappy at Newchurch, he asked him whether he would be interested in taking over, but purely on a temporary basis, the headship of Mayfield School in Manchester. The headmaster of that school, Mr A.J. Pope, was seriously ill and likely to be out of action for a good many months. A capable replacement was needed as a matter of urgency. Would William like to volunteer his services?

As in the case of Pwllheli, it was almost impossible to turn down such a request - and, of course, it was encouraging to know that he was held in such very high regard by officialdom. The upshot was, therefore, that on 20 September or thereabouts the George family moved to Manchester, taking up residence in 'a neat little house' [24] at 5 New York Place in an area then known as Chorlton-upon-Medlock (formerly known as Chorlton Row). It was the end house in a very short cul-de-sac leading off from the northern section of Robert Street (formerly known as Marsden Street) and in the north-eastern part of an estate of closely-packed terraced houses half-a-century old (formerly known as an open space). It was a bleak, rather dingy area, but things could have been much worse. [25] To the north, almost at the heart of the city and only half a mile away, was London Road station. There was, moreover, a remaining spot of open space at Ardwick Green, a short distance to the east, bordering the southern bank of the Medlock. 'It is not quite so good a house as we should choose if we expected to settle here,' William told Richard on 5 October, 'but the better class of houses are let by the quarter & then we should have to give notice on the day we took it, for we have no dependence upon staying here longer. This is a *weekly* house, so that we have only a week's notice to give.'

> You may be sure [he continued] that we were both very glad to leave Newchurch. The place itself we could do with very well - though cold & rather damp, it is healthy - the air is much purer there than at Manchester, & neither of us could hold out long without pure air. It was the Newchurch *school* & the people connected with it that did not suit me; & I need not say that I did not suit them. Nearly all the 'Directors' are rough working men who had not the means to act liberally even if disposed to do so - and besides, my temper is such that I would rather be the master of workpeople than their servant. I did not lose much in the way of bad debts - about £2, but I lost several pounds more owing to the

bad times. I daresay that made a difference of about £15.[26]

It seems improbable, in view of these sentiments, that he would ever have considered going back to Newchurch, but in theory he had only been seconded to Mayfield School and he retained a watching brief over the progress of his old school - where James Mellor now became the acting headmaster. One drawback was that it had been necessary to leave David behind in Newchurch for the time being. He could not remain by himself in Crabtree Buildings, but Mellor proposed that he should come and be a fellow-boarder with himself at the home of Mrs Ella Robinson at 146 Edgeside Holme. Mrs Robinson was a widow, with two daughters who were almost grown up. Richard thought that Mellor was being extremely thoughtful in helping out in this fashion, but William discerned an element of self-interest:

> I have no doubt that Mellor is kind to David because it is [in] his interest to be so, he knows that David is the best teacher he has & he would get on badly without him. Like yourself, I was very much pleased to see David is highly spoken of in the Inspector's report. I should very much like to have him here with us, but as he is an *apprentice* it would not do to take him away before having another school in view, to which he could be transferred at once.[27]

The inspection referred to had evidently been carried out during the final phase of William's headmastership, and he was pleased to learn that another pupil-teacher to whom he had given special tuition without holding out high prospects of success had managed to pass his test, 'with a warning that he must do much better next year.' David had done extremely well and now moved up from the first to the third year. William made him a present of the arrears that were due to himself, but feared that he would not get them unless trade revived. He reassured Richard about sixteen-year-old David's ability to cope on his own:

> You need not be uneasy on David's account; I do not think he will take any harm for a short time where he is. The worst part of this affair is the *hîraeth* [sudden loneliness], & that certainly is bad enough for a time, as I know from bitter experience. I went to London when I was younger than David, & I well remember how wretched I felt for the first few weeks - I got better then. All who go out to the world to fight their own way must go through this hardening process, & the sooner the better. The griefs of early life are often very bitter but they are almost always of very short duration in comparison with those of after years.

He mentioned that David would be coming to stay with them for most of the following weekend. 'If I saw any probability', he added, 'that this [absent] master would not be able to return for a long time or not at all I should like to have David here,' but with so much uncertainty about his own position it was difficult to make any plans for the future. [28]

Mellor married towards the end of 1862 and left the boarding-house, which rather worried Richard and Rebecca, but (writing on 12 January 1863) William reassured them that this might well be a blessing in disguise:

> I do not think that Mellor's marriage will be any loss to David, but on the contrary that it will be a gain. He will be rather less in Mellor's company no doubt but he will still have quite enough of it. I am glad for David's sake

that Mellor is married, for it seems that of late he was very fond of talk, to Mrs *Robinson's* daughters [Mary Ann and Eliza, aged 20 and 18 respectively], & even to David about the *young ladies* & about courting. He will have less of that sort of nonsense now. The Robinsons did not like Mellor at all. Mrs Robinson is really a nice sensible woman & I think very kind to David.

Reflecting in general on the subject of David, whom he and Betsy still saw quite often, he gave a cautiously encouraging report:

I think he has improved & continues to improve very much. If he keeps in good health I have no doubt he will get on well; he has very good natural ability & he has now a great desire to learn. He is greatly changed in that respect. Since he has been in England he has acquired a great taste for reading - especially for reading newspapers. I think it was the American war that first gave him an interest in newspapers, & now he reads all that comes his way in his way about them, leading articles & all. And he really understands a good deal about it, far more than many who are twice his years. The only cause I have to doubt David's success in life is his delicate health - for unfortunately we cannot conceal from ourselves that he is rather delicate. I advised him strongly the other day to take great care of his health now while he is growing - to rise early & take much outdoor exercise. The next three or four years will be his most trying time. [29]

Early in February, soon after the arrival of a new addition to the family (who would be bearing a very similar name), he ended his letter with a delighted postscript: 'David is here - he came over last evening - he is looking very well, and in good spirits.' [30] Later that year, he raised with Goffey on the possibility of David being taken on at the Hope Street school. He sent another relatively hopeful report to Llanystumdwy on 25 August 1863, while making no attempt to minimise the problems that might be caused by David's underlying poor state of health:

> Mr Goffey wrote to me a few days ago to say that there had not been a Committee meeting since I heard from him before but that he had spoken to the Chairman as well as Huxley [?], was quite agreeable that David should come to Hope St. School *on trial* as soon as he left Newchurch. Their reason for wishing him to come on trial is that they are in doubt about his health & they wish to see how he holds out during the month or so that will elapse before the inspection of their school. If he keeps pretty well there is no doubt that they will take him. I understand that their Master is anxious for him to come. He has a second master, an Irishman, who it seems is of very little use to him. Mr Goffey says that he has no command over the boys, & no wonder, for a master found him the other day *dancing* in the school for the amusement of the scholars in school hours!
>
> I wrote to David that his appointment to the Liverpool school is not yet settled. I think it best not to tell him that he will have to go to it when he leaves Newchurch that he may be able to say truly that he does not know. If the Master & Committee at Newchurch [know] that he is leaving them to go as pupil teacher to another school, they might throw difficulties in the way of his leaving & cause him much annoyance. And if he were to pass a very unhappy month there it might have

an injurious effect upon his health.... I think he ought
to go to Liverpool at once from Newchurch; if he settles
there he will have a worthy holiday at Christmas. [31]

At which point, as David Lloyd Jones virtually disappears from
this story, it is necessary to record, sadly, that the forebodings
about his poor state of health would prove to be justified. It is
highly probable, however, that he did indeed conclude his
pupil-teacher stint at the Hope Street school and, moreover (for
reasons which will become apparent shortly), that he followed
still further in William's footsteps by becoming a fully-fledged
teacher at the Troed-yr-Allt establishment.

William must have been excited to be working in Manchester,
now the second largest city in England and, suddenly, the true
heart of the British Empire. It was a town which had virtually
grown up with himself. From relatively humble beginnings,
'the greatest meer village in England' as Defoe had described
it, estimating that 'above fifty thousand people' lived there, it
was now the dominating metropolis of Lancashire and its
population had soared to more than half a million. [32] Its
existing rivers had been supplemented by canals, providing its
industrialists with easy contact with the rest of the country and
the all-important access to ports. 'Not only did the town's
major waterways reduce freight costs of coal, raw cotton,
foodstuffs, and manufactures,' it has recently been remarked,
'but they also determined the majority of the industrial sites
that allowed Manchester to become the world's leading factory
location in 1850.' [33] The scene of the Peterloo Massacre in
1819, the base camp not only of the textile industry and mid-
Victorian capitalism but also of Cobden and Bright and the
Anti-Corn Law League, the city which had witnessed the birth
of the Free Trade movement and spawned a renowned School

of Economists - providing, indeed, the impetus for the newly-created Liberal Party - existed as a state within a state and a virtual power-house of ideas. 'What Manchester thinks today, England will think tomorrow' is a statement attributed to Sir Robert Peel, and variations of this confident assertion would be echoed down the ages by its leading citizens. But, surprisingly, it had not received city status until 1853 - and, until transformed into a borough fifteen years before that, had consisted of five separate townships, namely Manchester, Hulme, Ardwick, Cheetham and Chorlton-upon-Medlock (a name which would eventually be shortened to Chorlton-on-Medlock).

Hippolyte Taine, visiting the city in 1859, described it in terms very similar to those which Hawthorne had used of Liverpool seven years earlier. 'What dreary streets!' he exclaimed. The poor, he found, were wretchedly poor while the rich flourished on a scale scarcely imaginable: 'they are the generals and rulers of human toil. Quarter of a million sterling, half a million sterling, such are the figures they deal in. . . . The warehouses of finished cotton goods and other fabrics are Babylonian monuments. One of them is two hundred yards long and the bales of cloth are handled by steam-driven machinery. A cotton mill may contain as many as three hundred thousand spindles.' 'But are work and power all that is required to make a man happy?' [34] Another resident of the city from time to time, also taking note of the abject poverty existing cheek by jowl with obscene prosperity (while, at the same time, reluctantly looking after his father's business interests), was Friedrich Engels - an observer approximately the same age as William himself.

But there were Quaker employers flourishing in Manchester, though perhaps fewer in number than those in Bristol and York, who took a paternal interest in heir employees' welfare. In the Mayfield district of Ardwick, just to the east of Chorlton-upon-Medlock, Thomas Hoyle (1739 - 1821) had established in 1782 the Mayfield Printing Works. His son, bearing the same name, assumed control of it after his father's death. He was generally known as 'Tommy' and, like his father, was a leading member of the Society of Friends and a well-known figure in the town. The firm produced an immensely popular range of patterns on calico known as Hoyle's Prints. It was, so William told his brother-in-law, 'the most celebrated works of the kind in the Kingdom.... Every draper tries to persuade his customer that their gown will wash well because it is one of Hoyle's Prints.' [35]

The second Thomas Hoyle died in 1834, at the age of sixty-nine. He had retired from the firm in 1828 or thereabouts and despite it bearing, by this time, the name of Thomas Hoyle *and Sons*, he had entrusted the management of the printing works to his three sons–in-law. Foremost among this trio was William Neild, who had married Mary Hoyle in 1816 and had been general manager since 1830. He would be in sole charge from the mid-1850s onwards. Like his father-in-law, he had been a member of the Society of Friends - but he resigned from the Society two years after that gentleman's death and developed an interest in local government, serving as mayor in 1841-2, and in the development of the city's police force. The firm continued to flourish. 'The prints of Thomas Hoyle and Sons achieved brand name status in mid-nineteenth century Britain,' writes Dr Phillip A. Sykas, 'and the firm's works at Mayfield ... was a "must" on the route of Victorian visitors to Manchester. They came to experience the spectacle of a mile of calico being printed in an hour- a symbol of industrial achievement through technology. Hoyle's purples became the standard day wear of middle-class Victorian women, and are preserved today in numerous antique patchwork quilts.' [36]

In 1825 the second Thomas Hoyle had apparently established, alongside the print works, an infants' school for the children of his employees. But subsequent developments are hazy and there seems to have been a situation, following William Neild's secession from the Society of Friends, when a *second* such school was established close to the gates of the print works. By the late 1840s similar schools had been established by firms elsewhere in the area but the two Mayfield schools continued to enjoy a high reputation. It is conceivable that, for all practical purposes, they fused into one - or became, at any rate, very closely linked. William Neild would state in 1853 that he and his partners 'had built two schools, which they supported', but with the passage of time the outside world seems to have regarded them (perhaps erroneously) as one single establishment. A Government report of 1847 certainly speaks in these terms, declaring that Manchester's Mayfield School was 'a school attached to Messrs. Hoyle's print works, and supported wholly by that firm. The boys and girls are taught together in a handsome school-room, well fitted up, and furnished besides with a good organ, which is used in teaching singing. The master and mistress have evidently bestowed much pains both upon the discipline and instruction of the children, and take a very proper pride in the clean, orderly, and neat appearance of the whole school.' [37]

One wonders, however, whether - by 1862 - it was invariably the case that the two sexes were taught as one large class, or it may be that they occupied the large school hall simultaneously while being sub-divided (with their backs to one another!) to receive separate tuition from their respective teachers. (It will be recalled that at Pwllheli the two sexes were taught separately.) It was the boys' half of the establishment of which William was now taking charge until such time as Mr Pope felt well enough to resume his duties. He told Richard, on 5 October 1862, that 'we' - by which he meant both himself and the mistress, whom he had mentioned earlier in the letter - were in charge of about 170 pupils with four pupil-teachers assisting. [38] This conjures up a notional image of 85 boys and 85 girls, with two pupil-teachers assigned to each group. Writing to Anne James a month later, however, William stated that he had 'almost 200 boys under my care'. [39] It may be that he had absent-mindedly written 'boys' instead of 'pupils', and totally blanked out the role of the mistress, in a conscious attempt to impress his niece - and he was presumably, it might be conceded, the senior partner in the management of the school - but this seems a little far-fetched. It is more probable that his realm of responsibility had in some way been extended.

William Neild was still the head of the firm but he was, by this time, quite elderly (he had been born in 1789). 'It his son, Mr Arthur Neild,' William explained to Richard, 'who is my Committee. I have heard them spoken of as very kind gentlemen, & liberal to those who please them, but if anyone displeases them once he may adopt the motto over the gates of Dante's hell, "Let all who enter here abandon hope." I hope for their own sakes that they are not quite so unforgiving as they are said to be. I believe they are very kind to the master of this school - I am afraid the poor fellow will need their kindness for some time.' [40]

Surprisingly, and most uncharacteristically, William seems to have been very timid during his stay at Mayfield School and perhaps somewhat in awe of his employer. His recent illness seems to have robbed him of his self-confidence. Arthur Neild, a year or two younger than himself, was much better educated and continued to take, indeed, a keen interest in the subject of education. It is recorded that he read widely in the fields of mathematics, classics and theology and was a very close friend of J.G. Greenwood, the first principal of Owens College, Manchester. He had been made a trustee of that college in 1858 and would clearly go on to still higher things thereafter. Having escaped from the management of 'rough working men' at Newchurch, whom he scorned and looked down upon, William now found himself confronted by someone who seems to have been (to his eyes, at any rate) a lofty martinet. He was very reluctant to speak up for himself and apparently developed something of an inferiority complex. 'I don't know anything more with respect to my position here,' he lamented to Richard on 5 October, 'I do not even know what they are going to pay me, though I have seen Mr Neild several times.' [41] One would have thought that this was something that would have been clear from the outset, when Morell first approached him, but the notion of actually *asking* Mr Neild what the position was evidently filled him with dread. He was discouraged, moreover, from making enquiries about the possibility of permanent posts at those three or four other schools which had been on his tentative short-list. As he did not know any of the masters at those schools, 'a letter to them would not answer so well as a personal interview. I have had my hands quite full [here] ... & besides, as these gentlemen [i.e., the two Mr Neilds] are so very exact I would not give anyone the chance to say that I was out on my own looking during school hours. I hope however to have an opportunity in the course of this week.' [42] But we hear nothing more about those other schools. Again, since he was only supposed to be at the school for a short time, one would have expected the Neilds to be understanding and sympathetic about his need to consider his future plans and make arrangements accordingly.

On the other hand, he rather liked Mayfield School and would not have been averse to staying there for a long period. 'This is a good school', he acknowledged, '& one where they are likely to offer a respectable man a good career for a master. I might remain here myself until next spring or early in the summer.' [43] He wished, as we have seen, that it could have been possible for David to join him

Good for morale, it seems, was 'the capital pair of boots' which Richard sent him a week or two later. 'They are first rate,' he declared, when he remembered to acknowledge their receipt, '& fit me very well. They are just the thing I wanted, an easy pair & not too heavy to wear in school all day. When I was at Newchurch I wore nothing but pegged boots & as I was obliged to have them strong for that wet cold place, they made my feet quite sore. I expect great comfort in wearing these shoes. I thank you very much for making me such a good pair & shall pay for them when I have an opportunity which I hope will be ere long.' [44]

Future plans depended, of course, on whether or not Mr Pope was going to shake off his illness. 'It appears', William explained to Richard in October 1862, with a certain degree of hopefulness,

> the poor man continues in a very weak state: for the last week or so he has had diarrhoea which of course will make him much weaker. Such extreme loosening is generally a bad symptom for a person in his state, but in his case it may be owing only to a change of air. He removed a few miles into the country the week before last. The mistress tells me that he is very fidgety & says he will come back into the school in a fortnight. That state of mind is not favourable to his recovery. [45]

Three months later, as a letter dated 12 January 1863 makes clear, the situation was very much in a state of flux:

> The master of this school is better - he came in twice last week, & was in the school for about 1½ hr. today. He seems in good spirits, & says he is all right, but I think he is very far from 'all right' and shall be greatly surprised if ever he gets strong and well again. Should

the weather be mild & dry he will probably come back soon to take charge of the school, that is if the managers will let him. I suspect however that they do not take so favourable a view of his case as he does himself. There is very little doubt that he is consumptive, but he is cheerful and almost free from pain as consumptive people often are, & also so blind to their own danger. Merciful blindness! When they are dying by inches, for months, perhaps years. I expect he will soon recover sufficiently to return to his duties *for a short* time, and then 'Cometh the end.' Poor fellow! I am very sorry for him. I may go before him, but it seems to me that his lease of life is almost certain to expire. [46]

William was virtually willing the wretched man to pull down the shutters, take to his bed and utter a groan or two before expiring, but on 6 February he was finally obliged to confess that the end of his Manchester sojourn was almost in sight:

I don't know exactly when we shall be leaving here or where we shall be going to next. The Master of the school is much better & thinks himself *almost* well enough to take charge of the school. He is however rather afraid of the month of March & he would I dare say like me to stay till it is nearly over. The weather has been so mild all this winter that he has not been seriously tested yet. As soon as I know for certain what our next move will be I shall let you know. If I take a school it will be only as temporary convenience - I shall give up teaching and get into the country as soon as I can. [47]

On the face of things, the cautious Albert James Pope had much in common with William and it could be argued that he was, indeed, almost a mirror-image of his temporary replacement. The census return for 1861 records that he too lived in Chorlton-upon-Medlock, that he too had been born in 1821 (or possibly 1820) and that he too had a small family to maintain - a wife aged 36, a daughter called Mary Anne aged 14 and two sons aged ten and seven - a third would arrive in 1862. By Victorian standards he was, like William, middle-aged. There is no mention of a bushy beard, for there is a limit to the amount of data that a census return can accommodate, but one strongly suspects that this also was something that he needed to maintain. Because the Mr James Pope who took on the headmastership of Mayfield School in 1859 or 1860, or whenever it might have been, was not quite what he seemed.

He was, in fact, newly manufactured, and so was his family. If the clock could be turned back to 1851 it would be found that he was then no more than a pupil-teacher aged fifteen. He was plain Albert Pope, the promising eldest son of a shoemaker called James Pope based in a village in Hampshire. He had two brothers and three sisters, the youngest of whom, Mary Anne, was aged four. Towards the end of 1858 he married a Manchester girl and settled down in that city, where Mary Anne joined them. He fathered two sons, the first born in 1859 and the second in 1861. He had signed his marriage certificate as Albert James Pope and these *may* have been the Christian names he used when applying for the post of headmaster at Mayfield School. But it could equally well have been nothing more than mere James, for this is how he features in that census return. It stated that his name was James - no more, no less - and left blank the column denoting his profession. He added fifteen years to his age and declared that Mary Anne was his daughter. By what manner of means he managed to convince the Neilds that he was a middle-aged gentleman with much teaching experience behind him must remain a matter for speculation, but the ruse was successful.

After the sudden death of the Prince Consort, he may have revealed to his pupils that his own first name happened to be Albert, for one of those pupils would remember him, sixty years later, as Mr A.J. Pope. The Neilds, in any case, would by this time not have been bothered by an initial veil drawn over that first name, for they were extremely pleased with his work and reluctant to contemplate the possibility of anyone else permanently replacing him. But by the time of the next census, in 1871, he would have left the school (for reasons unknown) and re-established himself as Albert James Pope aged 35, a draper based in Ormskirk, with a wife aged 37 (only a year older than in 1861) and three sons aged (correctly) eleven, ten and nine. Mary Anne, aged 24, became his sister once again and that putative beard may have been shaved off. His 'lease of life' proved much longer than his disgruntled temporary successor had expected: he would survive William by more than eleven years, though dying at the earlier age of forty, and the status of Gentleman would be solemnly conferred upon him so far as Probate records were concerned.

But William, of course, knew nothing of Mr Pope's curious past when he arrived in Manchester, nor would it ever occur to him to speculate on the subject. Betsy had meanwhile had her work cut out getting the little house in New York Place straight for both of them - or, rather, for all three of them, since Mary Ellen (sometimes referred to as 'Polly') was now a very distinct member of the household. Writing to his niece on 3 November 1862, William reported that Betsy 'has now much more than she can do every day. Her little girl is rather poorly & peevish with her teeth; & you know your Aunt won't let her cry a moment if she can prevent it. Between nursing & her other work, she is half killing herself.' [48] A fortnight later he told Richard that the weather was 'very cold & thick' and that, precisely because of this, 'Betsy & the little girl' were very fit. 'We had a long ramble & the young lady *a drive in her carriage* through the town on Saturday afternoon.' [49]

On 12 January 1863 William reported that Betsy was in fairly good health. 'The weather', he added, 'has been pretty fine here for the time of year. Little Mary still keeps the best of the family - it is wonderful she is so well considering that the teething is not yet nearly over. It is true her mother is very careful of her, that no doubt has much to do with her good health. I do not think she is naturally strong - how could she be? Can strength come out of weakness?' And in parenthesis, a little while later: 'Excuse these [three] blots. I did not see them till after I had begun to write. The paper had been with Baby & she put her coat of arms upon it.' [50]

'Can strength come out of weakness?'

It was a curious question to pose at that particular moment in time. Posterity, indeed, would have answered it with a resounding Yes! But William clearly had doubts on the matter and did not intend to provoke Providence. For the one thing he had not mentioned in his very long letter to his brother-in-law was the fact that Betsy was pregnant again and that the new baby was due in the very near future. It arrived, in fact, five days later, on Saturday, 17 January. It was a boy and they bestowed upon him the Christian names of his short-lived predecessor - David Lloyd. (David Lloyd Jones, when he visited them the following month, would have assumed that the names were chosen in honour of himself, and not for the worlds would they have disabused him of this belief.) To his niece (on the eve of her marriage), before the day was out, he excitedly announced that David was 'a sturdy healthy little fellow, stronger and much more lively than his sister, and he has fine curly hair.' [51]

Now it was safe to mention the subject of new arrivals in letters to Llanystumdwy! 'My dear Richard,' he wrote exultantly on 24 January, following up a preliminary announcement,

> I am happy very happy to say that Betsy and the young gentleman continue to get on very well. Betsy got up at about 5 this afternoon and she is still up, for which I am scolding her. I tell her she is overdoing it the first time.
>
> Little Mary is not thrown on one side although a son and *heir* (!!) has arrived. The dear little thing is getting more interesting every day. She is certainly a very sharp child, thank God for that. Although only just turned 14 months she seems to understand almost everything we say to her. She has taken wonderfully to little David. She calls him *boy, boy* and she gives us much amusement by mocking him when we ask her how does boy cry.
>
> The woman who is here to wait upon Betsy is very kind to Polly - almost the only thing that is in her favour. She is not a good hand at preparing a bite to eat - she used to work in a factory.

He wound up (on the assumption, evidently, that this was an issue that would still have been of vital importance to his readers) with the news that he himself felt better. 'My throat has not gathered as I feared. I have been poulticing it till it is nearly raw outside, but that is better than being inside.' [52]

A report written on 6 February was also reassuring:

> We are all pretty well. Betsy was rather weak the first fortnight [i.e., up until 31 January] but I think she is gaining strength fast strength now. She drinks bitter ale and finds it does her good. We cannot get milk and she was tired of drinking tea all the time, especially after some extraordinary tea the nurse gave her. She thinks it

must have been some cold tea boiled in a saucepan.
That dose was a *sickener*. [53]

'The maternity nurse who attended Mrs George on that
occasion', wrote J. Hugh Edwards, rather gushingly, in 1930,
'was an Irishwoman who seems to have been intensely imbued
with the traditional faith of her race in signs and omens.
Recalling the popular belief in her native land that "a child
with waves in his hair is sure of a living in two countries", she
was never tired of assuring the schoolmaster's wife, as with
true Hibernian fervour, she would lift the curly-headed babe in
her arms, that he was sure to make his mark in the world. So
confident a prediction made a deep impression upon the young
mother, for she appears to have treasured it in her heart. In
later years she frequently recalled it at every upward step in the
romantic career of her gifted son.' [54] William, one suspects,
would have fervently hoped that the new arrival would at least
be able to master the art of brewing a pot of tea successfully.

12 - BULFORD

Apologising for his delay in acknowledging receipt of that 'capital pair of shoes' in November 1862, William had explained that he frequently wrote his letters 'as soon as I come from school in the afternoon, the worst time of the day to do anything, as you can readily see. This fact will account for frequent omissions of importance & you must therefore please excuse them.' [1] A fortnight earlier, writing to his favourite niece, he had prefaced his remarks with what was almost a rebuke:

> Your letter with the interesting enclosure did not come to hand till this morning. I was not at the school on Saturday or yesterday, or else I might have had it sooner. Perhaps you had better direct your letters to the above address [i.e., No. 5 New York Place]. I wish we had the 'paper of Reason, etc' yesterday that we might read it more leisurely, than we can do today.
>
> You know that Monday is always an *extra* busy day with me; & as for your Aunt she has now much more than she can do every day.... And you may be sure that I am not very idle with almost 200 boys under my care. So you must bear in mind that all our letters must be *very hastily* written, & I hope you will make due allowance for their imperfections. [2]

His family correspondents, in short, were expected to thoroughly acquaint themselves with his routines and responsibilities and to bear them in mind when approaching him - but any shortcomings on his own part were to be automatically overlooked. It was a rather autocratic attitude (especially for someone who hesitated to speak out fully and frankly when, nursing a grievance, he encountered his immediate employer) and there is no way of knowing whether this was a recent development or whether William had always behaved in this manner. He felt overworked, certainly, and perhaps with good reason, but he evidently felt an ongoing need to assert himself within the family circle and to remind his relatives that, when all was said and done, he was really quite an important person. (And not somebody, as Richard was sharply reminded, who could be expected to pay tuppence on overdue postage - a rebuke sent at '8 o'clock Saturday evening', exactly a week after the birth of his son and heir and at a time when he might be expected to be overflowing with good spirits and geniality - as, indeed, he was in the rest of the letter.)[3]

At the end of 1862 and the beginning of 1863 he was, admittedly, preoccupied with family matters beyond the little circle at New York Place. One of them was agreeable while the other was far from pleasing.

On the agreeable side, there was his niece Anne James, who celebrated her twenty-fourth birthday in December 1862. It will be recalled that her mother (Mary, initially known as Gwenllian) had died in 1858. Levi, her father, was a prosperous farmer who would live on until 1884 but with at least seven other children to care for it may be that relations between him and Anne were not particularly close. Whatever the reason, a special bond seems to have developed between Anne and William and they evidently wrote to each other quite often. For some five or six years, Anne had been unofficially engaged to a sea captain called William Williams, three years older than herself, involved in trade on the west coast of Chile. He too had corresponded with William from time to time but there was considerable difficulty so far as her parents were concerned because William had lost an eye at some point in his career and they were, seemingly, uneasy about his appearance. At such times as he returned on leave to Wales, therefore, the

Captain was denied hospitality at the home of Mary's parents and obliged to lodge with a Mr and Mrs Hoad at their boarding-house in Fishguard, where William visited him on at least one occasion.

Mary's departure from the scene, looked at dispassionately, was one obstacle removed and the fact that Capt. Williams attained the status of Master Mariner clearly strengthened his standing in the world. In the autumn of 1862, despite continuing opposition from Levi James (exemplified by a string of letters), the young couple became officially engaged and Anne wasted no time in imparting the glad tidings to her uncle and aunt. A follow-up letter was despatched at the end of October, enclosing an essay on the subject of matrimony which her fiancée had composed. In a reply dated 3 November, William signified their full-hearted approval of the union - and captured, in passing, some lively remarks made by his wife, so that we have a rare glimpse of a momentarily elated Betsy:

> Your Aunt bids me say that she is very much pleased with Capt. W's Essay on the Marriage Ring; she thought highly of him before because you praised him; but now she thinks still more highly of him. The paper shows that Capt. W's ideas of the nature of the marriage union are far nobler than commonly entertained; that he possesses a mind & heart worthy of you. When I remarked that some of the comparisons are very pretty & that I wondered at the ingenuity & patience it exhibited she answered that she was not at all surprised at the patience for love has patience enough to hold out if it had been as long as the 119th Psalm! I cannot write down a hundredth part of the comments made while we were reading it - some of them were rather fancy, at least they made *me* laugh & I

think they would make you laugh too if you were here. That was your Aunt's constant exclamation, O how I wish that Anne was here, now. The paper suggested some serious, & [various ?] thought too. In short, as I said before, we are very much pleased - it shows that the writer is a refined, thoughtful & affectionate man - & I should think these three qualities will go very far towards making a good husband - one whom you can love & be proud of....

We were pleased to have the personal sketch in your last. Your Aunt *was* very curious to have some idea of his personal appearance. As for that one eye that is but a slight defect - especially as Capt. W. can make such a good use of the remaining one. That he can still see very clearly, your Aunt needs no better proof than his choosing you in preference to any of the eager beauties which surrounded him (you might almost take the words in their military meaning) at Fishguard....

Your Aunt is impatient to hear when the important day is to be, all about the wedding dress, etc etc. It would give me very great pleasure to be present on the happy occasion, but it will depend upon the time whether I can or not. I think I can say now that I shall not be able to come so far from home during the month of January and perhaps February, - before or after those months, if alive and well, nothing should prevent my coming.

There were a couple of passages which provide glimpses of both the humorous and the sanctimonious sides, respectively, of William's character.

In his earlier letter he had recalled the occasion of his encounter with Mrs Hoad, her fiancée's larger-than-life landlady. A gleeful Anne had asked for more information, but he was unable to satisfy her curiosity: 'I am sorry I cannot comply with your request to tell you much of what Mrs Hoad said to me. She rattled along so, & it is so long since, that I have nearly forgotten all. Her talk had much the same effect upon me as looking out of the carriage window of an *express train* - the objects succeed each other so rapidly that it is very difficult to receive much more to retain a distinct impression of them.'

He then commented on Anne's remarks about the shortcomings of her grandmother on the James side of the family, who was evidently another lady with much to say. 'Nanny *is* queer certainly,' he agreed. 'She has been so long used to gossiping about every body that she can't live without it. I suppose she does not mean mischief, though mischief is often done between friends where there is no mendacious intent. Poor Mother often used to wonder what pleasure I had in reading "that old newspaper" but I really think that it would be a great change for the better if women, & men too, were to talk more about the contents of newspapers & less about the private affairs of their neighbours & "dear friends".' [4]

He was unable, for obvious reasons, to attend Anne's wedding to Captain Williams on 18 January 1863 but continued to exchange letters with her during the months which followed. Those letters (and their many predecessors) do not now appear to be in existence, but it is just conceivable that they may surface one of these days.

'You can't tell us too much about yourself', he had concluded, 'but if you can bestow a word or two upon Trecoed etc etc all the better.' For the subject of the old family farm, and the question of what was to become of it, was very much on his mind. It will be recalled that in July 1861 he had attended the re-marriage of his step-father, Benjamin Williams, and that the wedding breakfast had been rendered memorable by the fact of the bride having accused him of stealing her chop while she was out of the room. Their relationship had not got off to a good start, therefore, and William would soon be nursing a grievance of his own so far as the lady was concerned. As recorded earlier, Benjamin had visited him at Newchurch on 18 November1861 and it has already been surmised that he drew William's attention on that occasion to two farms in Pembrokeshire which had come on to the market. But it is also very likely that this information was the sugar used to coat an unpalatable pill. For Benjamin, like William, was also thinking in terms of fathering a son and heir. His bride, Amy John, had been forty-two at the time of their wedding but was providing her husband (now in his mid-60s) with the fullest possible satisfaction and her ardour showed no sign of diminishing. She was evidently still capable of conceiving a child. Bearing in mind that the future management of Trecoed had always been a sensitive issue, Benjamin wanted William to be aware that there was the distinct possibility of a Benjamin Jnr making his appearance on the scene within the next year or two and that, obviously, the young man's future needs would have to be taken into account at such time as he drew up his next will.

William would not have been pleased at this news. A year went by, however, with no fresh developments and he may felt that it was a false alarm. But then, responding to the casual request he had made on 3 November for news about the folk at Trecoed, his niece plunged him into Monday-morning gloom with a vengeance. 'We had a letter today from Anne James', he wrote to Richard on 17 November, 'in which she tells us it's reported that the new Mary Williams Trecoed' - a sarcastic way of referring to Amy - 'is in the family way. If it proves true I don't know that it will make any difference to me, but it will be a great loss & disappointment for my young brother John.' [5] To see for himself, he went off to Trecoed for the usual Christmas festivities at the end of 1862 (leaving Betsy in Manchester) and came home in a very bad temper. The letter to Richard in which (one suspects) he relieved his feelings at considerable length has not been preserved, but the next one he sent (on 12 January) indicates that residual disgruntlement had not totally dispersed. 'I am glad to say', he reported, 'that we are both rather better than we were when I wrote last. I have had time to get over the bad effects of the journey - at least the travelling part of it - the annoyance I experienced while there still affects me occasionally. I try however not to fret about it, for I know *that* will not do me any good. Betsy is much better than she was on my return.'[6] (And he would have been gratified, as the year wore on, by finding that, in the event, the much-heralded birth had not materialised.)

With a view to taking his mind off the continuing ascendancy of the Williams clan at Trecoed, Richard had sent him a copy of the latest *Caernarvon Herald*. Thanking him, William remarked 'I suppose you meant to give me a chance of speculating in one of their small farms for sale. I have not however sufficient confidence in my judgment to *buy* - I would rather rent one.' And he reaffirmed, a month later, his definite desire to escape from both the classroom and the town: 'I shall give up teaching and get into the country as soon as I can.'[7]

We have already seen, from his letter to an unknown Pembrokeshire correspondent in November 1861, that he hoped to find somewhere in the 'old neighbourhood' and, to his great delight, he eventually discovered that the tenancy of an ideal farm had become available. It was located approximately midway between Merlin's Bridge (a large village immediately south-west of Haverfordwest) and Milford Haven, being roughly three miles from each of them. To be more precise, it was on the south side of a road running from Tiers Cross in the west to Johnston in the east and amounted to approximately 15 acres of meadow, pasture and arable land. Its name has been spelt in a variety of fashions - Bwlford, Bwllford, Bwlffordd and Bullford - but will be known, in these remaining pages, simply as Bulford. It was firmly in the southern half of the county, in 'Little England beyond Wales', so possessed the additional attraction of being a substantial distance away from Benjamin Williams and his new wife, the interlopers at Trecoed.

There is no precise indication of when the George family left Manchester for their new home but it is possible to make a reasonable guess. On 25 August 1863 he wrote as follows to Richard:

> You said something a week or two ago that you had often thought of coming to see us. My dear Brother I hope I need not say how delighted I should be to see [you] but I have given up asking you because I had no hope of succeeding. It would do you much good to go from home for two or three months, for I fear you are wearing yourself out. If I could say anything to induce you to come here, be sure I would soon say the word. Won't you give me a hint how to set about the formidable task of persuading you? [8]

This letter makes clear that he had written to Richard several times in the past, inviting him to come and stay, which obviously indicates that they had settled in at Bulford several months earlier than late August. The likelihood is, therefore, that they had left 5 New York Place early in April, in all probability immediately after Easter. The winter had been a mild one, and with the March winds having died down Mr Pope would have felt courageous enough to resume his place at the headmaster's desk at Mayfield.

One person who *did* pay them a visit was Anne Williams (the former Anne James). She stated in 1912 that she 'had the pleasure of seeing them settled in their new home at Bulford and of holding the infant David Lloyd George in my arms when he was three months old; his little sister Mary was then toddling about the room, being about fourteen or fifteen months old.' It was a claim which she repeated in a letter to her son-in-law ten years later, telling him that his father could not have been in Manchester very long 'because when I called at Bulford to wish them goodbye before going away to Chile in January 1863 - the little family, i.e., your parents and Mary and David - were *settled down* at the little farm very comfortably. Your brother was then a baby and I held him in my arms - Mary was very shy and kept running away from me.' [9]

There is something not quite right about this recollection. Anne had married William Williams on 18 January 1863, the day after David's birth. Mary was then fourteen months old. Anne could well have visited them late in January or early in February, but at that time they were still at Chorlton-upon-Medlock. If she called at Bulford in January 1864, on the other hand, David would have been a year old and Mary would have been more than two years old. But after half-a-century memory can play tricks, and it must be assumed that Anne visited 'the little farm' early in May 1863, when David and Mary would have been, respectively, four and eighteen months old: these ages equate, very roughly, with what she remembered.

Strictly speaking, although this may have been a purely local distinction, the farmlands now leased by William, surrounding a reasonably-sized house, were known as *Lower* Bulford and those on the north side of the road, farmed by a Mr John Phillips, were known as *Upper* Bulford. A plan dating from 1890 [10] shows that both areas consisted of half-a-dozen fields of varying shapes, a mill being located on the Upper

Bulford lands to which William may have had access, but those shapes could have altered over the years. Young David would remember that there was a green folding gate (i.e., one divisible into two separate parts) and trees on the short drive leading to their farm's front door. [11] To the east and to the north (beyond Upper Bulford) lay the Johnston Hall estate. Sunny Hill was to the west and Harmeston to the south, their locality being encompassed in the parish of Steynton (or Stainton). There was a congregational chapel at Tiers Cross, established in 1815, which William would attend quite regularly and he became friends with Evan Thomas, its Minister since 1847, who was almost the same age as himself. 'In the census of 1861,' so its website tells us, 'the total members of the Chapel amounted to 60, with 91 listeners [i.e., an attentive audience of potential converts] and a Sunday School of 100.' It is quite possible that William volunteered his services to help with the latter.

It was an isolated spot, but being located on a road carrying occasional traffic meant that they did receive the occasional visitor. 'We have heard', wrote William to Richard at the end of that letter of 25 August 1863 (the very last letter of his still in existence, it seems), 'that Lewis James was to preach in Haverfordwest yesterday; we hope he'll call before he goes back.'[12] We know that William had more than one horse - and he may also have had, primarily for the children's benefit, a donkey or pony as well - plus three or four cows. There were probably some chickens. He also had a carriage, as well as a cart in which to transport his crops to market. He invested in farming stock and husbandry implements, and he evidently employed at least one labourer (possibly two) - 'It is now they are sowing the turnips', Betsy noted in mid-June 1864, [13] and outstanding wages would have to be paid soon after that date. One of the labourers was forty-year-old William Edwards, living at a nearby cottage called Fernie

Castle, but that is really the full extent of our knowledge. Yet, despite the switch from an urban to a rural lifestyle, old habits would die hard. 'It is one of the family traditions', wrote J. Hugh Edwards in 1913 (acting on information supplied by Anne), 'that although William George relinquished the life of a schoolmaster, the student was in no way lost. His passion for reading continued with unabated force, and each day's tasks alternated between manual toil and mental studies. Within the domain of the little farm, books shared with agricultural implements the distinction of being necessary requisites, and however hard the day's toil, no day ended without seeing the schoolmaster-farmer deep in his books.' [14]

It must be surmised that the husband and wife settled down happily enough with their two young children and spent a contented family Christmas in close proximity to a roaring fire. They furnished the kitchen (which also served as a temporary living-room) and one bedroom, within which all four of them would have slept. But there was a crisis towards the end of January, for David succumbed to a viral infection known as croup. His throat swelled up and his cries became hoarse, and probably worse at night. It was a comparative commonplace ailment for children to suffer from at that time, in the days before vaccination became a routine precaution, but could sometimes prove fatal. A local physician, Dr James David Brown from Haverfordwest - William's contemporary, established in the town since 1844 or earlier, whom he would have known for many years - was called in and managed to restore the son to good health.

That, sadly, was more than he was able to do with the father.

In April the George family completed their first year of life at Bulford. The spring may have been raw but summer was on its way. Always susceptible to chills, however, William felt seriously unwell while working in the garden towards the end of May. He went to bed but the illness grew worse and he had great difficulty in breathing. Summoned to his bedside, Dr Brown told Betsy that the chill had turned to pneumonia. There was nothing he could do. William Edwards, abandoning his work in the fields, sat with him as a constant companion. William died five days later on Tuesday, 7 June. He was almost certainly unaware that he had, a little while earlier, fathered another child.

The event would have been a terrible shock for Betsy. But she rallied and managed, perhaps via Mr Edwards, to send a two-word telegram to her brother - '*Tyrd Richard*' ['Come Richard'] - which brought him hastening to Bulford as fast as the railway connections would permit. (It was, perhaps, the first occasion on which he had ever left his native county - and it would be virtually the last.) Once arrived he took charge of things and friends and neighbours rallied round with sympathy and advice. Edwards notified the Registrar of the death on the Thursday, the cause being described as inflammation of the lungs (not certified). William's age was said to be 42. Benjamin Williams came over on the Friday and, being a practical man of business, carried out a valuation of the premises. He told Betsy, in Richard's presence, that the small income in rent-money from her mother-in-law's cottage, previously forwarded to William (in theory, at any rate), would now be transferred to herself - and she would continue to receive it until such time as her children came of age. (Betsy hinted that it might be an even better arrangement if the money could be paid at the outset to her children rather than herself, but Benjamin appears to have become hard of hearing at this point.) [15] One assumes that John, her brother-in-law, also put in an appearance, as well as other members of the extended George family, but this is not certain.

Thomas Goffey, one of the first to be notified of William's death, offered to deal with all legal and financial matters on the family's behalf, an offer which was most gratefully accepted. William, it seems, had not had a favourable opinion of the Haverfordwest attorneys, so his widow recalled, and the making of a will - if he had ever considered it - was one of those tasks which, perhaps surprisingly, he had never tackled. She and Richard were only too glad for Mr Goffey to sort things out. But William had made, in the circumstances, extremely good provision for his family. The final balance sheet would show that his total estate amounted to almost a thousand pounds - £718 invested in the six building societies, £90 due to him as back-rent for the cottage (received from 'Mr L. James'), £64 for his crops and goodwill, £57 for his horses, carriages and farming implements, £34 for personal effects (as listed below) and cash in the house of £5, making a grand total of £968. From this there needed to be deducted expenses of £122, reducing the net value of his estate to £846 - £56 covering probate and administration costs, £34 in respect of rent and wages and, not least, £32 in respect of William's funeral.[16]

John Phillips, the lessee of Upper Bulford, took over the lease of William's fields with effect from 1 October and added them to his own. He was the purchaser, of course, of the crops and the goodwill, and had a small squad of young Phillipses to assist him in looking after his enhanced estate. (Betsy, who had an uncertain grasp of names, would always refer to him as 'Mr John' and this was the name by which her children, and their descendants, would remember him.)

There was a small green lawn in front of the house and it was here, on 15 August, that there took place the sale of what were officially defined as William's personal effects - namely furniture, plate, china, books, pictures, clothes, jewels and ornaments. 'The auctioneer at the sale', W.D. Phillips recalled in 1924, 'was the late Mr Henry Davies, of the Old Bridge Haverfordwest, and my fellow clerk, the late Mr J.M. Martin, managed and booked the sale. Having business in the neighbourhood, and passing from Tiers Cross to Johnston, I looked in ... I remember him [Mr Martin] remarking to me at the time, "Do you see that little chap swinging on the gate? He's a little terror. There was one lot being taken away just now, for which he evidently had a strong attachment, for he fiercely resisted it being taken away by the purchaser." As I passed out through the lawn gate, the boy referred to (Mr D. Lloyd George) was swinging on it with intense energy, and returned my look at him defiantly.' [17] David did indeed take strong exception to this raid on his family's possessions, and a little while later he persuaded his sister to join him in helping to pile stones against the gate. It was a last-ditch attempt to stop the intruders from making off with their ill-gotten gains. William would probably have been proud of them, but it was all to no avail.

It had been agreed that William should be buried in the churchyard at Jordanston, in close proximity to the graves of his parents. In all probability his departure from Bulford, under Benjamin's supervision, would have been on the Friday (10 June). Dr George has assumed that Betsy remained with the children at Bulford, for the churchyard was twenty miles away and it would have been a long and distressing journey for them all; Richard, certainly, would have attended on their behalf, and it is just possible that he was accompanied by Evan Thomas. William was buried either on that day or the one that followed. The tombstone recorded that William George (late of Trecoed) was aged 44 and there followed a heartfelt inscription -

Trwm fu'r tro wywo oi wedd - Gwr ydoedd
O gariadus - nodwedd.

Anwyl i'w deulu'n unwedd
Colled ei fyned i'w fedd.

William himself, perhaps in company with some of the readers of this present volume, might not have been able to interpret those words. Translated, they read: 'Heavy was that which wilted his face. He was a man of loving disposition beloved unanimously by his family. It is a great loss that he has gone to his grave.'

AFTERMATH

The sale of the personal possessions had taken place on Monday, 15 August 1864, and by the end of that week Richard Lloyd had brought Betsy and her two children back to Llanystumdwy. Betsy would have been aware, by now, that she was pregnant, and she gave birth to her third son on 23 February 1865. There was, of course, only one possible name that could be bestowed on him.

Somebody else who returned to Highgate, his childhood home, was David Lloyd Jones, but it is not known when he did so. It seems highly probable, as indicated earlier, that he had indeed completed his apprenticeship as a pupil-teacher at the Hope Street school in the autumn of 1863 and that he had thereafter (in 1864 or 1865, perhaps) moved on to become a fully-fledged teacher at the Troed-yr-Allt establishment at Pwllheli. But ill-health finally caught up with him and he was obliged to abandon his career. He was presumably company for the other David for a little while and celebrated his twentieth birthday on 30 January 1867, when his near-namesake would have been four years old, but he died seven months later on 2 September. He was described on his death certificate as a British School Teacher. (His cousin would have had a dim recollection of his presence at Highgate, although he never appears to have mentioned him.)

Benjamin Williams became a widower for a second time, but it is impossible to discover when this happened. He re-married on 8 February 1870, claiming to be sixty-eight rather than seventy-three. His latest bride, Maria Richards from Milford, was twenty-nine and she presented him with a daughter (Amy Anne) in March 1871. The proud father died in October 1875 and Trecoed at last passed into the care of John George, William's brother, who would die in 1907.

Rebecca Lloyd departed on 19 June 1868 and her son now assumed control of the Highgate household, acting as a father-figure in helping Betsy to bring up her three children. What followed thereafter is too well-known to bear repetition and lies, in any case, beyond the scope of this book. But it must be recorded that Betsy died on 19 June 1896 at the age of sixty-nine and that Mary Ellen, who had married Captain Philip Davies, died on 9 August 1909. Both of them were buried in the Criccieth churchyard and they would be joined in March 1917 by Richard Lloyd (a patriarchal figure in Lloyd Georgian mythology) who had died on the last day of February.

Little by little, looking beyond the immediate family circle, the people who had known William left the scene. Sir James Kay-Shuttleworth (diligent but depressed and, in some quarters, despised) took his leave in1877, Dr Morell (suffering from progressive dementia) went in 1891 and Dr Martineau (an awesome and austere living legend) at the great age of ninety-five in 1900. Thomas Goffey, whose name was revered at Highgate, lived on until 1915 but he never met Betsy or any of William's children and dispensed advice and assistance from afar. (In 1875 he investigated, without success, the claim that William had been entitled to a share in the proceeds from the sale of Tresinwen land in the vicinity of Strumble Head.)

The very last direct link with William was Anne Williams (née James), who survived her husband by nineteen years and died on 26 May 1928, seven months short of her ninetieth birthday. She had a double relationship with the George family, for her daughter Anita married William's third son in July 1910 and she thus became the mother-in-law of another William George. Anita presented her husband with twins in October 1912, one of them being christened David Lloyd and the other William Richard Phillip. Sadly, the first-named died three months before his second birthday. The surviving twin lived on until 2006, having been cited in the present volume as either W.R.P. George or Dr George. He would have been almost sixteen when Anne Williams died and thus, in his turn, would have been the very last direct link with her.

It must be borne in mind that, for more than a century, our perception of William as a personality has been subtly coloured by the words of this loving, loyal and devoted niece. In her eyes, he could do no wrong. She had an important input into the opening chapter of du Parcq's biography and also influenced, albeit less obviously, the phraseology employed in the one written by J. Hugh Edwards a couple of years later. The image that she conveyed to du Parcq, which subsequent biographers of David Lloyd George (including the present author) have drawn upon gratefully, was that of an outgoing, high-spirited, intelligent, quick-witted and very able young man who was greatly in demand in the family circle. The key paragraph in the account which she supplied to du Parcq is probably the one which runs as follows:

> He used to spend his holidays at his home at Trecoed, making a round of visits to his many relatives and friends around. He was well up in affairs of State and current events, and especially well versed in politics, and an excellent talker - in fact, a brilliant conversationalist, genial and humorous withal, and possessing a very engaging manner, so that he was much sought after by all, especially the well-educated families, throughout the whole of North Pembrokeshire. [1]

There is much in Anne's account which is still very valid and it should certainly not be denigrated. It is a testimony from someone who actually knew him. But she has drawn a veil over his moments of irritation, of which she had first-hand experience, and that avowed strong sense of humour will have to be taken largely on trust. William's humour, when we encounter it in his letters, is often of a rather ponderous, plodding variety, and his lack of tolerance when learning of that teacher at Pwllheli who had executed a few dance steps in order to entertain his pupils, is rather startling - the poor man is condemned on hearsay evidence, without William knowing anything about the context of the incident. A moment or two of levity or fooling-about in a classroom is often quite conducive to establishing a cheerful atmosphere and a good working relationship between teacher and pupils, followed by an increased willingness on the part of the latter to buckle down to a spot of hard grind. There are worse bases on which to proceed.

One can, if so inclined, chip away rather unfeelingly at the image which Anne had sought to foster, and it must be acknowledged that the temptation to challenge some of her statements is sometimes hard to resist. The stern disciplinarian depicted by Rees, for example, does not quite feature in du Parcq's Anne-inspired account. He was, certainly, a disciplinarian, du Parcq acknowledges, but he hastily adds that William was averse to corporal punishment and 'brought order out of chaos' by exercising his 'indefinable gifts'. [2] There is no glimpse here of the master who, according to Edwin John, laid about him with a cane to an unreasonable extent, and one wishes (with gross unfairness) that du Parcq had at least made a cursory attempt to define those indefinable gifts. And one suspects a slight element of exaggeration in the assertion that 'the well-educated families, throughout the whole of North Pembrokeshire', made a point of seeking him out - his death, it should be noted, went unreported in the local papers [3] - just as the statement that he was 'a great friend of Dr Henry Martineau and his daughter Harriet' needs to be taken with a grain of salt. (Dr James Martineau and his sister Harriet were barely on speaking terms when William was working in Liverpool - and Miss Martineau was a semi-permanent invalid, confined to the sickroom to a very great extent. She was also profoundly deaf, so that anyone seeking to engage the lady in conversation was obliged to shout down a large speaking-trumpet. The present writer strongly doubts whether William ever clapped eyes on her.)

And there were, of course, episodes that Anne suppressed. The shorthand notes made by her son-in-law on 6 November 1922 make it clear that she was aware that William had once been employed by Lady Byron and that she was also aware that, when based in Haverfordwest for a second time, he had married a Miss Huntley. This information had been withheld from both du Parq and Edwards, the most that was divulged to the latter about William's earlier career being that he had 'spent some years in London as a tutor in a private school'. [4] It was genuinely the case, one suspects, that Anne knew nothing about his stint at the pioneering Battersea establishment in 1841 and her knowledge of his connections with Lady Byron may have been very slight. She is, however, the only source for the statement that Miss Huntley was 'a chronic invalid who was madly in love with him' and that William 'married her to save her life!' [5] The statement may be correct, of course, or it may have been have been a deliberate attempt to minimise the importance of that first marriage and to convince her son-in-law that Betsy was the only woman whom his father had ever truly loved.

While loath to criticise too strongly that image of perfect rectitude created by the devoted niece - acting, as it were, in the role of Public Relations or Press Officer, anxious to burnish it to the best of her ability - we do need to set it gently aside. The reader now knows far more about her uncle than Anne ever did and a fresh, dispassionate assessment of William George needs to be attempted. But he occupies, it must be instantly acknowledged, a curious position. Posterity has remembered him as the father of a remarkable politician and statesman: if the fame of David Lloyd George had never dominated first Wales, then Britain and then the world, William would have been totally forgotten. He shares with Leopold Mozart and Isaac D'Israeli the distinction of having fathered a remarkable son, and retrospective lustre has been cast on his career purely for this reason.

But he deserves more attention than that. For the range and depth of that career has, until now, never been properly investigated or considered. It is clear that, while occupying a much smaller stage, William was a vital character in his own right and that his accomplishments during the first thirty-odd years of his life were almost as remarkable as those of his second son.

It was not previously realised, to begin with, that the innate gifts of this lad from a modest Pembrokeshire farm were so striking that it would have been considered a crime to deny him a first-rate education. Due almost certainly to the intervention of his grandfather, he had been sent to the local grammar school in the first instance - and the latter part of his schooling evidently took place somewhere in London. Nor was it realised that, after 'working his way through college' (at a location not yet identified) and passing some crucial exams, he went on to become the star pupil of the newly-established Battersea training institute for teachers. Nor, finally, was it realised that he had then been engaged by Lady Byron to play a leading role at *two* of her schools. And all this by the age of twenty-two! Had it not been for that strange and sudden departure from her employment (for which, with a twinge of conscience, she appears to have made amends some twelve years later) the inevitable ascent of the promotional ladder would doubtless have continued without pause. And, in fact, it was resumed four years later when he went to Liverpool and assumed control of the school attached to Dr Martineau's Paradise Street chapel - and then found himself charged with the task of helping to establish Sunday Schools at the new Hope Street premises, a commission which he evidently discharged with huge success and for which he earned Martineau's positively overwhelming gratitude. He, for his part, was massively grateful for having been granted more than a year's Sabbatical, a period of freedom and enterprise which he longingly recalled a little while later as a brief glimpse of Utopia - 'Remember Liverpool!' But the prospect of being enmeshed for ever more in the complexities of Unitarianism was not something to be welcomed, and he made his escape from Hope Street after devoting a year of his time to ensuring that the Schools had been firmly established.

After 1852, however, his increasingly poor state of health was a crucial factor. Periods of sustained activity were often followed by periods of sustained tiredness. He felt, moreover, that his creative talents had not been extended to their fullest capacity and that the time for deploying them was rapidly passing him by. A period of indecision resulted, eventually, in his returning to the tried and tested sphere of teaching, although his exceptional talents were noted by Dr Morell, who head-hunted him for two particular vacancies. Pwllheli had to be abandoned because of illness and by the end of his stint at Manchester he was physically weary and mentally tired. With a small family to support, prolonged illness kept at bay with difficulty, and wishing, for good or ill, to be his own master once again, the tenancy of a small farm seemed the only remaining option.

William's biographer is hampered, inevitably, by the fact that raw material for the life of his subject is in short supply. There is no mention of him in the Kay-Shuttleworth or Byron or Neild papers, although there may prove to be the occasional reference in the Martineau papers at such time as they are classified. Only at two phases in his life - first during the summer months of 1839, and secondly during the period running from 1861 to 1863 - can William be seen in close-up and his trains of thought followed to some extent. On other occasions, much has to be inferred or conjectured. It is possible that those missing sections of the *Journal*, still in existence when they were examined by W.R.P. George in 1976, will reappear and it may be that some of the letters written to his niece will eventually come to light, doubtless sealed in a large thick envelope tucked away at the back of a cupboard, but almost everything else currently available (including, where decipherable, expenditure records and private jottings included in the *Journal*) has been set out in the present volume.

How close is it possible to come, on the limited basis of that material, to re-creating the personality of William George and to discerning elements of continuity between the younger and the older versions?

The young man making those entries in the *Student's Journal* was, clearly, conscientious and sometimes self-conscious, a diligent worker but constantly rebuking and ridiculing himself for his short-comings. The subject of personal relationships troubles him - he is in search of the ideal woman, and not at all sure he will ever find her: soul-searching notes written many years later indicate that the hunt was still on. He was unsure of himself. Already, however, he is extremely well-read. Despondency alternates with high-spirits and those mysterious hieroglyphics at the beginning of July 1839 - a prolonged whoop of joy! - indicate that he was as capable of celebrating and enjoying himself as the next man.

His success at Battersea seems to have instilled a new confidence in him, and we see - in the drafts of the two speeches that have survived from that time - the development of a very capable young speaker, able to argue a case with conviction and with one or two of the orator's tricks already mastered. The draft of his farewell speech to the pupils at Pwllheli, twenty years later, is, admittedly, a sad, rambling and repetitive affair, but it was written at a time of illness. And we must remember those vivid words of the old man encountered by Herbert Lewis - 'When he was on his feet, the whole place was buzzing.' Apart from the comments of Anne Williams, those are the only words we possess of someone who *almost* saw William in action - for he was passing on, at one stage removed, what others had told him many years before.

He continued to be well-read during the years that followed his Battersea course. *Punch* was regularly purchased in his younger days and later on he would keep abreast of current events by investing in a weekly edition of *The Times*. Of standard hobbies as such there is no clue in the *Journal*, apart from that minor participation in amateur theatricals, but he was a compulsive purchaser of books and building-up his precious library was obviously a great passion. Much of his spare time was clearly taken up with reading but the jotting down of private reflections, either directly into his *Journal* or on spare scraps of paper thrust into its pages, became something of a reflex action.

He was a serious, brooding, introspective man and perhaps, in his later years, somewhat imperious and impatient. He claims that at one point he went through a Socialist phase, and some Owenite notions may have been picked up during his spell with Lady Byron, but his contemptuous remarks about the working-class men who were the school managers at Newchurch will be easily recalled: he resented being at the beck and call of such inferior people and he looked askance at the woman who had tended Betsy after David's birth - 'she used to work in a factory', so was clearly an inadequate type of person, incapable of providing a decent standard of service.

Basic Christian charity seems, by this time, to be in somewhat short supply.

But ever and again, one returns to the subject of his constant illnesses. He may have been something of a hypochondriac, but the concern for his health was obviously justified and it has long been generally accepted that he died at the appallingly early age of forty-four - two years sooner than his father and one year sooner than his sister. But (for the reasons set out in Appendix I) it was probably even *worse* than this, for his true age seems to have been no more than forty-two. The notion that his days were numbered lurked permanently in his self-consciousness during the final five years of his life, and this is a factor that must be borne in mind when trying to assess his character and achievements. He died a tired, frustrated, disappointed man, happy in his marriage and in the promising development of his two children, but always aware that, with his latent talents, he ought to have achieved something far greater than he actually managed. Even so, he did pretty well - and probably contributed, in the last analysis, far more to the world in which he lived than he could ever fully appreciate.

The first, most tangible legacy that he left to the boy whom he regarded as his one surviving son (for he could never have known that a *third* son, one much more like himself and one who would survive until 1967, was destined to appear) was that extensive library. That subject has been touched upon earlier, and it has been noted that there were several particular volumes which David evidently recalled - which suggests, perhaps, that he gave the rest of William's books only cursory attention. Rollin's *Ancient History* was one which he found hugely fascinating, but the credit for helping him to read this and other weighty volumes at an early age was given, quite naturally, to his uncle, Richard Lloyd. It is unlikely that second-hand bookshops held any great attraction for him. 'It is a mistake to purchase a quantity of books just for the sake of possession,' he told Sir George Riddell in September 1919. 'One never reads them. Of course, that does not apply to books of reference.' [6] While still a teenager, he went in for a spot of serious educational reading of his own volition, tackling A, M. Sullivan's *The Story of Ireland* (1867) and Henry George's *Progress and Poverty* (1879), both of which made a great impact on him, as well as Macaulay's works, but his subsequent 'serious' reading would prove to be somewhat erratic and he could never have been accused of being a bookworm. He evidently dipped into a vast number of biographies and history books, as the years went by, sometimes just to see what they said about himself, but the number which he consumed from cover to cover was probably very limited. (Reading official papers bored him immensely, for he always preferred to gain information by talking to and cross-examining sundry useful informants, listening intently to what they told him.) Thomas Jones, however, was surprised to discover in August 1921, from a publication called *Makers of the Modern World*, that David had been reading some works on ancient Rome by the eminent historian Theodor Mommsen. He checked the accuracy of this statement and David readily confirmed that this was the case, adding that he had also read 'Ferrero, Samuel Dill, [and] some Xenophon in the "Loeb" series; Thucydides entangled him by the number of small towns.' As always, he extolled the virtues of Rollin's *Ancient History*. The following day Jones noticed that *Letters of Luther* was included among the number of light novels which featured on David's bedroom bookshelf. [7]

Charles Read's *The Cloister and the Hearth* was a favourite fictional work, one to which he returned quite often, and other adventure stories which appealed to him were the tales emanating from Dumas and Stevenson. In later years David fell back upon those light novels spotted by Jones, which he himself described as 'shilling shockers'. Wild west stories by Ridgwell Cullum were devoured with great enthusiasm. Polite attention was paid to Dickens, it seems, but it is a moot point whether he ever read anything by Bulwer Lytton, or whether he would have been greatly inspired by it if he had. It is interesting to find, however, that he tackled Virginia Woolf's *Orlando* in January 1929, and thought it 'a very clever book'. [8]

So far as writing was concerned, on the other hand, David would attain a degree of excellence to which William had only aspired in his wildest dreams. Like William, he began by preparing short sermons and speeches, for delivery among largely domestic audiences or people who knew him well, but later on he would soar to levels unprecedented, even in Wales. When he had left high office (but was anxious to regain it), he would produce an endless stream of articles distinguished by vivid turns of phrase and much virulence. Later still, when his speaking powers had seemingly passed their prime, he would produce actual books (as distinct from collections of speeches), dealing with both peace and war, but what he hankered after, but never got round to achieving, was to pay homage to the world of his childhood and youth by writing a book about Welsh preachers and perhaps, with assistance, compiling a book of favourite Welsh hymns. This, certainly, was something of which William would have approved, and he would also have approved of those musical evenings in which David, in strong voice, would do vocal justice to some of those hymns. Eisteddfods strongly appealed to him, and as he grew older and more emotional the notion of obeisance to the Land of My Fathers held ever-stronger attractions. 'He wants to have a gathering in the autumn of Welsh poets and writers', noted Jones in June 1937, 'to read their own works and [tell] tales of the old preachers.' [9] (It would be atonement, in a sense, for many years of non-chapel going and for eventually, as he approached the age of sixty, playing golf on Sundays.)

The actual *sound* of Welsh hymns and Welsh poetry, irrespective of what the words meant, was something which he never tired of extolling. Like his father, on the other hand, he believed that the English wrote the best poetry (although William's grasp of Welsh had, admittedly, been very limited) and Dryden, as well as Byron, was one of his favourites.

And, also like his father, David had a strong admiration for Oliver Cromwell - an inflexible man of steel, a dictator who carried all before him and a man who got things done. David would have envied him his ability to ride roughshod over opponents. He came to believe, indeed, that there was much to be said for benevolent dictators. Theoretically a 'man of the people', a champion of the old and the poor and the sick, he believed in his heart of hearts that such people ought to know their place in the community and not seek to get above themselves. Organised labour, indeed, was a phenomenon which he regarded with acute distaste. Riddell noted in October 1919 that, 'with all his powers', David did 'not understand or sympathise with working men. His point of view is that of the solicitor or shopkeeper', regarding them as 'decent fellows, but unsophisticated, uneducated, and rather unreasonable on the whole.' [10] And one instantly recalls those contemptuous words about 'rough working men' uttered by William - 'My temper is such that I would rather be the master of workpeople than their servant.' These sentiments would have been warmly endorsed by his second son.

William's close attention to financial matters, if deemed inheritable, was a trait for which a future Chancellor of the Exchequer ought to have been eternally grateful. A question mark hangs over the issue of just how adept David was with figures, however, despite the skilful conjuror's patter which helped to conceal this fact, and it is difficult to draw any firm conclusions on the subject. Far more relevant to David's career was William's friendship with Thomas Goffey, for that gentleman (although never visiting either Llanystumdwy or Cricieth) was held up as a shining example of what could be achieved, in distinguished reputation and worldly goods, by becoming a practitioner of the law. It is highly improbable that David would ever have become a solicitor if Martha Goffey had not happened to be a teacher at Manesty Lane school.

When it came to the huge issue of sexual matters, father and son were poles apart. David, from the age of eighteen to that of eighty, always had an eye for the ladies and indulged, if he could, in numerous affairs. William, on the other hand, was very inhibited and cautious, treating the fair sex with respect and courtesy but always awaiting the appearance of that ideal woman. He married Betsy late in life but made up for lost time, as it were, by fathering four children in a marriage which lasted little more than four-and-a-half years: happiness, and sexual gratification, had been achieved but in an orthodox fashion. 'The best things in life', he might have proclaimed, 'are worth waiting for.' He would undoubtedly have been aghast at the 'loose' manner in which his second son - known, for much of his life, as 'the Goat' - would carry on.

The peripatetic nature of William's career certainly provided David with some useful assets. He would be forever associated with Llanystumdwy and Criccieth (and noted with glee, in later years, how well the sales of postcards of his childhood home were doing), but returning to the city of his birth he could also claim to be 'a native of Manchester' - and on visits to the county where his forbears had lived he would declare 'I am a Pembrokeshire lad. I come from Pembrokeshire stock and am proud of it.' Depending on how fast he was travelling in his electioneering campaigns, it was possible to establish direct personal contact with three very different communities almost simultaneously.

Occasionally, of course, his past caught up with him in unexpected fashion, but he usually managed to turn such encounters to his advantage. Someone at an election meeting apparently tried to cut him down to size. When the time came for questions from the audience, this gentleman delivered what might be regarded as a killer punch - 'Didn't your father have a small farm at Bulford, and didn't he have a donkey for drawing his cart?' David turned to the chairman of the meeting. 'Well, Mr Chairman,' was his response, 'I am very glad to have that question. I can tell you where the cart is - it is still in the barn at Bulford. And as for the donkey, I'm very glad to see that he is with us today' - a retort which produced roars of laughter, and the challenger himself seems to have been amused. [11] (It is a good story and just conceivable, bearing in mind the wiliness of the speaker – and the fact that such exchanges seem to have occurred more than once - that the question had been 'planted'.)

Visiting Pwllheli in 1922 he was greeted by a small group of his father's ex-pupils and that same year he received a letter from the Rev John Davies of Wigan, who recalled that he had served under William as a pupil-teacher at the Mayfield School in Manchester. 'Mr George,' he added, 'who had previously broken down in health but had somewhat recovered, became our headmaster during a serious breakdown of our head-master - Mr A.J. Pope.' [12]

But the paths of father and son also crossed in ways which the son never realised. In May 1897, urging his wife to come and join him in London, he suggested that they take a house in Ealing or Acton, 'Ealing for choice', where the air was 'quite as good as anything we can get in Wales'. [13] It is highly improbable that he realised that his father had ever had connections with that part of the world. Writing to Frances

Stevenson from Genoa, almost exactly twenty-five years later, he remarked that he was 'in a mood to chuck politics altogether and retire to Italy like Byron and Shelley who told work to go to the devil. I pass Byron's house every day.' [14] As a postscript to the same letter, he asked her to send him an unexpurgated edition of Byron's poems. Had he been aware of the relationship between his father and Lady Byron, and even perhaps with Lord Byron's daughter, he would scarcely have refrained from revealing this to his mistress.

In September 1905, with a long-awaited general election on the horizon, and every possibility that he would shortly become a Liberal Minister, David revisited his roots. He was accompanied by his eldest son and they were driven in a pony and trap hired in Haverfordwest for the day. After visiting Tiers Cross, they called in at Bulford. Mr Phillips, now a widower of 79, was there to greet them. His daughter Evelyn and two burly sons (Arthur and Walter), who had never fled the parental nest, were probably there as well, together with daughter-in-law Ann. The old gentleman may have been slightly surprised at being addressed by his guests as 'Mr John' (the name inadvertently bestowed on him by Betsy). David, gazing around, instantly spotted that one crucial feature had changed. 'The front gate!' he exclaimed. 'It used to be a green folding gate.' Mr Phillips explained that the old gate had recently been replaced by a larger one but that a section of it was still in use elsewhere, and led his visitors to the spot in question. He showed them round the rest of the farm and, as a memento of the occasion, presented David with the original lease-assignment document. After imbibing (one assumes) at least one cup of tea the visitors took their leave. 'Very nice little place,' David reported to his brother, 'with a touch of real style about it. Most untidily kept. Mr John told me that its present appearance gave no idea of what it looked like [in 1864]. The trees on the drive all cut down. I saw the gate

Mary and I carried stones to - not the old gate. That has been taken down and part of it put up elsewhere. Dick took photographs. It all rather saddened me.' [15]

He had not the remotest inkling, as he resumed his seat in the trap and the pony trotted away, of what the future held in store. He was leaving Bulford for the very last time at the age of forty-two. But if the statement on his father's death certificate (emanating from Betsy) is more accurate than the one twenty miles away chiselled on his tombstone (emanating from Benjamin), then William had *also* left Bulford for the very last time at the age of forty-two.

Such a coincidence could provide wonderful inspiration for a Celtic bard. He would be able to conjure up for us a God of Continuity, hovering benignly over that drab little farmstead and putting into effect a lease-transfer of his own. A torch, he would proclaim, now passed from father to son. William's career, after a dazzling start, had petered out in apparent obscurity; David's, after a long and gruelling apprenticeship, was about to assume epic proportions. Hazards of a complex and sometimes terrifying nature lay ahead. But the father's spirit would live on in the son, gathering renewed strength, and 'Onwards and upwards!' would once again be the order of the day. The intermission was over.

This is great Superman stuff, of course, but the sober biographer and historian, holding aloft his hands in horror, must shy away from such esoteric scenarios and simply leave the reader to draw his or her own conclusions, fanciful or otherwise, from the material assembled in this volume. It is hoped, however, that it will provide the basis for further and more detailed investigations by other hands in due course. Some useful and, at times, quite surprising information has come to light, and some long-established standard versions of events have now been superseded (not too ruthlessly, it is hoped), but - assuming that the relevant material for further research still exists - there is much that one would still like to know about William George and the intriguing and unexpected spheres in which he moved.

The question must be asked, finally, Was Lloyd George proud of his father? Sadly the answer would have to be No, not particularly. He would have acknowledged that William, with that vast library of books, was an erudite man, but the fact that he knew barely any Welsh rather astonished him. He did not despise school-mastering as a profession but did not hold it in especially high regard, tending to regard its practitioners as second-raters. He marvelled, in 1932, that a newly-deceased politician who had had 'a notable career & left his mark on the lives of millions' (T.J. Macnamara), should have started out as 'an ordinary school teacher'. [16]   Clearly, 'ordinary school teachers' came far behind 'ordinary solicitors' in the pecking order! But he had no true idea of what his father had achieved, the lavish praise of Anne Williams notwithstanding, because the details of William's career were largely unknown to him - and he had no desire to find out more. Lloyd George's tada, as the title of this book has indicated, was the one father whom Lloyd Gorge never knew.

Birth certificates did not come into general use until 1837, and the date on which William George was born is not known. His two marriage certificates (in 1855 and 1859) simply confirm that he was of 'full age' for entering into a state of matrimony.

William's death certificate states that he was 42 when he died on 7 June 1864. Without knowing the date on which he had celebrated his last birthday, this statement - if true - means that he had been born either in 1821 (during the period from 8 June to 31 December) or in 1822 (during the period from 1 January to 7 June).

But his gravestone claims, that he had reached the age of 44. If *this* statement is true, then the years quoted in the preceding sentence should be adjusted to 1819 and 1820.

However, it must be borne in mind that, even in the present day and age, and unless a birth certificate is readily available for consultation purposes, information about age that appears on death certificates and gravestones is not always totally reliable: it sometimes reflects what the deceased's nearest and dearest, to the best of their ability, believe to be the correct state of affairs.

The 'tombstone age' of 44 has been generally taken to mean, not unreasonably, that he was born in 1820. But, until now, the data on the death certificate does not appear to have been taken into account. William Edwards, a labourer on William's farm, was the source of this information when he visited the Registrar on 9 June - but the age of 42 would have been supplied to him by Betsy. It could equally well be the case, therefore, that he was born in 1822.

And, just to complicate the situation still further, a scrap of paper enclosed with his miscellaneous papers in the National Library of Wales, written in an unknown hand (that of Richard Lloyd, perhaps?), states that he was 41 when he died. [1] So *this* statement - if true - means that he was born either in 1822 (during the period from 8 June to 31 December) or in 1823 (during the period from 1 January to 7 June)

Census returns are usually (but not invariably) a better guide to the age of individuals, and William can be found in those for 1841, 1851 and 1861.

In the census for England taken on 6 June 1841, he is said to be twenty years old. This implies that he was born in 1820 (if his birthday was later than 6 June) or in 1821 (if his birthday actually occurred on 6 June itself or on one of the 156 preceding days of 1841). However, instructions had been given to the enumerators that they should round down the ages of persons aged more than 15 to the nearest five years. A true age of 21, 22, 23 or even (astonishingly) of 24 would thus have been recorded as one of 20. This raises the spectre of 'genuine' possible birth years ranging from 1816 to 1821: or, to be more precise, given such generous parameters as this, William could have been born at any time between 7 June 1816 and 6 June 1821. (But one is relieved to learn that, in many areas, those instructions were ignored by the enumerators!) In the census for England taken on 30 March 1851, William is said to be 33. This implies that he was born either in 1817 (during the period from 31 March to 31 December) or in 1818 (during the period from 1 January to 30 March).

In the census for Wales taken on 7 April 1861, William is said to be 39. This implies that he was born either in 1821 (during the period from 8 April to 31 December) or in 1822 (during the period from 1 January to 7 April).

On the basis of the wildly conflicting evidence set out above, William George could have been born at any point between 7 June 1816 and 7 June 1823. It could be argued that the 1861 census is perhaps the most accurate, for he would have had more of a direct input into his personal data (unlike the one of 1851, compiled by his landlord). And the age of 42 that appears on his death certificate is not in conflict with this statement. Nor is the age of 20 that is accorded him in the 1841 census. Until such time as fresh information comes to light, it is not unreasonable to assume that, in all probability, he was indeed born in 1821 rather than 1820.

APPENDIX II: A GUIDE TO THE CONTENTS OF WG'S 'STUDENT'S JOURNAL'

PART ONE: contents on a page-by-page basis

Page

1	Blank page
2	Diary entries for 3 - 6 June 1839
3	Diary entries for 7 - 9 June 1839
4	Diary entries for 10 - 13 June 1839
5	Diary entries for 14 - 16 June 1839
6	Diary entries for 17 - 20 June 1839
7	Diary entries for 21 - 23 June 1839
8	Diary entries for 24 - 26 June 1839
9	Blank page
10	Diary entries for 1 - 4 July 1839
11	Blank page
12	Cash in hand on 15 October 1841
13	Expenditure [on?] 15 October 1841
14	Crucial employment dates in 1842, 1843 and 1844; Books left behind at Newbold (items 1 to 12)

PART TWO: financial data (where extant) set out chronologically

- -

Diary page	Year	Months (expd)	Months (recd)
111	1843		June – Dec
112	1843		June
113	1843	June – Aug	
114	1843	Aug – Sept	
115	1843	Sept – Nov	
116	1843	Dec	

- -

111	1844		March – Nov
117	1844	Jan – March	

[WG left Newbold on 25 March 1844]

- -

Nothing for April – Dec 1844

- -

Nothing for 1845

- -

22	1846	July – Aug	
23	1846		July - Nov

Diary page	Year	Months (expd)	Months (recd)
24	1846	Aug – Oct	
25	1846		Sept - Nov
26	1846	Sept -Oct	

- -

Diary page	Year	Months (expd)	Months (recd)
28	1847		Feb – Dec
29	1847	Feb – mid-March	
30	1847	mid-March - April	
31	1847	April – mid-May	
32	1847	mid-May – mid-June	

[Pages 33/34 missing]

- -

Diary page	Year	Months (expd)	Months (recd)
28	1848		Jan
26	1848		Oct

- -

Diary page	Year	Months (expd)	Months (recd)
118	1849	Feb – March	
119	1849	March – April	
120	1849	April – May	

Diary page	Year	Months (expd)	Months (recd)
121	1849	June – July	
122	1849	Aug	
27	1849		Spring- Oct
123	1849	Sept - Dec	

- -

123		Brief 1850 entries	
35	1850	Jan & April	
27	1850		Feb

- -

Nothing for 1851

- -

36	1852		April – Dec

- -

To the editor of the *Carnarvon & Denbigh Herald*

Sir,

Happening to take up your impression of the 13th inst. today, I read a letter in it respecting the 'British' School at Pwllheli, in which I was sorry to observe a good deal of misunderstanding, respecting the relation of what is termed 'a British School' to the Committee of Council. It is in the hope of putting this matter right, and of uniting all parties in a good work, that I write these few lines, which I shall be glad for you to insert for the information of the persons concerned.

At the Council office, in London, all schools inspected in England are classed for convenience under three heads - National Schools, British Schools, and Roman Catholic Schools. The government takes no cognisance whatever of the particular principles, religious or otherwise, on which each individual school classed under the title of B.S., or British School, is carried on. The only point they insist on is, that the authorised version of the scriptures shall be read in it. Any amount or any description of religious instruction may be given, over and above this, *which the managers approve*. The government has nothing whatever to say in the question beyond the *one point* above mentioned. So long as the scriptures in the authorised version are read, you can teach a dozen different catechisms, *if the managers think fit* - or, at any rate as many as there are religious denominations attending the school.

This is the attitude which the government holds to the religious question, in so-termed British Schools. At the same time it is *usual* where schools are formed under committees consisting of various denominations, not to introduce any catechism at all, but to base the religious instruction entirely on the Bible, as being common ground to all. Many schools are under my inspection where this plan is working most satisfactorily; and many a clergyman has remarked to me, in connexion with such schools, how much to be regretted it is that, amongst a population of people belonging to different communities, such a system is not more generally adopted.

Might I take this opportunity of begging all concerned in the school at Pwllheli to lay aside their speculative differences, and unite in forming a vigorous school for the town, where a good secular education shall be supplemented by religious instruction, based upon the only Word of Life.

J.D. Morell,
Her Majesty's Inspector of Schools

Dolgelly, June 15th

[*Published 27 June 1858*]

APPENDIX IV: WHEN WILLIAM MET BETSY, 'THE GIRL NEXT DOOR'

In retrospect, it is clear that the first meeting between William George and Elizabeth Lloyd was as momentous as the first meeting between Mr Rolls and Mr Royce. And, since 1976 at any rate, the narrator's task has been greatly simplified and he or she can exclaim in jubilation that the fates have been kind. For it appears that, soon after the young widower from Wakefield took up residence in his new house (and unconsciously anticipating a favourite plot-line of *Peg's Paper* and other popular magazines of the early twentieth century), he happened to glance over his garden wall and was instantly smitten by the sight of a demure young lady walking in the grounds next door. The narrator can, certainly, allow himself to be carried away at this point, as the foregoing phraseology will have made clear. There is much scope for imagination and even, perhaps, for subsequent television treatment of such a scenario. But the historian needs to be a little more cautious.

How, in the first place, did this notion come about?

The fifth William was relatively circumspect when it came to describing the manner in which his parents met. In 1858, he tells us, Elizabeth Lloyd was 'in service as a lady's companion, in a country house situated about a mile outside the town' and it was 'more than likely' that they met each other as members of the congregation of the Pwllheli Baptist chapel. The sixth William, however, acting on fresh information, was able to be far more specific. He endorses the notion that it was the Baptist chapel that brought William and Elizabeth together, but has preceded this with the news that his grandmother, 'known to her contemporaries as Betsy Lloyd, was at the time in service with a Miss Evans who lived ay *Y Castell* (The Castle) in Pwllheli, next door to Troed-yr-Allt school.' [1]

Now most of this information, so far as one can check it, is very nearly correct. (Or, as Eddie Braben would have said - via the lips of Eric Morecambe - all the right notes are being played, but not necessarily in the right order.)

There was (and is) a house called *Y Castell* in Pwllheli, but it was located at some little distance from the school. Alongside the school, however, a castle of sorts did indeed exist. This was a splendid three-bed-roomed house equipped with actual battlements called Picton Castle (which, like *Y Castell*, is still there). And in Picton Castle, so the census returns tell us, there lived in the year 1871 a lady called Laura Evans (born in 1817) with her servant Jane Griffiths (born in 1852). This must surely be the Miss Evans to whom Dr George was referring.

Unfortunately, Miss Laura Evans was not living at Picton Castle in 1861, for the census return for *that* year shows her heading the team of 'house servants' at her uncle's small estate at Methlem, some twelve miles away. As it happens, we do know that Picton Castle was rented for five years during the 1850s by the widowed Mrs Ellen Lloyd, late of Ty Newydd (where David Lloyd George would live eighty-five years later)[2] but it has not proved possible to ascertain who took over the house after her death in April 1857. Miss Evans is unlikely to have moved there until the autumn of 1869 when, following the demise of her uncle Robert, she became relatively well-off and able to retire into private life, employing a servant of her own.

The present author is strongly inclined to discount the 'girl next door' story completely. But he has not been able to ascertain who, if anybody, was living at Picton Castle after April 1857. It is just conceivable that *another* Miss Evans moved into the house and did indeed employ Betsy as her servant, but - if so - her stay was of very short duration, since this 'second' Miss Evans does not appear in the census return for 1861. There are limits to which the long arm of coincidence can be stretched, but there may still be some who will be inclined (pending the discovery of fresh and conclusive information) to give Dr George the benefit of the doubt.

Returning to the statement that Betsy was 'in service as a lady's companion, in a country house situated about a mile outside the town' one has to acknowledge that this does, after a fashion fit the facts so far as 1851 was concerned. The census for that year shows that she was a housemaid (not a companion) at Trallwyn Hall, the home of a landed proprietor called John Lloyd (no relation) who was a magistrate and Deputy-Lieutenant, farming an estate of 190 acres and employing seven labourers - although only one other house servant is mentioned in the return (Lydia Morris, aged 33) which suggests that either that one or two more were away or that Betsy and Lydia had their work cut out in looking after the members of a large family. Trallwyn Hall is four miles north of Pwllheli. But there is no knowing how long Betsy was employed there and according to family tradition she was in domestic service at several different households prior to her marriage. It may indeed be the case that she was taken on at another country house in the area and served as a companion to the lady of that house, but proponents of this theory will need to produce evidence to support it.

NOTES

Abbreviations:

NBLFP   Noel, Buxton and Lovelace family papers ('the Lovelace-Byron Deposit') housed in the Bodleian Library, Oxford, which includes some of Lady Noel Byron's papers

NLW   National Library of Wales

ODNB   *Oxford Dictionary of National Biography*

OUP   Oxford University Press

PRO   Pembrokeshire Record Office

TMLG   *The Making of Lloyd George* by W.R.P. George (Faber & Faber, London, 1976)

WG   William George

WGSP   William George (Solicitor) Papers

Information about births, deaths and marriages has been taken, in the main, from the certificates issued by the General Register Office. Census returns, which are frequently referred to in the text, are made available by the National Archives for England and Wales. Useful supplementary material has been derived from the *Oxford Dictionary of National Biography* and Wikipedia.

PREFACE AND ACKNOWLEDGEMENTS

1   NLW, J. Herbert Lewis Papers D31, ff.62-63, 'LG's Early Life', 4 Dec. 1907.

2   *Pontypridd Chronicle* article reprinted 21 May 1890 in the *Haverfordwest & Milford Haven Telegraph* (an item very kindly brought to my attention by Mr Simon Hancock, Curtator of the Haverfordwest Town Museum).

3   NLW, J. Herbert Lewis Papers, as above. The full title of the Rollins work was *The Ancient History of the Egyptians, Carthaginians, Assyrians, Babylonians, Medes and Persians, Macedonians and Grecians*. It is conceivable that the *History of England* was Macaulay's, but - if so - one would have expected Herbert to identify it by name.

4   Ibid.

5   See *H.H. Asquith, Letters to Venetia Stanley*, selected and edited by Michael and Eleanor Brock (OUP, 1982), p.77 and Cameron Hazlehurst, *Politicians at War, July 1914 to May 1915* (Jonathan Cape, London, 1971), pp.129-30.

6   In a letter to the author dated 3 March 2010.

BY WAY OF INTRODUCTION

1   Letter from Macmillan Co. editor, 19 Nov. 1968.

2   Dr Johnson to Bennett Langton, Jan. 1759 (slightly adapted), *Boswell's Life of Johnson*, edited by G.B. Hill, revised by L.F. Powell (OUP, 1934), Vol. I, p.324.

3   David Benedictus, *Lloyd George* [a fictionalised biography] (Sphere Books Ltd, London, 1981), p.5; letter from Elaine Morgan, 13 Feb. 1980. In a letter to *Radio Times*, after the series had ended, I commented that much of it had been quite well done but that there had been considerable over-simplification and some serious factual distortions. In particular, Lloyd George and Lord Kitchener appeared to have swapped personalities - the first being morose and silent, the second being voluble and impassioned. The only person to draw attention to how things had evolved was *The Guardian*'s Norman Shrapnel, who reviewed the Benedictus book on 22 Jan. 1981. 'Eating people is no longer wrong,' he remarked; 'people do it all the time and in what looks like the friendliest of spirits. Cannibalistic banquets cause little surprise in the

285

most distinguished circles though it takes a bit of time to work out just who is eating whom; documentary fiction - in itself an ever-tantalising contradiction in terms - makes such confusions only to be expected.   In serving us *Lloyd George* David Benedictus is about as frank as you can get. Peter Rowland does a biography, Elaine Morgan draws on this substantially for a television treatment, and Mr Benedictus uses her scripts as a base for his novel.... [He] tells his (or Miss Morgan's, or Mr Rowland's) story with unfailingly brisk skill, yet the central problem is one of identity.'

4   William George, *My Brother and I* (Eyre & Spottiswoode, London, 1958), p.93.
5   *TMLG*, pp.50-51.
6   A brief note in the introduction to the schedule of documents deposited by his son in the PRO in 1984 (information supplied by Miss Nikki Bosworth of the PRO on 19 May 2010).
7   NLW, WGSP, notes made 7 Nov. 1922 enclosed in a folder, item 7942.

1 - THE FORERUNNERS

1   *Pontypridd Chronicle* article reprinted 21 May 1890 in the *Haverfordwest & Milford Haven Telegraph* .
2   Extract from 'Y Gwir Anrhydeddus David Lloyd George' by Henry Rees, *Seren Gomer*, Jan. 1909, pp.12-14 (translation from Welsh into English supplied by Cymen Translation Company, Caernarvon, Oct. 2012).
3   Herbert du Parcq, Life of *David Lloyd George* (Caxton Publishing Company Ltd, London, 1912), Vol I, pp.9-11.
4   J. Hugh Edwards, MP, *The Life Story of David Lloyd George with a short history of the Welsh People, Vol. I* (Waverley Book Co. Ltd, London, 1913), pp.270 and 263.
5   William George, op. cit., p.2.
6   W.R.D. Phillips, *Old Haverfordwest* (J.W. Hammond & Co. Ltd and *Pembroke County & West Wales Guardian*, Haverfordwest, 1925), p.23.
7   *TMLG*, p.36.
8   Email from Curator of the Haverfordwest Town Museum, 24 Aug. 2011.

9   H.W. Harrison, *Hanes Teulu Lloyd George Family History* (printed for private circulation in 1999, reprinted in 2010with minor amendments, St Albans, Herts), p.70. [No source for this statement is recorded, but Mr Harrison believes (in a letter dated 8 Sept. 2011) that it could only have come from Dr George, most probably at a meeting they had in April 1997.]

10   Robert Lloyd George, *David & Winston, How a Friendship Changed History* (John Murray, London, 2005), p.9.

2 - THE SON AND HEIR

1   For most of the family information in this chapter - and, indeed, for much of the detail on intricate relationships recorded elsewhere in this bok - I am hugely indebted to the monumental labours and knowledge of Mr Henry Harrison as embodied both in *Hanes Teulo Lloyd George Family History* and in subsequent clarification and advice which he has patiently and helpfully provided on several occasions.

2   See pages 208-10.

3   Francis Jones, 'Jordanston in Dewisland', *The Pembroke Historian,* 1974 (Vol. 5), p.97; see also Harrison, op. cit., p.51, for the conditions stipulated in 1842.

4   Samuel Lewis, *A Topographical Dictionary of Wales*, edited and published by Samuel Lewis (London, 1833), GENUKI extract.

5   *Pigot's Directory for South Wales* (Pigot & Co., London, 1835), p.1. For a modern equivalent, see *The Companion Guide to South Wales* by Peter Howell and Elizabeth Beazley (Collins, London, 1977) and its Pembrokeshire section, particularly pages 93 and 99-101.

6   Daniel Defoe, *A Tour through England and Wales* (from Vol. II, originally published in 1725), Everyman edition (J.M. Dent & Sons Ltd, London, 1928), Vol. 2, pp.57-8.

7   Richard Fenton, *A Historical Tour through Pembrokeshire* (Longman, Hurst, Rees, Orme & Co., London, 1811), pp.17, 108-9 and 204.

8   Virginia Woolf, *A Passionate Apprentice: The Early Journals*, ed. by Mitchell A. Leaska (the Hogarth Press, London, 1992), p.360; *The Sickle Side of the Moon, Collected Letters, Vol. V*, edited by Nigel Nicolson, p.297.

9   See Wikipedia for further details. The route of the Line had fluctuated from the Middle Ages onwards but appears to have stabilised by the nineteenth century, running eastwards from Newgale, situated on the coastline of St Brides Bay and close to Trefgarn Owen, passing a few miles to the north of Haverfordwest. It then veered off in a south-easterly direction, following a wobbly course into Carmarthenshire.

10   NLW, WGSP, item 7931 (WG to Anne James, 3 Nov. 1862).

3 - THE SCHOOLBOY AND THE APPRENTICE

1   Paul Langford, *A Polite and Commercial People: England 1727-1783* (Clarendon Press, Oxford, 1989), p.84.

2   Their findings were set out in the *Reports of the Commissioners of Inquiry into the State of Education in Wales* (known informally as 'the Blue Books'), published by the Government in 1847. Much of the information in this chapter is taken from those Reports, but for general background I am greatly indebted to *The History of Education in Wales*, edited by Jac L. Williams and Gwilym Rees Hughes (Christopher Davies, Swansea, 1978) - the first part of a projected two-volume work, of which the second, alas, never materialised - and to *A History of Education in Wales* by Gareth Elwyn Jones and Gordon Wynne Roderick (University of Wales Press, 2003).

3   *TMLG*, p.45.

4   NLW, WGSP, item 7930 (WG to Richard Lloyd, 5 Oct. 1862).

5   John Brown (writing as Christopher Cobbe-Webbe), *Haverfordwest and its Story, with Old Pembrokeshire Parishes, etc* (Llewellyn Brigstocke, Haverfordwest, 1882), pp.164-5.

6   Francis Bacon, a letter to Lord Burleigh in 1592 and *Meditationes Sacrae* (1597) - see *Bartlett's Familiar Quotations*, 14th edition (1968), p.206.

7   One notes, for what it is worth, that *The Cambrian* carried an advertisement on 5 Jan. 1839 stating that a draper's assistant was required by William Davis at his premises in Haverfordwest High Street.

1   NLW, WGSP, housed (with sundry enclosures) within item 7943 (a file of miscellaneous notes relating to George family history).

2   *TMLG*, pp.37-9, 41-4 and 48-51.

3   An offshoot, or local equivalent, of the British and Foreign Temperance Association, founded 1836.

4   Charles Macklin, *Four Comedies*, edited by J.O. Bartley (Sidgwick & Jackson, London, 1968), pp.250 and 270.

5   Lord Lytton, *Ernest Maltravers* (George Routledge & Sons, New York & London, 1840 edition), pp.41 and 66 (Book I, respective opening words of Chapters VII and XIV).

6   Entry dated 19 Dec. 1840 in 'Commonplace Book', *The Letters of Anthony Trollope*, edited by N. John Hall (Stanford University Press, 1983), p.1022.

7   John Brown states that Haverfordwest had a bowling green outside the castle until 1820, when the site was acquired for the erection of a gaol, and one assumes that a replacement green would have been provided elsewhere (Brown, op. cit., pp.71 and 142). The Curator of the Haverfordwest Town Museum, in an email dated 31 Oct. 2011, stated that he had been unable to find any record of special celebrations taking place on 5 June 1839.

8   See Cecil Price, *The English Theatre in Wales* (University of Wales Press, Cardiff, 1948), pp.99, 118, 129 and 174.

9   See Brown, op. cit., p.158 for details of 'the Bristol traders'.

10   *Pembroke County Guardian*, 21 March and 6 June 1924; Phillips, op. cit., pp.23 and 60.

11   Samuel Lewis, op. cit., GENUKI extract. Harrison, op. cit., records (p.60) that WG's sister Gwenllian and her husband Levi James lived at Llsyronen but that this was not until after 1851. It is conceivable, therefore, that WG's 'teaching activities' at Llysronen did not occur until 1852 or 1853 (years which are otherwise unaccounted for) and that he was boarding there at the time with Levi and Gwenllian, but Anne (Gwenllian's daughter), who would surely have remembered this, claims that he was teaching at Liverpool from 1852 onwards.

12   Philip Guedalla, *The Hundred Years* (Hodder & Stoughton, London, 1936), pp.14-15.

5 - 'NORMAL' LIFE AT BATTERSEA

1   NLW, WGSP, an undated draft speech enclosed within item 7943 (a file of miscellaneous notes relating to George family history).

2   Information in this paragraph, and in those which immediately follow, is taken primarily from *James Kay-Shuttleworth: Journey of an Outsider* by R.J.W. Selleck (The Woburn Press, Ilford, Essex, 1994). So far as later paragraphs are concerned, Kay-Shuttleworth's own *Four Periods* (cited below) proved indispensable. Also consulted have been 'Kay-Shuttleworth and the training of teachers for pauper schools' by Alexander M. Ross, *British Journal of Educational Studies*, Vol. 15, issue 3, Oct. 1967, pp.275-83, and an earlier biography of Kay-Shuttleworth by Frank Smith (cited below).

3   Selleck, op. cit., pp.132-3.

4   Ibid., p.148 (Kay to Lady Byron, 30 March 1839).

5   James Kay-Shuttleworth, *Four Periods of Public Education as Reviewed in 1832, 1839, 1846, 1862* (originally published 1862, reprinted by The Harvester Press, Brighton, 1973), p.179.

6   Ibid., p.311.

7   Ibid., pp.326-7.

8   Ibid., p.313.

9   Ibid., p.329 (see also p.325).

10   Quoted in Frank Smith's *The Life and Work of Sir James Kay-Shuttleworth* (John Murray, London, 1923), p.110.

11   Lytton Strachey and Roger Fulford, *The Greville Memoirs*, Vol. V (Macmillan & Co., London, 1938), p.15.

12   Smith, op. cit., pp.113-14.

13   NLW, WGSP, enclosed within the *Student's Journal* housed in item 7943 (a file of miscellaneous notes relating to George family history).

14   A slight misquotation of the final line of stanza 19 of Thomas Gray's *Elegy in a Country Churchyard* (1750), which runs 'They kept the noiseless tenor of their way.'

15   NLW, WGSP, an undated draft speech enclosed within item 7943 (a file of miscellaneous notes relating to George family history).

6 - A BYRONIC INTERLUDE

1   *TMLG*, p.41.
2   William Wordsworth, *Poems in Two Volumes* (Longman, Hurst, Rees & Orme, London, 1807), Vol. I, pp.14-15.
3   Lord Byron, *The Ravenna Journal* (First Edition Club, London, 1928), p.82.
4   First published by Moore in 1830 in his biography of Byron; absorbed into the *Collected Poems* from 1831 onwards.
5   Thomas Babington Macaulay, *Critical and Historical Essays* (Longmans, Brown, Green, and Longmans, London, 1844), Vol. I, p.314.
6   Leslie A. Marchand, *Byron, A Portrait* (John Murray, London, 1971), p.121.
7   Ibid., pp.122-3.
8   Ibid., p.166.
9   Macaulay, op. cit., p.318-19.
10 Marchand, op. cit., pp.260 and 267.
11 Macaulay, op. cit., p.319.
12 Quoted in *Shelley and His Circle, 1773-1822, Vol. VI*, edited by Donald H. Reiman (Harvard University Press, Cambridge, Massachusetts, 1973), p.757.
13 *Westminster Review for* the period June-Sept 1840, p.112. 'My book on de Fellenberg is out,' Lady Byron proudly informed her daughter - Joan Pierson, *The Real Lady Byron* (Robert Hale, London, 1992), p.207.
14 NBLFP, Box 119, folder (e), f.159.
15 Ibid.
16 Pierson, op. cit., pp.195-6. See also Doris Langley Moore, *Ada, Countess of Lovelace* (John Murray, London, 1977), pp.55-9, 'Ealing and Brentford: Education' in *A History of the County of Middlesex: Volume 7* (Victoria County History, London, 1982), pp.162-70, and Brian W. Taylor, 'Annabella, Lady Noel-Byron: A Study of Lady Byron in Education (*History of Education Quarterly*, Vol. 38, Winter 1998), pp.430-55.
17 He is mentioned in a letter which Kay sent Lady Byron on 30 July 1842 - NBLFP, Box 76, f.183.
18 Harriet Martineau, *The Collected Letters, Volume 2*, edited by Deborah Anna Logan (Pickering & Chatto, London, 2007), p.135; *Thomas and Jane Welsh Carlyle, Collected Letters, Vol.*

11, 1839, edited by C.R. Sanders & others (Duke University Press, Durham, North Carolina, 1985), p.157; *The Brownings' Correspondence, Vol. 7* (Wedgestone Press, Kansas, 1989), p.64.

19   *TMLG*, pp.40 and 44.

20   Referred to in William George's shorthand notes of 6 Nov. 1922 [transcribed for the author by Tracey Jennings] - NLW, WGSP, enclosed in a folder, item 7942.

21   *TMLG*, p.44.

22   Ibid., pp.42-4, passim.

23   Ibid., p.42.

24   Ibid., pp.42 and 44.

25   Ibid., p.41.

26   Ibid.

27   Ibid., pp.42 and 43.

28   Ibid., p.51.

29   The reference to Harrow is intriguing. Bearing in mind that WG had apparently been a boarder at a London-based school, for however short a period, is it remotely possible that he could have been re-visiting his old *alma mater?* The notion seemed wildly improbable, yet since his cousin, from a similar background, would be studying at Göttingen University, it was not altogether out of the question. Ms Anghared Meredith, Archivist and Research Manager at Harrow School, very helpfully checked their records but was unable to find any mention of WG having been a pupil there during the 1830s. (An email to the author dated 8 April 2013 refers.) It might be noted, on the other hand, that Lord Byron had been educated at Harrow and that its very name was anathema to his widow.

30   NBLFP, Box 119, folder (e), f.178 - undated memorandum entitled 'How to make Parents wish to send their Children to School, & keep them there as long as possible'.

31   Defoe, op. cit., pp.88-9.

32   www.leicestershirevillages.com/interviewsofframework-knitters.doc - Appendix to the report of the commissioners appointed to inquire into the conditions of the frame-work knitters, Part I, Leicestershire, 1845. (The units of land referred to are not clear.)

33   *TMLG*, p.45.

34   Ibid., p.44.

35   Benjamin Woolley, *The Bride of Science: Romance, Reason and Byron's Daughter* (Macmillan, London, 1999), p.2. See also the letter which she sent to Woronzow Greig early in 1845, quoted by Dorothy Stein in *Ada: A Life and Legacy* (MIT Press, Cambridge, Massachusetts, 1985), p.181.

7 - AN HONORARY 'SCOUSER'

1   NLW, WGSP, notes made 7 Nov. 1922 enclosed in a folder, item 7942.

2   Anne Williams conjectured, indeed, that he was there for as many as eight, acting on the assumption that he moved to Liverpool as soon as he left Lady Byron's employment.

3   Nathaniel Hawthorne, *The English Notebooks, 1853-1856*, edited by Thomas Woodson & Bill Ellis (Ohio State University Press, 1971), pp.12-13, 17, 18-19 and 77.

4   Information about Martha Goffey will be found on www.liverpool-schools.co.uk.

5   *TMLG*, p.46.

6   *Liverpool Mercury,* 10 Dec. 1847.

7   Hawthorne, op. cit., p.77.

8   *Liverpool Mercury,* 9 Oct. 1846.

9   Ibid., 12 May 1848.

10   *Liverpool Mercury,* 19 Oct. 1849 and an extract from a James Martineau bicentenary lecture delivered by Ralph Waller in 20005 (see users.ox.ac.uk/manc0395/jamesmartineau) which echoed his 2004 entry on Martineau in the *ODNB* - '... a beautiful Victorian-Gothic building, with statues, stained-glass windows, chair pews, and a high altar that was never used but which helped to create an atmosphere of medieval gloom, conducive to Martineau's ethereal voice and aesthetic sermons.'

11   *Liverpool Mercury,* 26 Dec. 1851.

12   du Parcq, op. cit., p.9.

13   *Liverpool Mercury,* 12 Dec. 1851.

14   *TMLG*, p.50.

15   William George, op. cit., p.2.

16   NLW, WGSP, enclosed in a folder, item 7942.

8 - HAVERFORDWEST REVISITED

1   *TMLG*, p.47.

2   Ibid., p.48 (long version) and *Haverfordwest & Milford Telegraph*, 22 March 1854 (short version).

3   M.R. James, 'A Neighbour's Landmark', *The Collected Ghost Stories* (Edward Arnold, London, 1964), p.530.

4   *TMLG*, p.48.

5   *The Cambrian,* 20 April 1855 (under 'Marriages') and 7 Dec. 1855 (under 'Deaths').

6   Phillips, op. cit., p23.

7   Michael Holroyd, *Augustus John* (Chatto & Windus, London, 1996), p.8.

8   NLW, WGSP, jottings in a folder, item 7943.

9   *TMLG*, p.49.

10   Ibid.

11   Information from parish records, accessed via ancestry.co.uk.

12   George Augustus Sala, *London Up to Date* (Adam & Charles Black, London, 1894), pp.16-17.

13   NLW, WGSP - William George's shorthand notes of 6 Nov. 1922 [transcribed for the author by Tracey Jennings], enclosed in a folder, item 7942; Selina's death certificate states that her malady had been identified two years earlier.

14   *The Cambrian*, 7 Dec. 1855; Michael Holroyd, *Augustus John: Vol. 1, The Years of Innocence* (Heinemann, London, 1974), p.9.

9 - A POSTING TO PWLLHELI

1   Miss Nikki Bosworth, of the PRO, has confirmed that there are no surviving records which could give any clue as to what became of WG's school after 1855. She adds that the 1861 census shows, seemingly, just one school in Upper Market Street 'and this was run by James David Ribbon, "Professor of Music", and two of his daughters who were each designated "schoolmistress". Mr Ribbon, then described as a "musician", was already living in Upper Market Street on the 1851 census, when the street was known as St Thomas Street, but I do not know whether he and his daughters might have taken over the school from WG.' (Email from Miss Bosworth dated 18 June 2013.)

2   NLW, WGSP, a letter contained in a folder, item 7942 - WG to Rev. W. Roberts, 21 Jan. 1857 (a photocopy supplied to Dr George in 1936). Reproduced, with very slight modifications, in *TMLG*, p.52. Miranda Tennant, PA to the Bursars of Wakefield's long- established Queen Elizabeth Grammar School, has confirmed that WG was *not* a member of their staff in the 1850s.

3   Ibid.

4   H.W. Harrison, op. cit., p.51.

5   *TMLG*, p.69.

6   See page 20.

7   *TMLG*, p.53.

8   Ibid., p.45.

9   I am indebted to the sixth chapter of *Pwllheli, An old Welsh town and its history* by D.G. Lloyd Hughes (Gomer Press, Llandysul, 1991) for much of the information in this paragraph,

10   D.G. Lloyd Hughes, op. cit., p.225.

11   du Parcq, op. cit., p.8.

12   *TMLG*, p.52-3.

13   NLW, WGSP, notes contained in a folder, item 7943.

14   *TMLG*, p.54.

15   Information very kindly supplied by Mr John Aaron via Mrs Shâron Barnes, Office Manager for the Evangelical Movement of Wales, Bridgend. He observes that Joseph Thomas and David Saunders 'had not quite reached their prime at that time' and that, 'throughout the period, the greatest gun of them all, by far, was certainly Henry Rees. The probability is that WG heard him on the evening of the 8th or the morning of the 10th.' He contends that all four of the men referred to 'were far greater preachers than either Humphrey Jones or David Morgan.' (Email from Mrs Barnes dated 19 June 2013.)

16   See Eifion Evans, *Two Welsh Revivalists* (Evangelical Library of Wales, Bridgend, 1985).

17   *TMLG*, p.55.

18   Ibid., p.54.

19   Ibid.

20   D.G. Lloyd Hughes, op. cit., p.228.

21   It was often the case, in the nineteenth century, that well-to-do members of the community employed some of their poor

relations as servants, though whether Jane was indeed a distant connection of the great shipbuilder will have to remain a matter for speculation: the name Jones' is, in itself, enough to daunt the most intrepid of family-researchers. (Another possibility to be borne in mind is that Jane and Betsy had been employed in the same household at some stage, but this too is something impossible to establish one way or the other.)

10 - RECUPERATING IN LLANYSTUMDWY

1   du Parcq, op. cit., p.10.
2   *TMLG*, p.28.
3   See pages 239-40.
4   du Parcq, op. cit., p.8; Lord Riddell, *War Diary, 1914-1918* (Ivor Nicholson & Watson Ltd, London, 1934), p.274; J. Hugh Edwards, *David Lloyd George, Vol I* (Waverley Book Co. Ltd, London, 1910), p.10.
5   NLW, WGSP - enclosed in a folder, item 7943. (Intended, apparently, for insertion in his *Journal*.)
6   *TMLG*, p.56.
7   NLW, WGSP - a scrap of paper thrust into his Journal (on the reverse side of which, as quoted on pages 161-2, he considers his future plans).
8   NLW, WGSP, item 7925.
9   *TMLG*, p.65.
10   In 1976 W.R.P. George discovered the fragment of a commiserating letter from Goffey written in the autumn of 1860. An allusion in a family Bible led him to conclude, erroneously, that the child had been a girl who 'could not have survived for more than a few weeks' and that the shortness of her life had prevented a name from being bestowed. (See *TMLG*, p.57.) His son, in February 2013, located a Peter Williams Bible mentioned earlier in *TMLG* (p.28) which is presumably the one now referred to. It contains some very faint entries in pencil which are difficult to decipher but they record the marriage between WG and Elizabeth and the death of their first-born, buried at Capel Ucha. He is unable to see anything in the entry which identified the gender of the child. (Email from Philip William George, forwarding a photocopy of the page in question, dated 5 Feb. 2013.)

11   NLW, WGSP - William George's shorthand notes of 6 Nov.
      1922 [transcribed for the author by Tracey Jennings], enclosed
      in a folder, item 7942.

11 - MARKING TIME IN NEWCHURCH AND MANCHESTER
1   John Marius Wilson, *Imperial Gazetteer of England and Wales*
      (1870-72). The authors of the Victoria County History would
      note in 1911 that Newchurch 'still remains for the most part
      desolate hill country ... but a populous manufacturing district
      has sprung up all along the narrow valley of the Irwell, which
      bounds the township on the south.'
2   NLW, WGSP, item 7927 (WG to Richard Lloyd,, 31 Aug.
      1861).
3   Ibid., items 7937, 7929 and 7930.
4   Ibid., item 7932.
5   The Rev. Henry Davies ('Davies Llangloffen'), who had died in
      August 1862, was a Baptist minister and the brother of WG's
      aunt Mary, the wife of Timothy George. (She followed her
      brother to the grave exactly five weeks after WG wrote this
      letter.)
6   NLW, WGSP, item 7933.
7   'Happy years spent there,' he later recalled, 'privileges enjoyed,
      friendships formed, struggles mental and spiritual ending in
      partial triumph, are not things to be forgotten' - Thomas
      Nicholas, *Dr Davidson's removal from the professorship of
      Biblical literature in the Lancashire independent college,
      Manchester etc* (Williams & Norgate, Edinburgh, 1860), p.6.
8   Iwan Morgan, 'Dr Thomas Nicholas and the U.C.W.' in *The
      College by the Sea*, edited by Iwan Morgan (Students'
      Representative Council, Aberystwyth, 1928), p.257.
9   NLW, WGSP, item 7936.
10   See Iwan Morgan, op. cit., pp.257-69.
11   NLW, WGSP, item 7936.
12   Ibid., item 7935 (WG to Richard Lloyd, 24 Jan. 1863).
13   Ibid., item 7927.
14   Ibid., item 7937 (WG to Richard Lloyd,, undated but perhaps
      Oct. 1861).
15   Ibid., item 7930 (WG to Richard Lloyd, 5 Oct. 1862).
16   Ibid., item 7933 (WG to Richard Lloyd, 12 Jan. 1863).

17   Ibid., item 7929 (WG to Richard Lloyd,, 10 June 1862).

18   Ibid., item 7927.

19   Ibid., letter from Benjamin Williams to WG 14 Nov. 1861, item 7926, referring to the visit.

20   Ibid., item 7928.

21   Ibid.

22   *TMLG*, p.65.

23   NLW, WGSP, item 7929.

24   Ibid., item 7930 (WG to Richard Lloyd,, 5 Oct. 1862).

25   'According to a survey of the district in 1854,' Chris Makepeace reports, 'there were 7,708 dwelling houses in Chorlton-on-Medlock and 39,962 individuals living there. The small houses were described as having two rooms on the ground floor, outside conveniences, deficient drains with no main sewer connection and drainage from the scullery going straight into the ashpit. In contrast, there were back-to-back houses, often three-storeyed, overcrowded and damp.' (Accompanying notes to *Old Survey Ordnance Maps*, 'The Godfrey Edition', Manchester (London Road) 1849, Manchester Sheet 34, 1988). Photographs suggest that 5 New York Place was a relatively large house but it does not appear to have been a back-to-back residence.

26   NLW, WGSP, item 7929.

27   Ibid., item 7930 (WG to Richard Lloyd, 5 Oct. 1862).

28   Ibid.

29   Ibid., item 7933.

30   Ibid., item 7936.

31   Ibid., item 7934.

32   Defoe, op. cit., pp.261-2. For a vivid depiction of the town in the mid-nineteenth century, see Mark Girouard, *Cities and People: a Social and Architectural History* (Yale University Press, New Haven and London, 1985), pp.257-70.

33   Peter Maw, Terry Wyke and Alan Kidd, 'Canals, rivers, and the industrial city: Manchester's industrial waterfront, 1790-1850', *Economic History Review* (Vol. 65, Issue 4, 2012), p.1521.

34   Quoted by Girouard, op. cit., p.258.

35   NLW, WGSP, item 7930 (WG to Richard Lloyd, 5 Oct. 1862).

36   Dr Philip A. Sykas of Manchester School of Art, 'Thomas Hoyle and Sons: Quality Prints for the Masses', one of the

many projects which he has pioneered (in this particular instance, in conjunction with Mr John Beckett), c/o Manchester Metropolitan University website.

37 Most of the material on which this paragraph is based has been very kindly supplied by Mr John Beckett, whose 'Thomas Hoyle and sons, calico printers, of Mayfield, Manchester, and Sandy Vale, Dukinfield, 1782-1809' appears in *Transactions of the Lancashire & Cheshire Antiquarian Society* (Vol. 108, *forthcoming*).

38 NLW, WGSP, item 7930.
39 Ibid., item 7931 (WG to Anne James, 3 Nov. 1862).
40 Ibid., item 7930 (WG to Richard Lloyd, 5 Oct. 1862).
41 Ibid.
42 Ibid.
43 Ibid.
44 Ibid., item 7932 (WG to Richard Lloyd, 17 Nov. 1862).
45 Ibid., item 7930.
46 Ibid., item 7933.
47 Ibid., item 7936.
48 Ibid., item 7931.
49 Ibid., item 7932.
50 Ibid., item 7933.
51 Edwards, *David Lloyd George, Vol. I* (1930), pp.11-12.
52 NLW, WGSP, item 7933.
53 Ibid., item 7936.
54 Edwards, *David Lloyd George, Vol. I* (1930), p.12.

12 - BULFORD

1 NLW, WGSP, item 7932.
2 Ibid., item 7931.
3 Ibid., item 7935 (WG to Richard Lloyd, 24 Jan. 1863).
4 Ibid., item 7931.
5 Ibid., item 7932.
6 Ibid., item 7933.
7 Ibid., items 7933 and 7936 (12 Jan. and 6 Feb. 1863).
8 Ibid., item 7934.
9 du Parcq, op. cit., p.11; NLW, LGSP, letter from Anne Williams to William George, 24 March 1922, enclosed in a folder, item 7942.

10   NLW, WGSP, enclosed in a folder, item 7941.

11   See *TMLG*, p.66.

12   NLW, WGSP, item 7934.

13   *TMLG*, p.65.

14   Edwards, *Life Story of David Lloyd George, etc, Vol.II* (Waverley Book Co. Ltd, London, 1914), p.4.

15   *TMLG*, p.65.

16   NLW, WGSP, item 7941 (details of WG's personal estate at the time of his death).

17   Phillips, op. cit., p.24. Betsy recalled, in later years, that Mary told a passer-by 'We are putting stones to prevent bad people taking away Mummy's furniture' (George, op. cit., p.5).

AFTERMATH

1   du Parcq, op. cit., p.10.

2   Ibid., p.8.

3   du Parcq, op. cit., p.10; Mr Simon Hancock, Curator of the Haverfordwest Town Museum, very helpfully checked the local newspapers and confirms that they carried no record of WG's death. (Letter dated 30 Nov. 2013 from Mr Hancock.).

4   Edwards, *Life Story of David Lloyd George, etc, Vol.I* (Waverley Book Co. Ltd, London, 1913), p.270.

5   See page 169.

6   Lord Riddell, *Intimate Diary of the Peace Conference and After, 1918-1923* (Victor Gollancz Ltd, London, 1933), p.120.

7   Thomas Jones, *Whitehall Diary, Vol. III: Ireland, 1918-25*, edited by Keith Middlemas (OUP, 1971), p.103.

8   See *My Darling Pussy: The Letters of Lloyd George and Frances Stevenson, 1913-41*, edited by A.J.P. Taylor (Weidenfeld & Nicholson, London, 1975), pp. 49 and 112.

9   Thomas Jones, *A Diary with Letters, 1931-1950* (OUP, 1954), pp.350-1.

10   J.M. McEwen, editor, *The Riddell Diaries, 1908-1923* (The Athlone Press, London and New Jersey, 1986), pp.293-4 passim.

11   Harrison, op. cit., p.147; another version of the story appears in Frank Owen's *Tempestuous Journey: Lloyd George, His Life and Times* (Hutchinson, London, 1954), p.41.

12   NLW, WGSP, a letter to Lloyd George dated 11 March 1922 enclosed in a folder, item 7942.

13   Quoted in J. Graham Jones, *David Lloyd George and Welsh Liberalism* (National Library of Wales, 2010), p.52.

14   *My Darling Pussy*, p.49.

15   *TMLG*, p.66.

16   *My Darling Pussy*, p.163.

APPENDIX I: THE AGE OF WILLIAM GEORGE

1   NLW, WGSP, enclosed in a folder, item 7943.

APPENDIX IV: WHEN WILLIAM MET BETSY, 'THE GIRL NEXT DOOR'

1   *TMLG*, p.56.

2   See John Dilwyn Williams, 'The Lloyds of Ty Newydd: A Study of a North Wales Family' (in *Second Stages in Researching Welsh Ancestry*, edited by John and Sheila Rowland, Federation of Family History Societies in conjunction with the University of Wales, 1999), p.306.

NB Photographs of the cottage at Llanystumdwy, No. 5 New York Place (Chorlton-upon-Medlock, Manchester) and the farm at Bulford will be found in the 'William George section' of the author's website - www.peter.rowland.org.uk

INDEX

120-9; his sudden flight from the latter , 129-33; perhaps teaching at Talgarth. 135; based primarily in Liverpool, 136–60 passim, but partly a free agent, 148-51; conconsiders other career options, 161-2, but establishes his own school in Haverfordwest, 162-5; his short-lived marriage to Selina Huntley, 167-70; teaching in Wakefield,171; in charge of British School in Pwllheli, 175, 178-9, 184; marries Betsy Lloyd, 185-9; poor health obliges him to resign, 195; lives with in-laws in Llanystumdwy, 195; suffers two bereavements, 198-9; resumes teaching, moving first to Newchurch, 202, and thence (on temporary basis) to Manchester, 218-19; likes the Mayfield school but strained relations with his employers, 228-31; delights in birth of daughter and son, 216, 233-6; retires from teaching and becomes a farmer at Bulford, 243-7; sudden illness and death, 248; assessment of his character, 254-61; book purchases: 119-20, 173; other purchases: 120, 126-7, 136-7, 148-9, 156; search for the perfect wife: 70, 101, 116-19, 127-8; thoughts on religious matters: 158-9, 179-80, 181-3, 199, 205-67, 210; variable nature of his links to David Lloyd George, 261-9

George, William (1865-1967), WG's third son: 5-6, 18, 22-3, 135, 252,   253, 281

George, Dr W.R.P. (1912-2006), WG's grandson: xii-xiii, 6, 9, 12 , 24-6, 27, 40, 53, 72, 111-12, 127, 129, 142, 159, 161-2, 164, 166, 173-4, 183, 193, 195, 250, 253-4, 259, 281

Goffey, Martha (1810-83): 142, 147, 160, 265

Goffey, Thomas (1836-1915): 142, 160, 193, 197, 203, 223, 249, 253, 265

Goodall, Mr: 113, 115, 116

Goodwick: 35, 36

Göttingen, University of: 60, 208

Granston: 43, 73

Grant, Breyn: 207

Gray, Thomas (1716-71): 98, 114

Greenwich: 126

Greenwood, J.G.: 228

Greville, Charles (1794-1865): 88-9

Grigg, John (1924-2001): 3

Guedalla, Philip (1889-1944): 74

Guizot, François (1787-1874): 88, 98

Halley, Edmund (1656-1742): 93, 95

Hanes Teulu Lloyd George Family History: xiii, 12

Harmonia Society: 55, 71

Harmony chapel: 34, 43, 71

Harrison, Henry: xiii - xiv, 12, 25

Harrow: 119

Haslingden: 216

Haverfordwest: 6, 8, 11, 12, 14, 15. 17, 18, 19, 35-6, 37, 46, 48, 49, 71, 72, 148, 162, 167, 243, 246; its Grammar School, 45-6

Hawthorne, Nathaniel (1806-64): 138–40, 145, 225

Haydon, Benjamin (1786-1846): 109

Heath, Joseph: 147

Henry VII (1457-1509): 33, 37